THE INTERNATIONAL HORSEMAN'S DICTIONARY

LEXIQUE INTERNATIONAL DU CAVALIER

INTERNATIONALES PFERDE-LEXIKON

LESSICO INTERNAZIONALE DEL CAVALIERE

DICCIONARIO INTERNACIONAL DEL JINETE

# THE INTERNATIONAL HORSEMAN 'S DICTIONARY
English – French – German – Italian – Spanish

# LEXIQUE INTERNATIONAL DU CAVALIER
anglais – français – allemand – italien – espagnol

# INTERNATIONALES PFERDE-LEXIKON
englisch – französisch – deutsch – italienisch – spanisch

# LESSICO INTERNAZIONALE DEL CAVALIERE
inglese – francese – tedesco – italiano – spagnuolo

# DICCIONARIO INTERNACIONAL DEL JINETE
inglés – francés – alemán – italiano – español

Translated by Christina Belton

J. A. ALLEN
London

British Library Cataloguing-in-Publication Data
A catalogue record for this book is available from the
British Library.

ISBN 0.85131.626.3

Published in Great Britain in 1996 by
J. A. Allen & Company Limited
1 Lower Grosvenor Place
London SW1W 0EL

Typeset by Setrite Typesetters Ltd, Hong Kong
Printed in Hong Kong

Illustrations by Dianne Breeze
Designed by Nancy Lawrence
Translated by Christina Belton
Edited by Elizabeth O'Beirne-Ranelagh

# Contents

# Table des matiéres

# Inhalt

List of illustrations   *page xii*
Signs and abbreviations   *xvi*
Introduction   *xix*
Acknowledgements   *xxi*

**THE HORSE   1**
Breeds, types   2
Breeding   4
The stud   8
Grassland   10
  Poisonous plants   10
Feed stuffs   12

Exterior of the horse   14
  Basic notions   14
  Nomenclature   16
  Points of the horse, conformation   20
  Conformation of the legs   32
  General descriptions   32
The colours   36
  Colours and shades   36
  Markings   40
Movement, the paces, the gaits   40
Miscellaneous   42
  The hoof, the foot   42
  The teeth   44
  Measurement, measures   44
Diseases and ailments   46
General veterinary terms   50

Liste des illustrations   *xii*
Signes et abréviations   *xvi*
Introduction   *xix*
Remerciements   *xxi*

**LE CHEVAL   1**
Les races, les types   2
L'élevage   4
Le haras   8
Les herbages   10
  Les plantes vénéneuses   10
Le fourrage, les denrées   12

L' extérieur du cheval   14
  Notions de base   14
  Nomenclature   16
  Caractéristiques, signalement   20
Les aplombs   32
  Descriptions générales   32
Les robes   36
  Robes et particularités   36
  Particularités des robes   40
Le mouvement, les allures   40
Divers   42
  Le sabot, le pied   42
  Les dents   44
  Mensuration, mesures   44
Maladies et tares   46
Termes vétérinaires généraux   50

Bilderverzeichnis   *xii*
Zeichen und Abkürzungen   *xvi*
Einleitung   *xix*
Danksagung   *xxi*

**DAS PFERD   1**
Die Rassen, die Typen   2
Die Zucht   4
Das Gestüt   8
Das Weideland   10
  Die Giftpflanzen   10
Das Futter, die
  Futtermittel   12
Das Exterieur des Pferdes   14
  Grundbegriffe   14
  Nomenklatur   16
  Charakteristik, Ansprechen   20
  Die Stellung der Gliedmassen   32
  Allgemeine Kennzeichen   32
Die Körperfarben   36
  Farben und Abarten   36
  Abzeichen   40
Die Bewegung, die Aktion, die Gangarten   40
Verschiedenes   42
  Der Huf, der Fuss   42
  Die Zähne   44
  Messung, Masse   44
Krankheiten und Mängel   46
Allgemeine tierärztliche Wörter   50

# Indice

*Elenco delle illustrazioni*   *xiii*
*Segni e abbreviazioni*   *xvii*
*Introduzione*   *xix*
*Ringraziamenti*   *xxi*

## IL CAVALLO   1

Le razze   3
L'allevamento   5
L'allevamento   9
Il pascolo   11
   Le piante velenose   11
I mangimi   13

Il corpo del cavallo   15
   Concetti di base   15
   La nomenclatura   17
   La caratteristiche   21
   Gli appiombi   33
   Caratteristiche generali   33
I mantelli   37
   Colori e gradazioni   37
   Particolarità   41
Il movimento, l'azione, le andature   41
Miscellanea   43
   Lo zoccolo, il piede   43
   I denti   45
   La misurazione, le misure   45
Malattie   47
Termini veterinari generali   51

# Indice de materias

*Lista de las ilustraciones*   *xiii*
*Señales y abreviaciones*   *xvii*
*Prefacio*   *xix*
*Agradecimiento*   *xxi*

## EL CABALLO   1

Las razas   3
La cría   5
La yeguada, el depósito, la ganadería   9
El pasto   11
   Las plantas venenosas   11
El pienso   13

El exterior   15
   Conceptos fundamentales   15
   La nomenclatura   17
   Las características   21
   Los aplomos   33
   Características generales   33
Las capas   37
   Capas y matices   37
   Particularidades   41
El movimiento, la acción, los aires   41
Miscelánea   43
   El casco, el pie   43
   Los dientes, la dentadura   45
   La medición, las medidas   45
Enfermedades y taras   47
Términos veterinarios generales   51

## HORSE AND RIDER   57

Schooling/dressage: basic notions   58
Character, temperament, degree
    of training, condition, form   64
Reactions of the ridden horse,
    evasions, disobedience   66

Riding technique   72
Classical equitation   76
General equitation   78
The school, the manège, school figures   80
    School paces   84
    Work on two tracks, lateral
        work   86
    Pirouettes and turns   86
    High school airs   86
Riders   90
The dressage test   90
Jumping   92
Horse trials/eventing   96
Driving   98
Hunting   102

## RACING   107

Racing personnel   108
Racing administration   108
Race categories   110
Race organisation   112
The going   114
Racing colours and designs   116
    Racing colour schemes   118
Training terms   118
Racing performance   120

## CHEVAL ET CAVALIER   57

Dressage: notions de base   58
Le caractère, le tempérament, degré de
    dressage, la forme   64
Réactions du cheval monté, les défenses,
    désobéissances   66

Technique de l'équitation   72
Équitation classique   76
Équitation pratique   78
Le manège, les figures de manège   80
    Les allures de l'école basse   84
    Travail de deux pistes,
        pas de côté   86
    Les pirouettes   86
    Les airs d'école   86
Cavaliers, écuyers   90
Le concours de dressage   90
Sauts d'obstacles   92
Le concours complet   96
L'attelage   98
Chasse à courre, vénerie   102

## LES COURSES   107

Le personnel de l'écurie de courses   108
L'administration des courses   108
Les catégories   110
L'organisation des courses   112
Le terrain   114
Les couleurs d'écurie et les dispositifs   116
    Dispositifs de couleurs   118
Vocabulaire d'entraînement   118
La performance   120

## PFERD UND REITER   57

Dressur: Grundbegriffe   58
Der Charakter, das Temperament, der
    Dressurgrad, die Form   64
Die Reaktion des
    Reitpferdes, der Ungehorsam,
    Widersetzlichkeit, Unarten   66
Reittechnik   72
Klassische Reitkunst   76
Angewandte Reitkunst   78
Die Reitbahn, die Hufschlagfiguren   80
    Die Gangarten der Kampagneschule   84
    Arbeit auf zwei Hufschlägen,
        Seitengänge   86
    Pirouetten und Wendungen   86
    Schulgänge   86
Reiter, Bereiter   90
Die Dressurprüfung   90
Springen   92
Vielseitigkeitsprüfungen   96
Das Fahren   98
Reitjagd   102

## DAS RENNEN   107

Der Rennverein   108
Die Verwaltung, die Rennbehörde   108
Art der Rennen   110
Die Rennorganisation   112
Das Geläuf   114
Das Renndress und Abzeichen   116
    Abzeichen/Rennfarben   118
Trainingsvokabeln   118
Die Rennleistung   120

## CAVALLO E CAVALIERE   57

Addestramento: nozioni di base   59
Il carattere, il temperamento,
    la forma   65
Le reazioni del cavallo montato,
    le difese, le disubbidienze   67

Tecnica equestre   73
L'equitazione classica   77
L'equitazione pratica   79
Il maneggio, le figure, gli esercizi   81
    Le andature della bassa scuola   85
    Il lavoro su due piste, i passi
        laterali   87
    Le piroette   87
    Le arie di scuola   87
Cavalieri   91
Il concorso di addestramento   91
Il salto ostacoli   93
Il concorso completo   97
Gli attacchi, la guida   99
La caccia a cavallo   103

## LA CORSA   107

Il personale della scuderia da corsa   109
L'amministrazione   109
Le categorie   111
L'organizzazione delle corse   113
Il terreno   115
I colori di scuderia, i colori delle giubbe   117
    Disegni dei colori   119
Vocabolario di allenamento   119
La prestazione   121

## CABALLO Y JINETE   57

Doma: conceptos fundamentales   59
El carácter, el temperamento, el nivel de doma,
    la forma   65
Reacciones del caballo montado, las defensas,
    las desobediencias   67

Técnicas de equitación   73
La equitación clásica   77
La equitación práctica   79
El picadero, las figuras   81
    Los aires básicos de escuela   85
    El trabajo en dos pistas, los pasos de
        costado   87
    Piruetas   87
    Los aires de alta escuela   87
Jinetes   91
La prueba de doma   91
Obstáculos   93
El concurso completo   97
Los enganches   99
La cacería a caballo   103

## LA CARRERA   107

Gente del turf   109
La administración   109
Las categorías   111
La organización de las carreras   113
El terreno, el piso   115
Los colores de cuadra y los dibujos   117
    Dibujos de los colores   119
Terminología de entrenadores   119
Los resultados   121

# EQUIPMENT   125

The stable and equipment   126
Horse transport   128
Stable management   130
Trimming   130
Tack, saddlery   132
   The saddle   132
   The bridle   140
   Bits   140
   Martingales and lungeing
     gear   144
   Whips and spurs   144
Riding wear   148
Obstacles, jumps   154

*Indexes*   **159**
   *English*   160
   *French*   173
   *German*   185
   *Italian*   197
   *Spanish*   209

# LE MATÉRIEL   125

L'écurie, les accessoires   126
Le transport de chevaux   128
Soins à l'écurie   130
La toilette   130
La sellerie   132
   La selle   132
   La bride   140
   Les embouchures   140
   Martingales, enrênements,
     matériel de dressage   144
   Fouets et éperons   144
La tenue du cavalier   148
Les obstacles   154

*Index*   **159**
   *anglais*   160
   *français*   173
   *allemand*   185
   *italien*   197
   *espagnol*   209

# DAS MATERIAL   125

Stall, Stallgerät   126
Der Pferdetransport   128
Stalldienst   130
Frisieren   130
Das Sattelzeug   132
   Der Sattel   132
   Das Zaumzeug   140
   Die Gebisse   140
   Hilfszügel, Longier- und
     Dressurzeug   144
   Peitschen und Sporen   144
Die Reitkleidung   148
Die Hindernisse   154

*Register*   **159**
   *englisch*   160
   *französisch*   173
   *deutsch*   185
   *italienisch*   197
   *spanisch*   209

## GLI ATTREZZI 125

La scuderia, gli utensili 127
Il trasporto dei cavalli 129
Le cure in scuderia 131
La toeletta 131
La selleria (il materiale) 133
   La sella 133
   La bardatura della testa 141
   Le imboccature 141
   Martingale, redini speciali 145

   Fruste e speroni 145
La tenuta del cavaliere 149
Gli ostacoli 155

*Indici* 159
   *inglese* 160
   *francese* 173
   *tedesco* 185
   *italiano* 197
   *spagnuolo* 209

## EL EQUIPO, LOS UTENSILIOS 125

La caballeriza y el equipo 127
El transporte de caballos 129
El mantenimiento, el cuidado 131
Recortar 131
Los atreos, la guarnicionería 133
   La montura, la silla 133
   La brida 141
   Las embocaduras 141
   Martingalas, rendajes y equipo para el
      trabajo a la cuerda 145
   Fustas y espuelas 145
Los trajes de jinete 149
Los obstáculos 155

*Indices* 159
   *inglés* 160
   *francés* 173
   *alemán* 185
   *italiano* 197
   *español* 209

# List of illustrations

1 Points of the horse *page 18*
2 Skeleton 19
3 Head and neck 21–23
4 Back and croup 25–27
5 Conformation of forelegs 34
6 Conformation of hindlegs 35
7 Diseases and ailments 56
8 Principal parts of the horse 59
9 The legs and their action 59
10 Lateral flexion ('position') and bend 62
11 Different degrees of contact and
    collection 62
12 Taking the rein down and
    self-carriage 63
13 Positions of head and neck 70
14 Rein effects 71
15 School figures, changes of
    direction 82
16 Serpentines, voltes, circles 83
17 Shoulder in, *travers* 88
18 Renvers, half-pass 88

19 Half-turn on the haunches 89
20 Turn on the haunches, pirouette 89
21 Single turnout 106
22 Racing colour schemes 119
23 Stable equipment 127
24 Trimming 134
25 Saddles 135
26 Parts of the saddle 138
27 Bridles 139
28 Nosebands 142
29 Bits 143
30 Martingales, lungeing gear,
    draw-reins 146

# Liste des illustrations

L'extérieur du cheval 18
Le squelette 19
Têtes et encolures 21–23
Dos et croupes 25–27
Les aplombs antérieurs 34
Les aplombs postérieurs 35
Maladies et tares 56
Les régions principales du cheval 59
Nomenclature et jeu des membres 59
Le pli, le placer, l'incurvation 62
Appui, ramener, rassembler 62

Extension de l'encolure et
    descente de main 63
Position de tête et d'encolure 70
Effets de rênes 71
Figures de manège,
    changements de main 82
Serpentines, voltes, cercles 83
Epaule en dedans, tête au mur 88
La croupe en dehors, appuyer sur la
    diagonale 88
Demi-pirouette 89
Pirouette ordinaire 89
L'attelage simple 106
Dispositifs de couleurs 119
Accessoires d'écurie 127
Toilette du cheval 134
Selles 135
Parties de la selle, accessoires 138
Brides 139
Muserolles 142
Embouchures 143
Martingales, enrênements 146

# Bilderverzeichnis

Das Exterieur 18
Das Knochengerüst 19
Kopf- und Halsformen 21–23
Rücken- und Kruppenformen 25–27
Stellungen der Vordergliedmassen 34
Stellungen der Hintergliedmassen 35
Krankheiten und Mängel 56
Grundeinteilung des Pferdes 59
Benennung und Spiel der Beine 59
Die Stellung, die Biegung 62
Anlehnung, Beizäumung, Versammlung 62

Strecken und Selbsthaltung 63

Kopf- und Halshaltung 70
Zügeleffekte 71
Hufschlagfiguren, Wechsel 82

Schlangenlinien, Volten, Zirkel 83
Schulterherein, Travers 88
Renvers, Traversale 88

Kehrtwendung 89
Wendung auf der Hinterhand, Pirouette 89
Der Einspänner 106
Abzeichen/Rennfarben 119
Stallgerät 127
Frisieren 134
Sättel 135
Bestandteile des Sattels, Zubehör 138
Zäume 139
Reithalfter 142
Gebisse 143
Hilfszügel, Longier- und Dressurzeug 146

# Elencio delle illustrazioni   Lista de las illustraciones

| | | | |
|---|---|---|---|
| 1 | L'esteriore 18 | El exterior 18 | |
| 2 | Lo scheletro 19 | El esqueleto 19 | |
| 3 | La testa, l'incollatura 21–23 | La cabeza, el cuello 21–23 | |
| 4 | Il dorso, la groppa 25–27 | El lomo, la grupa 25–27 | |
| 5 | Gli appiombi anteriori 34 | Los aplomos anteriores 34 | |
| 6 | Gli appiombi posteriori 35 | Los aplomos posteriores 35 | |
| 7 | Malattie 56 | Enfermedades y taras 56 | |
| 8 | Le parti principali del cavallo 59 | Las regiones principales del caballo 59 | |
| 9 | Gli arti 59 | Los miembros 59 | |
| 10 | Il piego laterale, l'incurvamento 62 | El pliegue lateral, la incurvación 62 | |
| 11 | Dall'appoggio alla messa in mano 62 | El apoyo, el 'recoger', la puesta en mano 62 | |
| 12 | L'estensione dell'incollatura e la discesa della mano 63 | Descenso del cuello y descenso de mano 63 | |
| 13 | Posizione della testa 70 | Posición de la cabeza 70 | |
| 14 | Effetti delle redini 71 | Efectos de las riendas 71 | |
| 15 | Le figure, gli cambiamenti di direzione 82 | Las figuras, los cambios de dirección 82 | |
| 16 | Serpentine, volte, circoli 83 | Serpentinas, vueltas, circulos 83 | |
| 17 | Spalla in dentro, testa al muro 88 | Espalda adentro, 'travers' 88 | |
| 18 | La groppa in fuori, appoggiare sulla diagonale 88 | La grupa al muro, apoyo sobre la diagonal 88 | |
| 19 | Mezza piroetta 89 | Media pirueta 89 | |
| 20 | Girare intorno alle anche, piroetta 89 | Pirueta directa 89 | |
| 21 | L'attacco del singolo 106 | La limonera 106 | |
| 22 | Disegni dei colori 119 | Dibujos de los colores 119 | |
| 23 | Utensili di scuderia 127 | El equipo de la caballeriza 127 | |
| 24 | La toeletta 134 | Recortar 134 | |
| 25 | Selle 135 | Monturas 135 | |
| 26 | Parti della sella, accessori 138 | Las partes de una montura, equipo adicional 138 | |
| 27 | La bardatura della testa 139 | Bridas 139 | |
| 28 | Capezzine 142 | Muserolas 142 | |
| 29 | Imboccature 143 | Embocaduras 143 | |
| 30 | Martingale, redini speciali 146 | Martingalas, rendajes 146 | |

## SIGNS and ABBREVIATIONS

- characteristic expression used only in the given language
○ an equivalent expression does not exist in the given language
(12.4) see illustration 12.4
*m.* masculine
*f.* feminine
*n.* neuter
*pl.* plural

## SIGNES et ABBREVIATIONS

expression propre exclusivement à la langue donnée
expression équivalente manque dans la langue donnée
V. dessin 12.4
masculin
féminin
neutre
pluriel

## ZEICHEN u. ABKÜRZUNGEN

charakteristischer nur der gegebenen Sprache eigener Begriff
ein gleichwertiger Ausdruck fehlt in der gegebenen Sprache
s. Zeichnung 12.4
männlich
weiblich
sächlich
Mehrzahl

# SEGNI e ABBREVIAZIONI

espressione caratteristica della data lingua
espressione equivalente non esiste nella data
    lingua
vedi illustrazione 12.4
maschile
femminile
neutro
plurale

# SEÑALES y ABREVIACIONES

expresión característica de dicho idioma
expresión equivalente no existe en dicho
    idioma
mirar grabado 12.4
masculino
femenino
neutro
plural

# INTRODUCTION
## Antony Wakeham

I well remember sitting on the Hunter's Improvement Society (HIS) stand at the 1977 Equitana in Essen and listening to the late General Sir Evelyn Fanshawe explaining the intricacies of how to breed the British hunter to some German visitors. The conversation, as you might imagine, was conducted in English of some technicality. Things went swimmingly until the General came to his explanation of the HIS position on artificial insemination, in short, that the Society was against it. This was a point of view which the Germans clearly could not understand. No amount of graphic gesticulation from another stalwart Englishman, the late 'Tub' Ivens, really got the message home. To this day I believe that those visitors left the stand labouring under a misconception, not to put too fine a point on it.

The English are notorious for their inability to speak languages and the genial General was the epitome of the Englishman abroad: a perfect ambassador who nonetheless expected people to speak plain English. How useful this dictionary would have been on that occasion. It is regrettable but true that, in general conversation, most people get by in English. However, technicalities do not succumb so easily to the onslaught of a loud voice and gesticulation. The lack of the *mot juste* can land both parties in difficulties they never envisaged.

So here is the horseman's technical guide to French, German, Italian and Spanish brought up to date and much improved. If you aspire to course building in Spain or horse dealing in France your life will take on a new dimension with the Dictionary to guide you. It is to state the obvious that many horsemen have been Europeans for years—well before the European Union was conceived, racing people, showjumpers, breeders and saddle makers have done business in Europe with more or less success. Since horses are responsible in large measure for the development of Europe the only real surprise is that there is no universal equestrian language.

French was always the language of the horse trainer and a piaffe is still a piaffe in any language. But if you think French will get you out of trouble giving a riding lesson to an Italian, do not believe for one moment that 'doubler' (to turn across the school/down the centre line) will absolve you from 'tagliare'. Since the first edition in 1955, the language has moved on, not so much in the age-old lexicon of equestrian terms but in equipment, particularly clothing. New words now command space in the Dictionary. Shopping at the Salon du Cheval or the Essen Equitana need hold no more terrors for the horseman. The jockey helmet and the riding cap make separate appearances, and if the body protector is described as a back protector, that is to quibble; the German 'die Schutzweste' does not require further refinement.

The illustrations are a fall-back for anyone in need of further help. The businessman selling equipment in Spain does not necessarily have to get his tongue round 'el bocado de doma clásica'; pointing to the picture of the Weymouth curb will do the job nicely. Should he finally overcome his reticence he will be relieved to know that a Pelham is a Pelham anywhere in Europe.

The next challenge to the meticulous team producing this remarkable Dictionary may well be a Chinese and Japanese edition. These countries are now the source of most of our equipment if not our horses. However, in spite of an equestrian tradition even more ancient than ours it seems unlikely that the Horseman's Dictionary will ever become redundant, if only because the European tradition has just one real competitor—the Western tradition—and the Dictionary is reassuring in the matter. In France, Germany and Italy the word 'cowboy' is used to describe the Western saddle, though not apparently in Spain, where 'Western' is the word. In equestrian language Europe is the place that matters most and the English would do well to remember that theirs is not the dominant tongue. The Horseman's Dictionary is a salutary reminder of that.

**Antony Wakeham**
Wothersome
Christmas 1995

Antony Wakeham is Publisher of the British Equestrian Directory and Equestrian Trade News. Secretary of BETA (the British Equestrian Trade Association). Organiser of the BETA International Trade Fair.

# Acknowledgements: Remerciements: Danksagung: Ringraziamenti: Agradecimiento

My thanks to the following:

**France:**
The Directeur of the École Nationale d'Équitation: Monsieur Jean-Luc L'HEMANNE, and the Écuyer en Chef of the Cadre Noir: Colonel de BEAUREGARD.
M.Patrice FRANCHET D'ESPÈREY.
M. Vital le POURIEL.
Madame le Docteur-Vétérinaire Marlène FRANCQUEVILLE, Clinique vétérinaire de Saumur.

Mlle Delphine SAUDO;
the SAUDO family for their support and hospitality.

**Germany:**
The Deutsche Reiterliche Vereinigung;
Erhard T. VOGT.

Klaus and Sylvia BEESE of Agrarflug Ahlen GMbH for their hospitality and the use of their airstrip.

**Italy:**
Col. Paolo ANGIONI for placing at my complete disposal his expertise and that of his circle of acquaintances, and for his hospitality and that of Elisabetta zu STOLBERG;

The Director of the Museo di Cavalleria at Pinerolo.

**Spain:**
Sr Josep PUIG I PARAIRE and his colleagues and associates of the Federación Hípica Catalana, the Club de Enganches y Equitación de Cataluña, and the Veterinary Faculty of the Universidad Autónoma de Barcelona; Sra Maria José CHARLO; Brigitte WAGNER.

For their hospitality: Jose LOPEZ CASAL of the International Police Association, together with his wife Rosa; and Miguel-Luis TORRENTS FONT.

**England:**
Don Enrico Incisa Della Rochetta.

I also owe thanks to people too numerous to mention individually, or whose names I have forgotten or never knew, who contributed words, or whose expertise or hospitality I prevailed upon in almost every country of Europe.

Chris Belton

**The Horse**

**Le Cheval**

**Das Pferd**

**Il Cavallo**

**El Caballo**

| BREEDS, TYPES | LES RACES, LES TYPES | DIE RASSEN, DIE TYPEN |
|---|---|---|
| pure-bred Arab | le pur sang arabe | der Vollblut-Araber |
| English Thoroughbred | le pur sang anglais | das (englische) Vollblut |
| Anglo-Arab | l'anglo-arabe (*m.*) | der Anglo-Araber |
| native breed | la race indigène | die bodenständige Rasse |
| Oriental horse | le cheval oriental | das orientalische/morgenländische Pferd |
| Warmblood | le demi-sang | das Warmblutpferd |
| pony | le poney | das Kleinpferd, das Pony |
| cob | le demi-trait | der Cob, das Robustpferd |
| race horse | le galopeur, le cheval de course | das Rennpferd |
| hunter | le cheval de chasse, le hunter, le demi-sang | das Jagdpferd |
| hack | le hack, le cheval de selle léger | das Gebrauchspferd |
| cart horse, draught horse | le cheval de trait | das Kaltblutpferd |
| donkey | l'âne (*m.*) | der Esel |
| mule | le mulet | der Maulesel |
| jumper, show jumper | le cheval d'obstacle, — de concours d'obstacle | das Springpferd |
| eventer | le cheval de concours complet | das Vielseitigkeitspferd |
| dressage horse | le cheval de dressage | das Dressurpferd |
| carriage horse | le cheval d'attelage | das Wagenpferd |
| trotter | le trotteur, le cheval de course | der Traber, das Trabpferd |
| pacer, ambler | l'ambleur (*m.*) | der Passgänger, der Zelter |
| riding horse, saddle horse | le cheval de selle | das Reitpferd |
| ride and drive horse, dual-purpose horse | le cheval à deux fins | das Reit- und Wagenpferd |
| pack horse | le cheval de bât, — de somme | das Tragferd, das Packpferd |
| heavy horse, cold-blooded | le cheval de trait | der schwere, kaltblütige Schlag |
| light horse, warm-blooded | le demi-sang | der leichte, warmblütige Schlag |
| •lightweight horse | °le cheval pour cavalier de poids léger | °das Reitpferd für leichtes Gewicht |
| •middleweight horse | °le cheval pour cavalier de poids moyen | °das Reitpferd für mittleres Gewicht |
| •heavyweight horse | °le cheval pour cavalier de poids lourd | °das Reitpferd für schweres Gewicht |
| general utility horse | le cheval à toute fin | das Gebrauchspferd |
| breeding stock | le reproducteur (jument/entier) | das Zuchtpferd |

## LE RAZZE

il purosangue arabo
il purosangue inglese
l'anglo-arabo (*m.*)
la razza indigena
il cavallo orientale

il mezzosangue
il pony, il cavallino, il cavallo piccino
il cavallo di bassa taglia e robusto
il cavallo da corsa
l'hunter, il cavallo da caccia
l'hack (*m.*), il cavallo da passeggio
il cavallo da tiro pesante
l'asino (*m.*)
il mulo, la mula
il cavallo da salto ostacoli
il cavallo da concorso completo
il cavallo da dressage, — da
   concorsi di addestramento
il carrozziere
il trottatore
l'ambiatore (*m.*)
il cavallo da sella
il cavallo a doppio uso, —
   da sella e da carrozza
il cavallo da soma
il cavallo da tiro
il cavallo leggero, il mezzosangue
°il cavallo da sella leggero
°il cavallo da sella medio
°il cavallo da sella pesante
il cavallo a doppio uso
il riproduttore, la riproduttrice

## LAS RAZAS

el pura sangre árabe
el pura sangre (inglés)
el anglo-árabe
la raza indígena
el caballo árabe

el media-sangre
el pony
el caballo semi-pesado
el caballo de carrera
el caballo de caza, el media-sangre
el caballo de paseo; — de silla
el caballo de tiro, — pesado
el burro
el mulo, la mula
el caballo de salto
el caballo de concurso completo
el caballo de doma

el caballo de enganches
el caballo de trote, el trotón
el caballo de andadura
el caballo de silla
el caballo de montura y de enganche

el caballo de baste
el caballo de tiro, el caballo pesado
el media-sangre
°el caballo para jinete ligero
°el caballo para jinete de peso medio
°el caballo para jinete pesado
el caballo para todo
el caballo de cría

| BREEDING | L'ÉLEVAGE | DIE ZUCHT |
|---|---|---|
| breeding, breeding industry | l'élevage (*m.*) | die Zucht |
| rearing, raising | l'élève (*m.*) | die Aufzucht |
| breeder | le naisseur | der Züchter |
| rearer, raiser | l'éleveur (*m.*) | der Aufzüchter |
| species | l'espèce (*f.*) | die Gattung |
| variety | la variété | die Art |
| breed | la race | die Rasse |
| family | la famille | die Familie |
| stud (farm) | le haras | das Gestüt |
| dam | la mère | die Mutter |
| granddam | la grand-mère | die Grossmutter |
| grandsire | le grand-père | der Grossvater |
| daughter | la fille | die Tochter |
| son | le fils | der Sohn |
| brother | le frère | der Bruder |
| full brother | le propre frère | der Vollbruder |
| half brother | le demi-frère | der Halbbruder |
| sister | la soeur | die Schwester |
| full sister | la propre soeur | die Vollschwester |
| half sister | la demi-soeur | die Halbschwester |
| granddaughter | la petite-fille | die Enkelin |
| grandson | le petit-fils | der Enkel |
| foundation stock | la souche | der Stamm |
| line | la branche | der Zweig, der Schlag |
| individual | l'individu (*m.*) | das Einzelwesen |
| produce, offspring | le produit | das Produkt, die Nachzucht |
| type | le type | der Typ |
| origin | l'origine (*f.*) | der Ursprung, die Abstammung |
| ancestors, ancestry | l'ascendance (*f.*) | die Vorfahren, die Ahnen |
| descendants, offspring | la descendance | die Nachkommenschaft |
| strain, lineage | la lignée | die Nachkommenschaft, der Blutstrom |
| bloodline | la lignée | die Blutlinie |
| tail line | la famille | die Familie |
| consanguinity | la consanguinité | die Blutgemeinschaft |
| affinity | la parenté | die Verwandtschaft |
| degree | le degré | der Grad |

| L'ALLEVAMENTO | LA CRÍA |
|---|---|
| l'allevamento (*m.*) | la cría |
| allevare | la cría |
| l'allevatore (*m.*) | el criador, el ganadero |
| l'allevatore (*m.*) | el criador, el ganadero |
| la specie | la especie |
| la varietà | la variedad |
| la razza | la raza |
| la famiglia | la familia |
| l'allevamento (*m.*) | la yeguada |
| la madre | la madre |
| la nonna | la abuela |
| il nonno | el abuelo |
| la figlia | la hija |
| il figlio | el hijo |
| il fratello | el hermano |
| il fratello pieno | el propio hermano |
| il mezzo fratello | el medio hermano |
| la sorella | la hermana |
| la sorella piena | la propia hermana |
| la mezza sorella | la media hermana |
| la nipote | la nieta |
| il nipote | el nieto |
| l'origine (*f.*) | el origen |
| la linea | la línea |
| l'individuo (*m.*) | el individuo |
| il prodotto | el producto |
| il tipo | el tipo |
| l'origine (*f.*) | el origen |
| gli antenati, l'ascendenza (*f.*) | los ascendientes |
| i discendenti, la progenie | los descendientes |
| la famiglia, la linea | la línea, el linaje |
| la famiglia, la linea | la línea sanguínea |
| la famiglia | la familia |
| la consanguineità | la consanguinedad |
| l'affinità (*f.*) | la afinidad |
| il grado | el grado |

| | | |
|---|---|---|
| homogeneous | homogène | homogen, gleichartig |
| heterogeneous | hétérogène | heterogen, andersartig |
| mixed | métis | gemischt |
| pedigree | le papier, le pedigree, le certificat d'origine | die Abstammung, der Stammbaum, der Abstammungsnachweis |
| | | |
| hybrid | hybride | hybrid, fremdartig |
| typical | typique, typé | typisch |
| not true to type | dépourvu de type | typlos |
| potency | la puissance de génération | die Zeugungsfähigkeit, die Potenz |
| heredity | l'hérédité (f.) | die Erblichkeit |
| inheritance | le pouvoir héréditaire (f.) | die Erbanlage |
| prepotency | l'excellence héréditaire (f.) | die Vererbungsfähigkeit |
| innate defect | la tare héréditaire | der Erbfehler |
| throw-back | le retour de race | der Rückschlag |
| retrogressive | en régression | rückschlägig |
| degenerate | dégénéré | entartet |
| improve a breed | améliorer une race | eine Rasse verbessern, veredeln |
| create a breed | faire souche | einen Stamm gründen, bodenständig machen |
| constancy, stability | la stabilité | die Beständigkeit, die Konstanz |
| breeding selection | la sélection | die Auslese, die Zuchtwahl |
| crossing | le croisement | die Kreuzung, -zucht |
| intermediary produce | le produit intermédiaire | das Zwischenprodukt |
| utility cross-breeding | le métissage, la métisation | die Gebrauchskreuzung |
| mixed breed | le métis, le cheval croisé | der Mischling, das Mischblut |
| pure breeding | l'élevage (m.) dans la pureté de race, l'alliance (f.) | die Reinzucht |
| | | |
| inbreeding | l'élevage dans la consanguinité, en —, de —, dans de — | die Verwandtschaftszucht, die Inzucht |
| | | |
| inbreeding, close breeding | l'élevage en proche parenté | die enge Verwandtschaftszucht |
| incest breeding | l'union incestueuse | die Inzestzucht |
| free generation | la génération libre (de consanguinité) | die inzuchtfreien Ahnenreihen |
| outbreeding, outcrossing | le croisement irrégulier, le brassage de sang, l'outcrossing (m.) | die Fremdzucht, die 'bunte' Mischung |
| | | |
| line breeding | l'élevage en lignée (m.) | die Linienzucht |
| admixture of new blood | le renouvellement du sang | die Blutauffrischung |
| prototype of the species | le prototype de l'espèce | der Prototyp der Gattung |
| tap-root strain | la branche-maîtresse | der Hauptstamm |
| foundation sire | le cheval-père | der Stammvater, -grunder |

| | |
|---|---|
| omogeneo | homogéneo |
| eterogeneo | heterogéneo |
| misto | cruzado |
| l'albero genealogico, il pedigree | el pedigree, la carta genealógica, el certificado de origen |
| | |
| ibrido | híbrido |
| tipico | típico |
| atipico | atípico |
| la potenza | la potencia genealógica |
| l'ereditarietà | la herencia |
| il patrimonio ereditario | la herencia |
| il dominio | el poder hereditario; raceador |
| il difetto ereditario | la tara hereditaria |
| il ritorno indietro | el salto atrás hereditario |
| regressivo | el salto atrás hereditario |
| degenerato | la degeneración |
| migliorare una razza | mejorar una raza |
| creare una razza | crear una raza |
| la costanza | las características fijadas |
| la riproduzione per selezione | la selección |
| l'incrociamento (*m.*) | el cruce |
| il prodotto intermedio | el producto intermedio |
| il mezzosangue per lavoro | el cruce mestizo |
| il meticcio | el caballo cruzado |
| l'incrocio (*m.*) puro | la cría de pura raza |
| | |
| la riproduzione per consanguinità | el cruce de consanguinidad, el inbreeding incestuoso |
| l'allevamento (*m.*) in stretta parentela | el inbreeding |
| l'incrocio incestuoso | el inbreeding incestuoso |
| la generazione libera | la generación libre (sin consanguinidad) |
| l'outcross (*m.*), l'incrocio (*m.*) tra non parenti | el cruce con raza distinta, — con línea distinta |
| | |
| l'allevamento secondo la famiglia | el cruce siguiendo una línea |
| l'immettere (*m.*) nuovo sangue | el refrescamiento/la renovación de sangre |
| il prototipo della specie | el prototipo de especie |
| la linea d'origine | la línea principal |
| lo stallone di origine | el padre de una raza |

| | | |
|---|---|---|
| tap-root mare | la jument-mère | die Stammstute, -mutter |
| sire | le père, l'auteur | das Vatertier, der Vater |
| stallion | le producteur, le reproducteur | der Beschaler, der Hengst |
| brood mare | la reproductrice, la poulinière | die Zuchtstute |
| mating, serving, covering | l'accouplement (*m.*), la monte, la saillie | der Deckvorgang, Deckakt |
| beget, procreate, engender | procréer, engendrer | zeugen, befruchten |
| inseminate | inséminer | besamen |
| artificial insemination | l'insémination artificielle | die künstliche Besamung |
| prolific, productive | prolifique | zeugungsfähig, fruchtbar |
| sterile | stérile | unfruchtbar, steril |
| quality | la qualité | die Qualität, die Klasse |
| balance | l'équilibre (*m.*) | das Gleichgewicht |
| temperament | le tempérament | das Temperament |
| action, movement | l'action (*f.*) | die Aktion, die Bewegung |
| conformation | la conformation, le modèle | der Körperbau, das Exterieur |
| constitution | la constitution | die Konstitution |
| soundness, health | la santé | die Gesundheit |

| **THE STUD** | **LE HARAS** | **DAS GESTÜT** |
|---|---|---|
| stud farm[1] | le dépôt d'étalons | das Hengstdepot (Landgestüt) |
| stud farm[2] | la jumenterie, le haras | die Stuterei, das (Haupt-) Gestüt |
| young stock | les produits | die Nachzucht |
| stallion | l'étalon | der Beschäler |
| entire | le cheval entier | der Hengst |
| colt | le poulain | der Junghengst |
| teaser | l'étalon d'essai, boute-en-train | der Probierhengst |
| rig, cryptorchid | le cryptorchide, le cheval pif | der Klopphengst |
| mare | la jument | die Stute |
| filly (maiden) | la pouliche | die junge Stute |
| served mare | la jument saillie | die gedeckte Stute |
| in-foal mare | la jument pleine | die tragende Stute |
| foaling mare, dam | la poulinière | die Mutterstute |
| mare with foal at foot | la jument suitée | Stute mit Fohlen bei Fuss |
| barren mare | la jument vide | die güsste Stute |

1 A centre, in continental Europe, where 'travelling' stallions are gathered together.    2 A National Stud, or an important private one.

| | |
|---|---|
| la fattrice | la yegua madre, origen de una raza |
| il padre | el padre de un producto |
| lo stallone | el semental, el caballo entero |
| la fattrice | la yegua madre, — de vientre |
| la monta | el salto, la monta, el servicio |
| procreare | procrear |
| l'inseminare (*m.*) | inseminar |
| l'inseminazione (*f.*) artificiale | la inseminación artificial |
| prolifico | prolífico |
| sterile | estéril |
| la qualità | la calidad |
| l'equilibrio (*m.*) | el equilibrio |
| il temperamento | el temperamento |
| l'azione (*f.*) | la acción |
| la conformazione | la conformación |
| la costituzione | la constitución |
| la salute | la salud |

## L'ALLEVAMENTO

## LA YEGUADA, EL DEPÓSITO, LA GANADERÍA

| | |
|---|---|
| il deposito stalloni | el depósito de sementales |
| l'allevamento | la yeguada, la ganadería |
| i prodotti giovani | los productos |
| lo stallone | el semental, el garañón |
| il cavallo intero | el caballo entero |
| il puledro | el potro, el potrillo macho |
| l'esploratore (*m.*) | el recela |
| il criptorchide | el criptórquido |
| la fattrice | la yegua |
| la puledra | la potra |
| la fattrice coperta | la yegua servida, — cubierta |
| la fattrice piena | la yegua llena, — preñada |
| la fattrice | la yegua de vientre |
| la fattrice con puledro | la yegua con potro |
| la fattrice vuota | la yegua vacía |

| | | |
|---|---|---|
| the season | les chaleurs | die Rosse |
| covering, service | la monte | der Deckvorgang |
| period of gestation | la gestation | die Trächtigkeit |
| parturition, foaling | la mise-bas, le poulinage | die Geburt |
| foal | le poulain | das Fohlen |
| suck | l'allaitement (*m.*) | das Säugen |
| weaning a foal | le sevrage | das Absetzen |
| stud manager | le directeur de haras | der Gestütsleiter |
| stud groom | le palefrenier-chef | der Stutmeister |
| stallion man | l'étalonnier | der Hengstwärter |
| groom | le palefrenier | der Gestütswärter |
| stud-book | le registre général, stud-book | das Gestütsbuch, das Stutbuch |
| brand | la marque (extérieure) de haras apposée au fer rouge | der Gestütsbrand |
| identification document | le signalement | das Signalement |

## GRASSLAND

## LES HERBAGES

## DAS WEIDELAND

| | | |
|---|---|---|
| meadow | la prairie | die Wiese |
| pasture | la pâturage, le pré | die Weide |
| turning out to grass | la mise à l'herbe | der Weidegang |
| paddock | l'enclos (*m.*), le paddock, l'enceinte (*f.*) | die Koppel, der Paddock, der Auslauf |
| fencing | la clôture | die Umzäunung, der Zaun |
| gate | la barrière | das Tor |
| to graze | brouter | grasen |
| shelter | l'abri (*m.*) | die Schutzhütte |

**Poisonous plants**

**Les plantes (*f. pl.*) vénéneuses**

**Die Giftpflanzen (*f. pl.*)**

| | | |
|---|---|---|
| autumn crocus, meadow saffron (*Colchicum autumnale*) | le safran des prés, le colchique, le tue-chien | die Herbstzeitlose |
| box (*Buxus*) | le buis | der Buchsbaum |
| bracken (*Pteridium aquilinum*) | la fougère | der Adlerfarn |
| buttercup (*Ranunculus*) | le bouton d'or | der Hahnenfuss |
| deadly nightshade (*Atropa belladonna*) | la belladonne, le bouton noir | schwarze Tollkirsche |
| foxglove (*Digitalis purpurea*) | la digitale pourprée | roter Fingerhut |
| hemlock (*Conium maculatum, Cicuta virosa*) | la ciguë | der Schierling |
| henbane (*Hyoscyamus niger*) | la jusquiame (noire) | schwarzes Bilsenkraut |
| horsetails (*Equisetum*) | la prèle des marais | der Sumpf-Schachtelhalm |

| | |
|---|---|
| i calori, l'estro (*m.*) | los celos |
| la monta | el servicio, la monta, el salto |
| il periodo di gestazione | la gestación |
| il parto | el parto |
| il puledro | el potrillo |
| l'allattamento, allattare | la lactancia, mamar |
| slattare | el destete |
| il direttore dell'allevamento | el directtor de la yegua |
| il capo palafreniere | el primer mozo |
| il caporazza | el paradista |
| il ragazzo di scuderia | el mozo, el palafrenero |
| il libro genealogico | el registro matrícula |
| il marchio | el hierro |
| | |
| lo stato segnaletico | la reseña |

## IL PASCOLO / EL PASTO

| | |
|---|---|
| il prato | el prado |
| il pascolo | el prado, el pasto |
| mettere al prato | dejar el caballo en un prado |
| il paddock, il recinto | el cercado, el potrero |
| la recinzione | el vallado |
| il cancello | la barrera |
| brucare l'erba (*f.*), pascolare | pastar, triscar |
| la tettoia, il ricovero | el cobertizo, el refugio |

**Le piante velenose** / **Las plantas venenosas**

| | |
|---|---|
| il colchico | el cólquico, la quitameriendas |
| | |
| il bosso | el tejo |
| la felce aquilina | el helecho |
| il ranuncolo | el ranúnculo, el botón de oro |
| il solano insano, (l'erba (*f.*)) belladonna | la belladonna, el solano furioso |
| il digitale | el digital, la dedalera |
| la cicuta | la cicuta |
| la fava porcina, la morte delle galline | el beleño |
| l'equiseto (*m.*) | el equiseto, la cola de caballo |

| | | |
|---|---|---|
| laburnum (*Laburnum*) | le cytise, le faux ébénier | der Goldregen |
| lupin (*Lupinus*) | le lupin | die Bitterlupine |
| privet (*Ligustrum*) | le troène | der Liguster |
| ragwort (*Senecio jacobea*) | le séneçon, la jacobée | das Kreuzkraut |
| robinia, false acacia (*Robinia pseudoacacia*) | le robinier faux acacia | weisse Robinie |
| St John's wort, rose of Sharon (*Hypericum*) | le millepertuis, l'herbe (*f.*) de Saint-Jean | das Johanniskraut |
| yew (*Taxus baccata*) | l'if (*m.*) | die (Beeren-) Eibe |

## FEED STUFFS / LE FOURRAGE, LES DENRÉES / DAS FUTTER, DIE FUTTERMITTEL (*n. pl.*)

| | | |
|---|---|---|
| corn | les grains | das Korn-, Hardfutter |
| dry food, roughage | le fourrage 'sec' | das Rauhfutter |
| green fodder | le vert | das Grünfutter |
| compound feed | la nourriture composée | das Mischfutter |
| oats | l'avoine (*f.*) | der Hafer |
| barley | l'orge (*f.*) | die Gerste |
| crushed, rolled | concassé | gequetscht, geschrotet |
| sugar-beet | la betterave | die Trockenschnitzel (*m.pl.*) |
| maize | le maïs | der Mais |
| straw | la paille | das Stroh |
| chaff | la paille hâchée, le foin hâché | der Häcksel |
| nuts, cubes | les granulés | die 'Pellets' (*n. pl.*), das pelletiertes Futter |
| coarse mix | le floconné | das Mischfutter |
| hay (first cut) | le foin (1ère coupe) | das Heu (1 Schnitt) |
| hay (second cut) | le foin, le regain | das Grummet (2 Schnitt) |
| •haylage | °un produit intermédiaire entre le foin et l'ensilage | die Anwelksilage |
| grass | l'herbe (*f.*) | das Gras |
| lucerne, alfalfa | la luzerne | die Luzerne |
| clover | le trèfle | der Klee |
| carrot | la carotte | die Mohrrübe |
| bran | le son | die Kleie |
| linseed | la graine de lin | die Leinsamen |
| molasses | la mélasse | die Melasse |
| sugar | le sucre | der Zucker |

| | |
|---|---|
| il laburno, il maggiociondolo | el codeso |
| il lupino | el lupino |
| il ligustro | la alheña |
| il senecio, il senecione | la hierba cana, — de Santiago, el zuzón |
| la robinia, la falsa acacia | la acacia falsa |
| l'iperico (*m.*) | la hierba de San Juan |
| il tasso | el tejo |

## I MANGIMI

## EL PIENSO

| | |
|---|---|
| i grani | los granos |
| il foraggio | el forraje seco |
| il foraggio verde | el forraje verde, el alimento verde |
| i mangimi composti | el pienso compuesto |
| l'avena (*f.*) | la avena |
| l'orzo (*m.*) | la cebada |
| schiacciato | triturado, aplastado |
| la barbabietola | la remolacha |
| il granoturco | el maíz |
| la paglia | la paja |
| la paglia tritata, il fieno tritato | la paja corta, el heno corto |
| i pellettati | los gránulos |
| la mescolanza | la mezcla de pienso |
| il fieno, il maggengo | el heno (el primer corte) |
| il fieno (secondo taglio), il lugliatico, l'agostano (*m.*) | el heno (el segundo corte) |
| °un prodotto intermedio tra fieno e foraggio insilato | °un producto intermedio entre el heno y el ensilado |
| l'erba (*f.*) | la hierba |
| l'erba (*f.*) medica | la alfalfa |
| il trifoglio | el trébol |
| la carota | la zanahoria |
| la crusca | el salvado |
| il seme di lino | la linaza |
| la melassa | la melaza |
| lo zucchero | el azúcar |

| | | |
|---|---|---|
| oil | l'huile (*f.*) | das Öl |
| salt, salt lick | le sel, bloc de sel | das Salz, der Leckstein |
| mash | le mash, le barbotage | der Mash |
| water | l'eau (*f.*) | das Wasser |
| daily ration | la ration journalière | die Tages-ration, -norm |
| maintenance ration | la ration d'entretien | die Erhaltungs-, Grund-ration |
| working ration | la ration de travail | die Artbeits-ration |
| supplementary ration | la ration de croissance, — supplémentaire | die Jungpferde-, zusätzliche Ration |
| titbit | la friandise | der Leckerbissen |

## EXTERIOR OF THE HORSE — L'EXTÉRIEUR DU CHEVAL — DAS EXTERIEUR DES PFERDES

| **Basic notions** | **Notions de base** | **Grundbegriffe** |
|---|---|---|
| conformation | la conformation du cheval | der Körperbau des Pferdes |
| skeleton | le squelette | das Skelett, Knochengerüst |
| bone | l'os (*m.*), l'ossature (*f.*) | die Knochen (*m.pl.*) |
| joint | l'articulation (*f.*) | das Gelenk |
| spine | le rachis, la colonne vertébrale | die Wirbelsäule |
| vertebra | la vertèbre | der Wirbel |
| thorax | le thorax | der Brustkorb |
| ribs | les côtes (*f.pl.*) | die Rippen (*f.pl.*) |
| pelvis | le bassin | das Becken |
| organs | les organes (*m.pl.*) | die Organe (*n.pl.*) |
| muscles | les muscles (*m.pl.*) | die Muskeln (*f.pl.*) |
| tendons | les tendons (*m.pl.*) | die Sehnen (*f. pl.*) |
| ligament | le ligament | das Band |
| nerves | les nerfs (*m.pl.*) | die Nerven (*m.pl.*) |
| skin | la peau | die Haut |
| coat | le poil, la robe | die Behaarung |
| hair | les poils, les crins (*m.pl.*) | das Haar |
| colour | la robe | das Haarkleid, die Farbe |
| head | la tête | der Kopf |
| trunk | le tronc | der Rumpf |
| limbs | les membres (*m.pl.*) | die Gliedmassen (*n.pl.*) |
| exterior, points of the horse | l'extérieur du cheval (*m.*) | das Exterieur, die äussere Form |
| conformation of the legs, set of the legs | les aplombs (*m.pl.*) | die Stellung der Gliedmassen |

| | |
|---|---|
| l'olio (*m.*) | el aceite |
| il sale, il rullo di sale minerale | la sal, la bola de sal |
| il pastone, il beverone | el pienso caliente |
| l'acqua (*f.*) | el agua (*f.*) |
| la razione giornaliera | la ración diaria |
| la razione di mantenimento | la ración de mantenimiento, — de entretenimiento |
| la razione di lavoro | la ración de trabajo |
| la razione supplementare | la ración de crecimiento, el supplemento |
| la leccornia | la golosina |

## IL CORPO DEL CAVALLO

### Concetti di base

| | |
|---|---|
| le caratteristiche | la conformación, la morfología |
| lo scheletro | el esqueleto |
| l'osso (*m.*) | el hueso |
| l'articolazione (*f.*) | la articulación |
| il rachide, la colonna vertebrale | la columna vertebral |
| la vertebra | la vértebra |
| il torace | el tórax |
| le costole | las costillas |
| il bacino, i cosciali | la pelvis |
| gli organi | los órganos |
| i muscoli | los músculos |
| i tendini | los tendones |
| il legamento | il ligamento |
| i nervi | los nervios |
| la pelle | la piel |
| il mantello | el pelaje, la capa |
| i peli, i crini | el pelo, la crin |
| il colore | la capa |
| la testa | la cabeza |
| il tronco | el tronco |
| gli arti | los miembros |
| la nomenclatura, l'esteriore | el exterior |
| gli appiombi | los aplomos |

## EL EXTERIOR

### Conceptos fundamentales

## Nomenclature
### Key to illustrations 1 and 2
1. poll
2. ear
3. forehead
4. eye
5. nose
6. nostrils
7. mouth
8. curb groove, chin groove
9. lower jaw
10. throat
11. neck
12. crest
13. chest
14. ribs
15. back
16. withers
17. belly
18. flank
19. loins
20. croup
21. point of hip
22. dock

23. tail
24. sheath
25. navel
26. shoulder
27. point of shoulder
28. upper arm
29. elbow
30. forearm
31. chestnut
32. knee

33. cannon bone
34. fetlock

## Nomenclature
### Légende des illustrations 1 et 2
1. la nuque
2. l'oreille ( f.)
3. le front
4. l'oeil (m.)
5. le chanfrein
6. les naseaux (m.pl.)
7. la bouche
8. le passage de gourmette
9. la ganache, la mâchoire inférieure
10. la gorge
11. l'encolure ( f.)
12. le bord supérieur de l'encolure
13. le poitrail
14. les côtes ( f.pl.)
15. le dos
16. le garrot
17. le ventre
18. le flanc
19. le rein
20. la croupe
21. la pointe de la hanche
22. le coir

23. la queue
24. le fourreau
25. le nombril
26. l'épaule ( f.)
27. la pointe d'épaule
28. le bras
29. le coude
30. l'avant-bras (m.)
31. la châtaigne
32. le genou

33. le canon
34. le boulet

## Nomenklatur
### Legende der Bilder 1 und 2
1. das Genick
2. das Ohr
3. die Stirn
4. das Auge
5. der Nasenrücken, das Untergesicht
6. die Nüstern ( f.pl.)
7. das Maul
8. die Kinnkettengrube
9. die Kinnbacke, die Ganasche
10. der Kehlkopf
11. der Hals
12. der Mähnenkamm
13. die Brust
14. die Rippen ( f.pl.)
15. der Rücken
16. der Widerrist
17. der Bauch
18. die Flanke
19. die Lende, die Niere
20. die Kruppe
21. der Hüfthocker
22. die Schweifrübe

23. der Schweif
24. der Schlauch
25. der Nabel
26. die Schulter
27. das Buggelenk
28. der Oberarm
29. der Ellbogen
30. der Vorarm
31. die Kastanie
32. das Vorderfusswurzelgelenk, das Vorderknie

33. das Rohrbein, die Röhre
34. das Fesselgelenk, der Fesselkopf

**La nomenclatura**
*Leggenda delle illustrazioni 1 e 2*
1. la nuca
2. l'orecchio (*m.*)
3. la fronte
4. l'occhio (*m.*)
5. il dorso del naso
6. le narici, le nari
7. la bocca
8. la barbozza
9. la ganascia, la mascella inferiore
10. la gola
11. il collo, l'incollatura (*f.*)
12. il bordo superiore dell'incollatura
13. il petto
14. le costole
15. il dorso
16. il garrese
17. il ventre
18. il fianco
19. le reni, i lombi
20. la groppa
21. la punta dell'anca
22. la base della coda, il fusto, il torso della coda
23. la coda
24. il prepuzio
25. l'ombelico (*m.*)
26. la spalla
27. la punta della spalla
28. il braccio
29. il gomito
30. l'avambraccio
31. la castagna
32. il ginocchio

33. lo stinco
34. il nodello

**La nomenclatura**
*Leyenda de las descripciones 1 y 2*
1. la nuca
2. la oreja
3. la frente
4. el ojo
5. el hocico
6. las narices, los ollares
7. la boca
8. el canal de babilla
9. la quijada inferior
10. la garganta
11. el cuello
12. la cerviz
13. el pecho
14. las costillas
15. el lomo, el dorso
16. la cruz
17. el vientre
18. la ijada
19. los riñones
20. la grupa
21. la cadera
22. el maslo

23. la cola
24. la vaina
25. el ombligo
26. la espalda
27. la punta de espalda
28. el brazo
29. el codillo
30. el antebrazo, el brazuelo
31. el espejuelo, la castaña
32. la rodilla

33. la caña
34. el menudillo

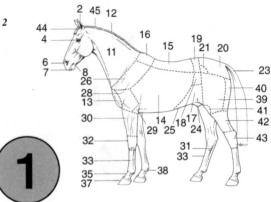

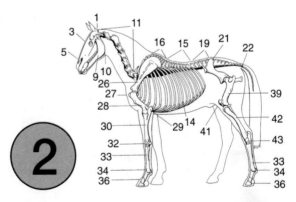

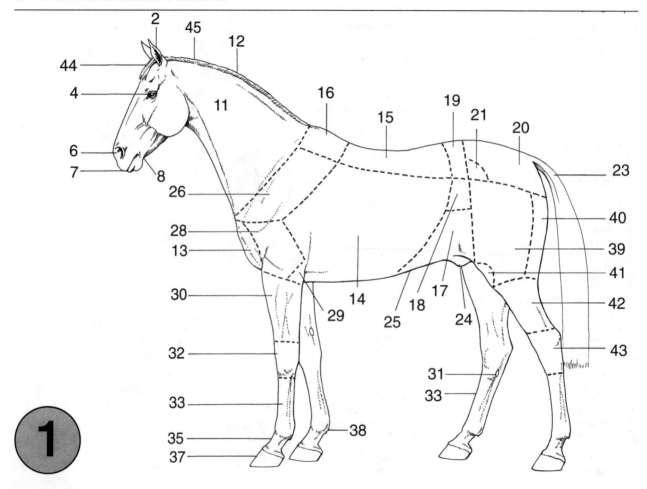

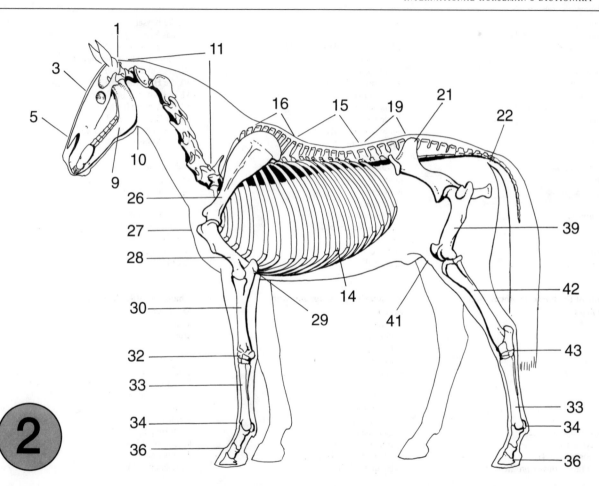

| | | |
|---|---|---|
| 35. pastern | 35. le paturon | 35. die Fessel |
| 36. coronet | 36. la couronne | 36. das Kronengelenk |
| 37. foot, hoof | 37. le pied, le sabot | 37. der Fuss, der Huf |
| 38. ergot | 38. l'ergot (*m.*) | 38. die Afterklaue, der Sporn |
| 39. thigh | 39. la cuisse | 39. der Oberschenkel |
| 40. buttock | 40. la fesse | 40. die Hinterbacke |
| 41. stifle | 41. le grasset | 41. das Knie, Hinterknie |
| 42. second thigh, gaskin | 42. la jambe | 42. der Unterschenkel |
| 43. hock | 43. le jarret | 43. das Sprunggelenk |
| 44. forelock | 44. le toupet | 44. der Schopf, die Schubrine |
| 45. mane | 45. la crinière | 45. die Mähne |

| ***Additional points*** | ***Supplément*** | ***Weitere Körperteile*** |
|---|---|---|
| head | la tête | der Kopf |
| feather, hairy heel | le fanon | der Kötenbehand |
| anus | l'anus (*m.*) | der After |
| scrotum | les bourses (*f.pl.*) | der Holdensack |
| testicles | les testicules (*m.pl.*) | die Holden (*f.pl.*) |
| penis | la verge | die Rute |
| vulva | la vulve | die Scheide |
| udder | la mamelle | das Euter |

| **Points of the horse, conformation** | **Caractéristiques, signalement** | **Charakteristik, Ansprechen** |
|---|---|---|
| ***The head*** | ***La tête*** | ***Der Kopf*** |
| small — | — petite | kleiner — |
| big — | — grande | grosser — |
| light — | — légère | leichter — |
| heavy — | — grosse | schwerer — |
| lean, dry — | — sèche | trockener — |
| coarse — | — charnue | fleischiger — |
| expressive, noble — | — expressive | ausdrucksvoller, edler — |
| common — | — commune | gemeiner — |
| straight — (3.1) | — droite (3.1) | gerader — (3.1) |
| wedge-shaped — (3.2) | — conique (3.2) | keilförmiger — (3.2) |
| concave — (3.3) | — concave, camuse (3.3) | konkaver— (3.3) |
| dish-nosed — (3.4) | — de brochet (3.4) | Hechtskopf (3.4) |
| arched face, convex profile (3.5) | — busquée (3.5) | Ramskopf (3.5) |

35. il pastorale
36. la corona
37. il piede, lo zoccolo
38. lo sperone
39. la coscia
40. la natica
41. la grassella
42. la gamba
43. il garretto
44. il ciuffo
45. la criniera

*Altre regioni*
la testa
il fiocco
l'ano (*m.*)
lo scroto
i testicoli
il pene
la vulva
la mammella

### Le caratteristiche
*La testa*
—piccola
—grande
—leggera
—pesante
—asciutta
—carnosa
—espressiva, nobile
—volgare
—dritta (3.1)
—conica (3.2)
—concava (3.3)
—camusa (3.4)
il profilo convesso, la testa arcata (3.5)

35. la cuartilla
36. la corona
37. el pie, el casco
38. la cerneja
39. el muslo
40. la nalga
41. la rodilla
42. la babilla
43. el corvejón
44. el copete
45. la crin

*Otras características*
la cabeza
el pelo de la cerneja
el ano
el escroto
los testículos
el pene
la vulva
la ubre, la mama

### Las características
*La cabeza*
—pequeña
—grande
—ligera
—pesada
—seca
—pastosa
—expresiva
—común
—recta (3.1)
—cónica (3.2)
—cóncava (3.3)
—cóncava (3.4)
—convexa (3.5)

1

2

| | | |
|---|---|---|
| Roman-nosed (3.6) | — de mouton (3.6) | Schafskopf (3.6) |
| well, badly set on head | bonne, mauvaise attache de la tête | gut, schlecht aufgesetzter Kopf |

| *The neck* | *L'encolure ( f.)* | *Der Hals* |
|---|---|---|
| short — | — courte | kurzer — |
| well-proportioned — | — proportionnée | proportionierter — |
| long — | — longue | langer — |
| narrow — | — étroite, grêle | schmaler — |
| light, fine — | — légère, fine | leichter —, feiner — |
| thick, strong — | — grosse | dicker — |
| heavy neck, bull-necked | — lourde | schwerer — |
| low set — (3.7) | — horizontale (3.7) | waagerechter — (3.7) |
| straight — (3.8) | — droite (3.8) | gerade verlaufender (3.8) |
| sloping, oblique — | — oblique | schräggestellter —, (steilgestellter —) |
| arched — (3.9) | — rouée (3.9) | gebogener— (3.9) |
| swan-necked | — de cygne | Schwanenhals |
| ewe-necked[1] (3.10) | — de chèvre (3.10) | Bretthals (3.10) |
| ewe-necked[2] (3.10) | — de cerf, —renversée (3.10) | Hirschhals (3.10) |
| low, high set-on neck | — bas, haut greffée/plantée | tief-, hochangesetzter — |
| badly, well-muscled up — | — mal, bien musclée | schwach, gut bemuskelter— |

| *The chest* | *Le poitrail* | *Die Brust* |
|---|---|---|
| narrow — | — étroit, serré | schmale, enge — |
| well-proportioned — | — proportionné | proportionierte — |
| wide — | — large | breite — |
| hollow — | — creux | hohe —, flache — |
| deep — | — profond | tiefe — |
| chicken-breasted | — saillant | Habichtsbrust |
| pigeon-breasted | — de chèvre | Ziegenbrust |
| thick in front, carty chested | — de lion | Löwenbrust |

| *The ribs* | *Les côtes* | *Die Rippen ( f.pl.)* |
|---|---|---|
| short — | — courtes | kurze — |
| long — | — longues | lange — |
| flat — | — plates | flache — |
| curved, well-sprung — | — arrondies, convexes | gewölbte — |

la testa montonina (3.6)
una buona/cattiva attaccatura

*L'incollatura (f.)*
— corta
— proporzionata
— lunga
— stretta
— leggera
— grossa
— pesante
— orizzontale (3.7)
— dritta (3.8)
— obliqua
— arcuata (3.9)
il collo di cigno
l'incollatura rovesciata (3.10)
— di cervo (3.10)
— attaccata bassa,— alta
— male/bene muscolata

*Il petto*
— stretto
— proporzionato
— largo
— incavato
— profondo
— carenato
a petto di pollo
grosso davanti

*Le costole*
— corte
— lunghe
— piatte
— convesse

— acarnedada (3.6)
una buena/mala unión cabeza-cuello

*El cuello*
— corto
— proporcionado
— largo
— estrecho
— ligero
— grueso
— pesado
— horizontal (3.7)
— recto (3.8)
— oblicuo
— arqueado (3.9)
— de cisne
— de cabra (3.10)
— de ciervo (3.10)
inserción baja/alta del cuello
el cuello bien/poco musculado

*El pecho*
— estrecho
— proporcionado
— ancho
— hundido
— profundo
— en punta
— de cabra
— de león

*Las costillas*
— cortas
— largas
— planas
— curvadas

3

4

5

6

7

8

9

10

3

*The back*
short —
long —
straight — (4.1)
dipped, sway, hollow — (4.2)
arched back (4.3)
roach-backed
weak —
strong, well-coupled up —

*The withers*
short —
long —
low —
high —
lean —
thin, bony —
thick —
pronounced —
poorly defined —

*The belly*
normal —
pendulous —
pot-bellied
cow-bellied
tucked-up —
herring-gutted, greyhound-like

*The loins*
short —
long —
narrow —
wide —
level —
sunken —
weak —
strong —

*Le dos*
— court
— long
— droit (4.1)
— ensellé (4.2)
— vouté (4.3)
— de carpe, de mulet
— faible
— solide, fort

*Le garrot*
— court
— prolongé
— bas
— saillant
— tranchant
— maigre, décharné
— épais
— prononcé
— noyé

*Le ventre*
— normal
— descendu
— rond
— rond
— retroussé
— levretté

*Le rein, les lombes*
— court
— long
— étroit
— large
— horizontal
— descendu
— creux
— ferme

*Der Rücken*
kurzer —
langer —
— gerader (4.1)
gesenkter —, Senkrücken (4.2)
gewölbter — (4.3)
Karpfenrücken
schwacher, weicher —
starker —

*Der Widerrist*
kurzer —
langer —
niedriger —
hoher —
scharfer —
magerer —
dicker —
ausdrucksvoller, trockener —
verschwommener —

*Der Bauch*
normaler —
hängender, gesenkter —
Heubauch
(Kuh-) Heubauch
aufgezogener —
aufgeschürzter —

*Die Niere (Lende)*
kurze —
lange —
schmale —
breite —
gerade —
gesenkte —
hohle —
geschlossene —

**Il dorso**
—corto
—lungo
—dritto, orizzontale (4.1)
—insellato, concavo (4.2)
—convesso (4.3)
—di mulo
—debole
—robusto

**Il garrese**
—corto
—lungo
—basso
—elevato
—tagliente
—asciutto
—grasso
—pronunciato
—piatto

**Il ventre**
—normale
—pendente
—avvallato
—di mulo
—retratto, contratto
—di levriero

**Le reni, i lombi**
—brevi
—lunghe (i)
—strette (i)
—larghe (i)
—orizzontali
—in pendenza
—depresse (i)
—forti

**El lomo**
—corto
—largo
—recto (4.1)
—ensillado (4.2)
—convexo (4.3)
—de mulo
—débil
—fuerte

**La cruz**
—corta
—larga
—baja
—alta
—fina
—delgada
—empastada
—destacada
—plana

**El vientre**
—normal
—caído
—de vaca
—de vaca
—contraído
—de liebre

**Los riñones**
—cortos
—largos
—estrechos
—anchos
—horizontales
—caídos
—hundidos
—fuertes

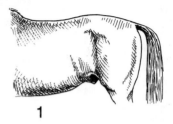

1

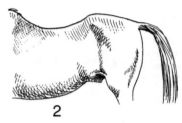

2

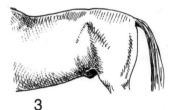

3

*The croup*
short —
long —
narrow —
broad —
flat — (4.4)
sloping —, goose-rumped (4.5)
sharp —
oval —
too high, overbuilt —
weak —
strong —

*The hip*
normal —
pointed, ragged —
prominent —

*The tail*
high-set — (4.6)
low-set — (4.7)
deep-set —
rat —
tail carriage —

*The shoulder*
short —
long —
straight, upright —
oblique —
sloping —
lean, clean —
pronounced —
loaded, coarse —
loose, weak —

*The (upper) arm*
short —

*La croupe*
—courte
—longue
—étroite
—large
—horizontale (4.4)
—inclinée, avalée (4.5)
—tranchante, de mulet
—ovale
—(trop) haute, bâti en descendant
—faible
—puissante

*La hanche*
—normale
—pointue
—proéminante, saillante

*La queue*
—haut plantée (4.6)
—bas plantée (4.7)
—enfoncée
—de rat
—le port de queue

*L'épaule ( f.)*
—courte
—longue
—verticale, droite
—oblique
—inclinée, couchée
—sèche, fine
—prononcée, bien dessinée
—charnue
—relâchée, faible

*Le bras*
—court

*Die Kruppe*
kurze —
lange —
schmale —
breite —
waagerechte — (4.4)
abfallende, abschüssige — (4.5)
abgedachte —, Eselskruppe
ovale —
hohe, überbaute —
schwache —
starke —

*Die Hüfte*
normale —
spitze —
ausgeprägte —, (hüftige —)

*Der Schweif*
hoch angesetzter — (4.6)
tief angesetzter — (4.7)
eingeklemmter —
Rattenschweif
das Tragen des Schweifes

*Die Schulter*
kurze —
lange —
steile —
schräge —
schräge abfallende —
trockene —
ausdrucksvolle —
überladene —
lose —

*Der Oberarm*
kurzer —

*La groppa*
—corta, breve
—lunga
—stretta
—larga
—orizzontale (4.4)
—obliqua, avvallata, bassa (4.5)
—scesa tagliente, di mulo
—a mandorla
—troppo alta
—debole
—forte

*L' anca ( f.)*
—normale
—cornuta
—sporgente

*La coda*
—attaccata alta (4.6)
—attaccata bassa (4.7)
—serrata
—di sorcio
il portamento della coda

*La spalla*
—corta
—lunga
—dritta
—obliqua
—inclinata
—asciutta
—pronunciata, ben disegnata
—carica di carne; —massiccia
—debole

*Il braccio*
—corto

*La grupa*
—corta
—larga
—estrecha
—ancha
—plana (4.4)
—caída (4.5)
—de mulo
—oval
—alta
—débil
—fuerte

*La cadera*
—normal
—en punta
—prominente

*La cola*
—de inserción alta (4.6)
—de inserción baja (4.7)
—hundida
—de rata
el porte de la cola

*La espalda*
—corta
—larga
—derecha
—oblicua
—inclinada
—seca
—pronunciada
—pastosa
—débil

*El brazo*
—corto

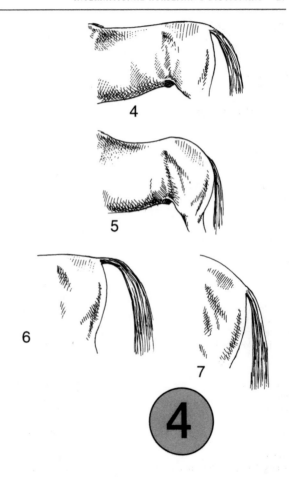

4

5

6

7

4

long —
straight —
sloping —

— long
— vertical
— oblique

langer —
steiler —
schräger —

**The elbow**
loose, weak —
— inclined outwards
— inclined inwards
tied-in —

*Le coude*
— faible
— écarté
— serré
— plaqué

*Der Ellbogen*
loser —
abstehender —
angedrückter —
gebundener —

**The forearm**
short —
long —
wide, large —
flat —
narrow —

*L'avant-bras*
— court
— long
— large
— plat
— étroit

*Der Vorarm*
kurzer —
langer —
breiter —
flacher —
schmaler —

**The knee**
large —
wide —
long —
rounded —
lean —
well-defined —
flat —
knotted —
tied-in below the knee

*Le genou*
— grand
— large
— long
— bombé
— net
— bien sculpté
— plat
— noué
— chevillé

*Das Vorderfusswurzelgelenk*
grosses —
breites —
langes —
gewölbtes —
trockenes —
ausgeprägtes —
flaches —
geschnürtes —
gedrosseltes —

**The cannon**
long —
round —
weak —
short —
wide —
strong —
clearly defined —, free from gumminess

*Le canon*
— long
— rond
— faible
— court
— large
— solide
— dégagé

*Die Röhre (Vorder-), (Hinter-)*
lange —
runde —
schwache —
kurze —
breite —
starke —
gut eingeschiente —

—lungo
—dritto
—obliquo

**Il gomito**
—debole
aperto di gomiti
serrato ai gomiti
—attaccato al torace

**L'avambraccio (m.)**
—corto
—lungo
—largo
—piatto
—sottile

**Il ginocchio**
—grande
—largo
—lungo
—arrotondato
—asciutto, netto
—ben scolpito
—piatto
—affunato
—strozzato

**Lo stinco**
—lungo
—tondo
—debole
—corto
—largo
—solido
—netto

—largo
—recto
—oblicuo

**El codo**
—débil
abierto de codos
cerrado de codos
cerrado de codos

**El antebrazo**
—corto
—largo
—ancho
—plano
—estrecho

**La rodilla**
—grande
—ancha
—larga
—globosa
—fina
—ben definida
—plana
—acodada
un estrechamiento debajo de
la rodilla

**La caña**
—larga
—redonda
—débil
—corta
—ancha
—fuerte
—bien definida

**The pastern**
short —
long —
upright —
sloping —
weak —
too long — [1]
too long — [2]

**Le paturon**
— court
— long
— droit jointé
— incliné
— long jointé
— bas jointé
— en patte d'ours

**Die Fessel**
kurze —
lange —
steile —
schräge —
weiche —
durchgetretene —
bärentatzige —

**The thigh**
long —
sloping —
well-muscled —

**La cuisse**
— longue
— inclinée
— bien musclée

**Der Oberschenkel**
langer —
schräger —
gut bemuskelter —

**The stifle**
large —
lean —
open —

**Le grasset**
— grand
— net
— ouvert

**Das Knie, das Hinterknie**
grosses —
ausgeprägtes —
offenwinkeliges —

**The second thigh, gaskin**
long —
strong —
clearly defined —
well-muscled —
full —

**La jambe**
— longue
— solide
— bien sculptée
— bien musclée
— culottée

**Der Unterschenkel**
langer —
kräftiger —
ausdrucksvoller —
gut, lang bemuskelter —
behoster —

**The hock**
long —
wide —
large —
well-defined —
lean —
— close to the ground
— at an open angle
straight —
poorly defined —
spongy —
woolly outline

**Le jarret**
— long
— large
— grand
— saillant, tranchant
— sec, net
— bas, près de terre
— droit
— droit
— estompé
— empaté
— empaté

**Das Sprunggelenk**
langes —
breites —
grosses —
kantiges —
trockenes —
tief am Boden —
offenes, abstehendes —
steiles —
verschwommenes —
schwammiges —
ausdrucksloses —

*Il pastorale, la pastoia*
—corto (a)
—lungo (a)
—dritto-giuntato (a)
—inclinato (a)
—lungo-giuntato (a)
—basso-giuntato (a)
—lungo (a) e basso (a)

*La coscia*
—lunga
—inclinata
—muscolosa

*La grassella*
—grande
—asciutta, netta
—aperta

*La gamba*
—lunga
—forte
—ben definita
—muscolosa
—piena

*Il garretto*
—lungo
—largo
—grande
—ben definito
—asciutto, netto
—vicino a terra, —basso
—aperto
—dritto
—mal definito
—spugnoso
il contorno confuso

*La cuartilla*
—corta
—larga
—vertical
—inclinada
—débil
largo de cuartilla
cuartillón

*El muslo*
—largo
—inclinado
—bien musculado

*La babilla*
—grande
—nítida
—abierta

*La pierna*
—larga
—fuerte
—bien definida
—bien musculada
—bien musculada

*El corvejón*
—largo
—ancho
—grande
—bien definido
—nítido
—bajo
—abierto
—derecho, recto
—mal definido
—empastado
—mal definido

| | | |
|---|---|---|
| weak — | — pauvre, faible | schwaches — |
| strong — | — solide | kräftiges — |
| sickle — | — coudé | säbelbeinig; zu stark gewinkeltes — |

## Conformation of the legs / Les aplombs / Die Stellung der Gliedmassen

| Conformation of the legs | Les aplombs | Die Stellung der Gliedmassen |
|---|---|---|
| normal (5.1, 5.4, 5.7, 6.1) | normal, régulier (5.1, 5.4, 5.7, 6.1) | normal (5.1, 5.4, 5.7, 6.1) |
| defective | défectueux | fehlerhaft |
| narrow at the chest (5.8) | trop serré de devant (5.8) | brusteng (5.8) |
| wide at the chest (5.9) | trop ouvert de devant (5.9) | brustweit (5.9) |
| knock-kneed [1] | genoux-clos | knieeng |
| knock-kneed [2] | genoux déviés en dedans | knieeng |
| wide at the knees (5.11) | trop ouvert de genoux (5.11) | knieweit (5.11) |
| pigeon-toed (5.10, 5.13, 6.7) | cagneux (5.10, 5.13, 6.7) | zeheneng (5.10, 5.13, 6.7) |
| feet turned out (5.12, 6.5, 6.6) | panard (5.12, 6.5, 6.6) | zehenweit (5.12, 6.5, 6.6) |
| over at the knee (5.6) | arqué, brassicourt (5.6) | vorbiegig (5.6) |
| calf-kneed, back at the knee (5.5) | genoux creux (5.5) | rückbiegig (5.5) |
| overshot fetlock (5.2) | bouleté (5.2) | steilgefesselt, kurzegefesselt (5.2) |
| undershot fetlock (5.3) | bas-jointé, long jointé (5.3) | weichgefesselt (5.3) |
| narrow behind, at the hocks (6.2) | trop serré de derrière (6.2) | Sprunggelenke zu eng (6.2) |
| wide behind, at the hocks (6.3) | trop ouvert de derrière (6.3) | Sprunggelenke zu weit (6.3) |
| cow-hocked (6.4) | panard (de derrière) (6.4) | kuhhessig (6.4) |
| bow-legged, bow-hocked (6.7) | les jarrets cambrés (6.7) | fassbeinig, 'o'-beinig (6.7) |
| standing under (6.8) | sous lui (6.8) | überständig (6.8) |
| standing stretched, open outline (6.9) | campé (6.9) | gestreckt (6.9) |

## General descriptions / Descriptions générales / Allgemeine Kennzeichen

| General descriptions | Descriptions générales | Allgemeine Kennzeichen |
|---|---|---|
| height (at withers) | la taille (au garrot ) | die Widerristhöhe |
| depth, girth | la profondeur | die Tiefe |
| | | |
| compact | uni | geschlossen |
| stocky, thick set | trapu | gedrungen |
| sturdy | costaud | stark |
| with good bone | de bonne ossature | viel Knochen |
| close to the ground | près de terre | bodennahe, kurzbeinig |
| standing over a lot of ground | la base de sustentation large | viel Boden deckend |
| lines, outlines | les contours (*m.pl.*) | die äussere Linien |
| angles | les angles (*m.pl.*) | die Winkelung |
| levers | les leviers (*m.pl.*) | die Hebel (*m.pl.*) |

il garretto debole
— solido
— a falce

**Gli appiombi**
normale (5.1, 5.4, 5.7, 6.1)
difettoso
serrato davanti (5.8)
aperto davanti (5.9)
le ginocchia chiuse
le ginocchia valghe
aperto davanti (5.11)
cagnolo (5.10, 5.13, 6.7)
mancino (5.12, 6.5, 6.6)
le ginocchia arcate (5.6)
le ginocchia da montone (5.5)
dritto giuntato (5.2)
obliquo giuntato (5.3)
i garretti stretti (6.2)
i garretti larghi (6.3)
i garretti valghi (6.4)
i garretti vari (6.7)
sotto di sé dietro e davanti (6.8)
disteso anteriormente e posteriormente (6.9)

**Caratteristiche generali**
l'altezza ( *f.*) al garrese
il perimetro toracico; la profondità del torace,
    la lunghezza —
compatto
grosso
potente
con buona ossatura
vicino a terra
la base di appoggio larga
i contorni
gli angoli
le leve

— débil
— fuerte
remetido de atrás

**Los aplomos**
normal (5.1, 5.4, 5.7, 6.1)
defectuoso
estrecho de pecho (5.8)
amplio de pecho (5.9)
cerrado de rodillas
cerrado de rodillas
patiabierto (5.11)
estevado (5.10, 5.13, 6.7)
izquierdo (5.12, 6.5, 6.6)
corvo (5.6)
transcorvo (5.5)
recto de cuartilla (5.2)
pando (5.3)
cerrado de corvejones (6.2)
hueco de corvejones (6.3)
cerrado de corvejones (6.4)
estevado (6.7)
remetido de atrás, — de delante (6.8)
plantado (6.9)

**Características generales**
la alzada
el tórax

compacto
grueso
fuerte
con buenos huesos
cerca de tierra
largo
los contornos
los ángulos
las palancas

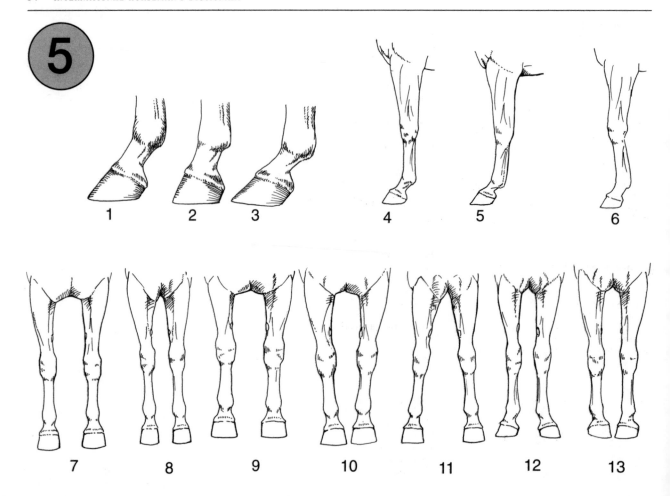

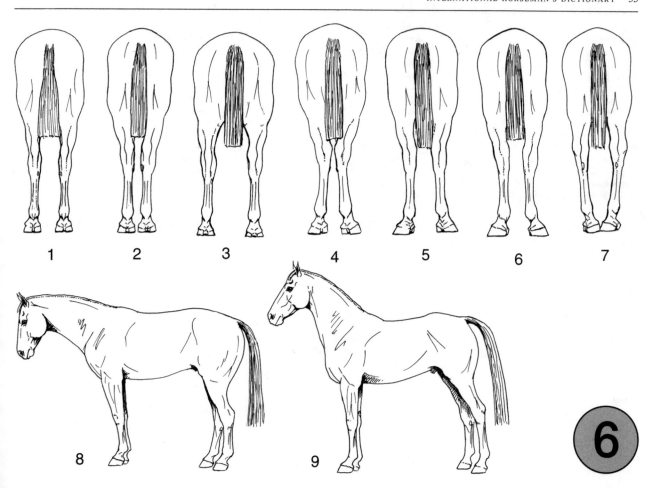

| | | |
|---|---|---|
| forehand | le devant | das Vorderteil |
| body, barrel | le milieu | das Mittelstück |
| hindquarters | l'arrière-train (*m.*) | das Hinterteil |
| upper part | le dessus | der Oberbau |
| lower part | le dessous | der Unterbau |
| frame | le cadre | der Rahmen |
| dimensions | le format | das Format |
| set four-square | carré | quadratisch |
| rectangular | rectangulaire | rechteckig |
| too high at withers | bâti en montant | vorn zu hoch |
| croup-high | haut de croupe, bâti en descendant | überbaut |
| balanced | équilibré | im Gleichgewicht |
| in proportion | proportionné | proportioniert |
| harmonious | harmonieux | harmonisch, wohlgeformt |
| noble, highly bred, quality | noble | edel |

## THE COLOURS

## LES ROBES

## DIE KÖRPERFARBEN

| | | |
|---|---|---|
| foundation | primitives | angeborene |
| simple | simples | einfache |
| composite | composées | zusammengesetzte |
| mixed | mélangées | gemischte |
| derived | dérivées | abgeleitete |

**Colours and shades**

**Robes et particularités**

**Farben und Abarten**

| | | |
|---|---|---|
| *White ( foaled)* | *Blanc (de naissance)* | *Schimmel (weissgeboren)* |
| cream, cremello | —rosé, isabelle aux crins blancs | Milch-, Blassisabel |
| porcelain —, blue-grey | —porcelaine | Porzellan- |
| dirty — | —sale | Gelb- |
| | | |
| *Black* | *Noir* | *Rappe* |
| jet —, coal — | —de jais | Glanz- |
| dull —, rusty — | —mal teint | Sommer- |
| | | |
| *Chestnut* | *Alezan* | *Fuchs* |
| light — | —clair, café au lait | Hell- |
| dark —, liver — | —foncé, — brûlé | Dunkel- |

l'anteriore (*m.*)
il tronco
il posteriore
la parte superiore
la parte inferiore
l'intelaiatura
la conformazione, le dimensioni
quadrato
rettangolare
troppo alto davanti
troppo alto dietro
ben bilanciato
proporzionato
armonioso
nobile

el tercio anterior
el tronco
el tercio posterior
la parte superior
la parte inferior
el cuadro
las dimensiones
cuadrado
rectangular
demasiado alto de la cruz
demasiado alto de la grupa
equilibrado
proporcionado, proporcional
armonioso
noble

# I MANTELLI

originari
semplici
composti
mescolati
derivati

# LAS CAPAS

primitivas
simples
compuestas
mezcladas
derivadas

**Colori e gradazioni**

*bianco (albino)*
sauro isabella
bianco porcellana
— sporco

**Capas y matices**

*albino, blanco*
cremello
blanco porcelana
blanco sucio

*Morello*
— corvino
— maltinto, — affumicato

*Negro*
— azabache
— morcillo

*Sauro*
— chiaro; caffelatte
— scuro, — bruciato

*Alazán*
— claro; pelo de vaca
— oscuro, — tostado

| | | |
|---|---|---|
| washed-out — | —lavé | Lehm- |
| dark red, reddish liver — | —brûlé | Kohl- |
| golden — | —doré | Gold- |

**Palomino** | **Palomino** | **Palomino**

**Bay (*and brown*)** | **Bai** | **Braun**
| | | |
|---|---|---|
| light — | —clair | Hell- |
| bright, clear, golden — | —doré | Gold- |
| fawn —, tawny —, bronze — | —fauve | Reh- |
| dark — | —foncé | Rot- |
| blood — | —cerise | Kirsch- |
| brown | —brun | Schwarz- |

**Dun** | **Isabelle (*aux crins noirs*)** | **Falbe**
| | | |
|---|---|---|
| yellow —, buckskin | —ordinaire | Falbe |
| blue —, mouse —, grey — | souris | Mausgrau |
| light blue — | souris clair | Aschfalb |
| dark blue — | souris foncé | Mausfalb |

**Skewbald, piebald** | **Pie** | **Schecke**
| | | |
|---|---|---|
| skewbald (chestnut and white) | —alezan | Gelb- |
| —(brown and white) | —bai | Rot- |
| piebald (black and white) | —noir | Schwarz- |

**Spotted** | **Tigré** | **Tiger**

**Roan** | **Rouan et aubère** | **Schimmel (*Stichelhaar*)**
| | | |
|---|---|---|
| strawberry —, chestnut — | aubère | Fuchsschimmel |
| red — | rouan | Braun- |
| blue — | —foncé | Rapp- |

**Grey** | **Gris** | **Schimmel (*veränderlich*)**
| | | |
|---|---|---|
| slaty blue — | —ardoise; bleu gris | Grau-, Blau- |
| dark — | —foncé | Schwarz- |
| iron — | —fer | Eisen- |
| fleabitten — | —moucheté | Fliegen- |
| speckled — | —truité | Forellen - |

—lavato
—ciliegia, — scuro, — bruciato
—dorato

*Palomino*

*Baio*
—lavato
—dorato
—fulvo
—scuro
—ciliegia
—oscuro

*Isabella (con crini neri)*
isabella (con crini neri)
sorcino
sorcino chiaro
sorcino scuro, — nero, — maltinto

*Pezzato*
sauro pezzato
baio pezzato
nero pezzato

*Tigrato*

*Roano e ubero*
ubero
roano
grigionato

*Grigio*
—ardesia
—scuro
—ferro
—moscato
—trotinato

—claro, —lavado
—oscuro, —cereza
—encendido, —guinda

*Palomino, isabelo*

*Castaño*
—claro
—normal, — giunda, — encendido
—claro
—oscuro
—cereza
—oscuro

*Bayo*
bayo
ratonero
lobero
ratonero oscuro

*Pío*
—alazán
—castaño
—negro

*Manchado*

*Overo y roano*
overo
roano (vinoso)
roano, moro (pelos negros y blancos)

*Tordo*
—pizarra
—oscuro
—muy oscuro
—mosqueado
—picazo, —atruchado

| | | |
|---|---|---|
| dappled — | — pommelé | Apfel- |

| | | |
|---|---|---|
| °*Wolf-coloured* | *Louvet* | *Wolfsfarbe* |
| (yellow and black mixed hairs, or black tipped yellow hairs and black points) | | |

| **Markings** | **Particularités des robes** | **Abzeichen** |
|---|---|---|
| *Head* | *Tête* | *Kopf* |
| 'some white hairs' | quelques poils (*m.pl.*) en tête | die Flocke |
| star | l'étoile ( *f.*) en tête, la pelote en tête | der Stern, die Blume |
| blaze | la liste large | die Blesse |
| stripe | la liste étroite | der Strich |
| bald face | la belle face | die Laterne |
| snip | le bout de nez, le ladre | die Schnippe |
| white muzzle | boit dans son blanc | das Milchmaul |

| *Limbs* | *Membres* | *Beine* |
|---|---|---|
| white markings at front of coronet | les principes (*m.pl.*) de balzane | Krone ( *f.*) weiss gesaumt |
| white markings at back of coronet | la trace de balzane | Ballen (*m.pl.*) weiss gesaumt |
| sock | la petite balzane | Vorderfessel (*m.*) weiss, Hinterfessel — |
| stocking | la grande balzane | Vorderfuss (*m.*) hoch weiss, Hinterfuss — |
| stocking rising above knee (hock) | la balzane haut-chaussée | Vorderbein (*n.*) weiss, Hinterbein — |

| *Miscellaneous* | *Divers* | *Verschiedene* |
|---|---|---|
| wall eye, silver eye | l'oeil (*m.*) vairon | das Glasauge, das Kakerlakenauge |
| dark head | le cape de maure | der Mohrenkopf |
| eel stripe, dorsal band, list | la raie de mulet | der Aalstrich |
| prophet's thumb mark | le coup de lance | der Lanzenstich |
| whorl, parting, ridge (of hair) | l'épi | der Haarwirbel |
| whole-coloured, without markings | zain | ohne jegliche Abzeichen |

## MOVEMENT, THE PACES, THE GAITS[1]

movement, action

## LE MOUVEMENT, LES ALLURES[1]

le mouvement

## DIE BEWEGUNG, DIE AKTION, DIE GANGARTEN[1]

die Bewegung

[1] *See also* p. 84.

[1] *V. aussi* p. 84.

[1] *S. auch* S. 84.

—pomellato

*Falbo, cervato*


**Particolarità**
*Testa*
alcuni peli bianchi
la stella, il fiore
la lista (larga)
la lista (stretta)
bella faccia
il liscio fra le nari
bevente in bianco

*Gambe*
la traccia di balzana davanti
la traccia di balzana al tallone
la balzana
la balzana calzata
la balzana alto calzata

*Miscellanea*
l'occhio (*m.*) gazzuolo
la capezza di moro
la riga mulina
il colpo di lancia
il remolino
zaino

# IL MOVIMENTO, L'AZIONE (*f.*), LE ANDATURE[1]

il movimento, l'azione (*f.*)

—rodado

*Lobero*
(mezcla de negro y alazán, o alazán en
   la base y negro en su extremo)

**Particularidades**
*Cabeza*
algunos pelos blancos
el lunar, el lucero
el cordón corrido
la raya
el careto
el lunar entre ollares
el belfo blanco

*Extremidades*
la corona blanca
el nudo blanco
el calzado bajo
el calzado alto
el calzado alto hasta la pierna, — la babilla

*Miscelánea*
el ojo de perdiz
la cabeza de moro, —negra
la raya de mulo
la huella dactilar
el remolino
de pelo uniforme

# EL MOVIMIENTO, LA ACCIÓN, LOS AIRES[1]

el movimiento

[1] *Vedi anche* p. 85.

[1] *Mirar también* p. 85.

| | | |
|---|---|---|
| paces, gaits | les allures (*f.pl.*) | die Gangarten (*f.pl.*) |
| tempo, cadence | la cadence | das Tempo |
| natural paces/gaits | les allures (*f.pl.*) naturelles | die natürlichen Gangarten (*f.pl.*) |
| school 'airs' | les allures (*f.pl.*) d'école | die Schulgangarten (*f.pl.*) |
| artificial 'airs' | les allures (*f.pl.*) artificielles, les airs (*m.pl.*) de fantaisie | die künstlichen Gangarten (*f.pl.*) |
| regular paces/gaits | les allures (*f.pl.*) régulières | die regelmässigen Gangarten (*f.pl.*) |
| irregular paces/gaits | les allures (*f.pl.*) irrégulières | die unregelmässigen Gangarten (*f.pl.*) |
| free, extended paces/gaits | les allures (*f.pl.*) vives, libres, étendues | die schnellen, freien, gestreckten Gangarten (*f.pl.*) |
| collected paces/gaits | les allures (*f.pl.*) raccourcies, rassemblées | die verkürzten, versammelten Gangarten (*f.pl.*) |
| principal paces/gaits | les allures (*f.pl.*) principales | die Hauptgangarten (*f.pl.*) |
| the walk | les pas | der Schritt |
| the trot | le trot | der Trab |
| the canter (gallop) | le galop | der Galopp |
| the pace (the amble) | l'amble (*m.*) | der Passgang |

## MISCELLANEOUS

**The hoof, the foot**

## DIVERS

**Le sabot, le pied**

## VERSCHIEDENES

**Der Huf, der Fuss**

| | | |
|---|---|---|
| horny wall | la paroi | die Hornwand |
| toe | la pince | die Zehe |
| heel | le talon, le glome | der Ballen |
| sole | la sole | die Sohle |
| frog | la fourchette | der Strahl |
| flat foot, dropped sole | le pied plat | der Flachhuf |
| club foot | le pied de rampin | der Bockhuf |
| hoof-bound, contracted foot | le pied encastelé | der Zwanghuf |
| sandcrack | la seime | die (durchgehende) Hornspalte |
| prick by farrier | la piqûre | das Vernageln |
| a picked-up nail | le clou de rue | der Nageltritt |
| the farrier, blacksmith | le maréchal ferrant | der Beschlagschmied |
| farriery, forge, smithy | la forge | die Schmiede |
| shoe | le fer à cheval | das Hufeisen |
| nail | le clou à ferrer | der Hufnagel |
| clench | le rivet | die Niete |
| rasp | la râpe | die Hufraspel |

le andature

il tempo, la cadenza

le andature naturali

le arie di scuola, le andature —

le andature artificiali


le andature regolari

le andature irregolari

le andature libere, allungate


le andature corte, riunite

le andature principali

il passo

il trotto

il galoppo

l'ambio (*m.*)

los aires

la cadencia

los aires naturales

los aires de escuela

los aires de fantasía, la equitación de adorno


los aires regulares

los aires irregulares

los aires libres, largos


los aires cortos, reunidos

los aires principales

el paso

el trote

el galope

el paso de andadura


## MISCELLANEA

**Lo zoccolo, il piede**

la muraglia, la parete

la punta

il tallone

la suola

la forchetta

il piede piatto

il piede rampino

il piede incastellato

la setola

l'inchiodatura (*f.*)

il chiodo da strada

il maniscalco

la forgia

il ferro

il chiodo

la ribattitura

la raspa


## MISCELÁNEA

**El casco, el pie**

la pared

las lumbres

el talón

la suela, la palma

la ranilla

palmitieso, la palma plana

el topino

el casco encastillado/amulado

la grieta en el casco (comenzando en la corona)

pinchar, la clavadura

el punzamiento, la herida punzante

el herrador

la fragua, la herrería

la herradura

el clavo

la pestaña

la escofina

| | | |
|---|---|---|
| to pare the hoof | parer le pied | den Huf richten |
| to shoe a horse | ferrer le pied | den Huf beschlagen |
| remove the shoe | déferrer le pied | das Eisen abnehmen |
| stud | le crampon | die Stolle |

**The teeth** / **Les dents** (*f.pl.*) / **Die Zähne** (*m.pl.*)

| | | |
|---|---|---|
| milk teeth [1] | les dents de lait | die Milchzähne |
| milk teeth [2] | les dents de poulain | die Fohlenzähne |
| permanent teeth | les dents de remplacement | die Ersatzzähne |
| changing the teeth | l'éruption (*f.*)/la chute des dents | der Zahnwechsel |
| incisors, biting teeth | les incisives (*f.pl.*) | die Schneidezähne |
| molars, grinding teeth | les molaires (*f.pl.*) | die Backenzähne |
| tushes, canine teeth | les crochets (*m.pl.*) | die Hakenzähne (*m.pl.*) |
| central incisors | les pinces (*f.pl.*) | die Zangen (*f.pl.*) |
| lateral incisors | les mitoyennes (*f.pl.*) | die Mittelzähne |
| corner incisors | les coins (*m.pl.*) | die Eckzähne |
| grinding surface, table | la surface de frottement | die Reibfläche |
| infundibulum, black centre | le germe de fêves, le cornet dentaire externe | die Kunde |
| periods | les périodes (*f.pl.*) | die Perioden (*f.pl.*) |
| hook, dovetail | la queue d'aronde | der Einbiss |

**Measurement, measures** / **Mensuration, mesures** / **Messung, Masse**

| | | |
|---|---|---|
| the height (at withers) | la taille au garrot | die Widerristhöhe |
| girth circumference | le tour de sangle | der Gurtumfang |
| cannon circumference, bone (measurement) | le tour du canon | der Röhrbeinumfang |
| measurement taken with tape | la mesure souple, à la chaîne | das Bandmass |
| measurement taken with stick | la mesure rigide, sous potence | das Stockmass |
| measuring tape | le ruban/la chaîne métrique | das Messband |
| measuring stick | la canne à toise | der Messtock |
| measuring unit | l'unité de mesure (*f.*) | die Messeinheit |
| •hand = 4 in. = 10.16 cm (English measure for horses) | °'hand' (main) = 4 in. (pouces) = 10, 16 cm (unité de mesure anglaise pour chevaux) | °'Hand' = 4 engl. Zoll = 10, 16 cm (engl. Messeinheit für Pferde) |
| •stone = 14 lb = 6.3 kg (English weight for riders) | °'stone' = 14 livres angl. = 6, 3 kg (unité de poids anglaise pour cavaliers) | °'Stone' = 14 engl. Pfund = 6, 3 kg (englische Gewichtseinheit für Reiter) |

| | |
|---|---|
| pareggiare il piede | recortar |
| ferrare | herrar un caballo |
| sferrare | desherrar, quitar la herradura |
| il rampone | el ramplón |

**I denti**

| | |
|---|---|
| i denti da latte | los dientes de leche |
| i denti decidui | los dientes temporales |
| i denti permanenti | los dientes definitivos |
| l'eruzione, la caduta | el cambio de dientes |
| i denti incisivi | los incisivos |
| i molari | los molares |
| gli scaglioni | los colmillos |
| i picozzi | las pinzas, las palas |
| i mezzani, i mediani | los medianos |
| i cantoni | los extremos |
| la superficie masticatoria | la tabla |
| il germe di fava | la negrilla |
| i periodi | los períodos |
| la coda di rondine | el pico de gavilán |

**La misurazione, le misure** — **La medición, las medidas**

| | |
|---|---|
| l'altezza ( *f.* ) al garrese | la alzada |
| la circonferenza al torace, il passaggio delle cinghie | el perímetro del tórax |
| la circonferenza dello stinco, — del canone | el perímetro de la caña |
| la misurazione con metro di stoffa | la medición con la cinta |
| la misurazione con metro rigido | la medición con el bastón |
| il metro di stoffa | la cinta métrica |
| l'ippometro ( *m.* ) | el bastón de medir |
| l'unità ( *f.* ) di misura | la unidad de medida |
| •'hand' = 4 pollici = 10, 16 cm (l'unità inglese di misura per cavalli) | •'hand' = 4 pulgadas = 10, 16 cm (la unidad inglesa de medida para caballos) |
| •'stone' = 14 libbre inglesi = 6, 3 kg (l'unità di peso inglese per cavalieri) | •'stone' = 14 libras inglesas = 6, 3 kg (la unidad de peso inglés para jinetes) |

| *Metric and English measures* | *Mesures métriques et anglaises* | *Metrische und englische Masse* |
|---|---|---|
| metre | mètre | Meter |
| inch | pouce | Zoll |
| foot | pied | Fuss |
| yard | yard | Yard |
| furlong | furlong | Achtelmeile |
| mile | mile | Meile |

## DISEASES AND AILMENTS

## MALADIES ET TARES

## KRANKHEITEN UND MÄNGEL

| | | |
|---|---|---|
| abscess | l'abcès (*m.*) | der Abszess |
| African horse sickness | la peste équine | die afrikanische Pferdepest |
| anaemia | l'anémie (*f.*) | die Blutarmut |
| ascarids | les ascarides (*m.pl.*) | die Spulwürmer (*m.pl.*) |
| arthritis | l'arthrite (*f.*) | die Gelenkentzündung |
| azoturia, Monday morning disease | l'hémoglobinurie (*f.*), le coup de sang, la maladie du lundi | die Feiertagskrankheit, der Kreuzverschlag, die schwarze Harnwinde |
| back sores | la pression, blessure, de selle; la plaie du garrot | der Satteldruck |
| blindness | la cécité | die Blindheit |
| bog spavin (7a) | le vessignon articulaire (au jarret) (7a) | die Kreuzgalle (7a) |
| bone spavin (7b) | l'éparvin (*m.*) (7b) | der Spat (7b) |
| bots | les gastérophiles (*m.pl.*) | die Magenbremsen (*f.pl.*) |
| broken knees (7c) | les genoux couronnés (7c) | die haarlosen Vorderfusswurzelgelenke (*n.pl.*) (7c) |
| broken wind | la pousse, l'emphysème (*m.*) pulmonaire | der Dampf |
| capped hock, capped elbow (7d) | le capelet, l'éponge (*f.*) (7d) | die Piephacke, die Stollbeule (7d) |
| cancer | le cancer | der Krebs |
| chronic obstructive pulmonary disease (COPD) | la bronchiolite chronique obstructive | die chronische obstruktive Bronchiolitis |
| colic | la colique | die Kolik |
| conjunctivitis (7e) | la conjonctivite (7e) | die Lidbindehautentzündung (7e) |
| contagious equine metritis | le métrite equine contagieuse | die kontagiöse equine Metritis |
| corns (7f) | les bleimes (*f.pl.*) (7f) | die Steingallen (*f.pl.*) (7f) |
| cough | la toux | der Husten |
| cracked heels (7g) | les crevasses (*f.pl.*) (7g) | die Mauke, das Ekzem (7g) |
| curb (7h) | la jarde (7h) | die Hasenhacke, die verletzte Linie (7h) |
| diarrhoea | la diarrhée | der Durchfall |

| *Misure metriche e inglesi* | *Medidas métricas y inglesas* | inch | foot | yard | furlong | mile |
|---|---|---|---|---|---|---|
| metro | metro | 0.0254 | 0.3048 | 0.9144 | 201.168 | 1609.3 |
| pollice | pulgada | 1 | 12 | 36 | | |
| piede | pie | | 1 | 3 | | |
| iardo | yarda | | | 1 | | |
| stadio | estadio | | | 220 | 1 | |
| miglia | milla | | | 1760 | 8 | 1 |

## MALATTIE

l'ascesso
la pesta equina
l'anemia ( *f.*)
gli ascaridi
l'artrite ( *f.*)
l'azoturia ( *f.*)

la fiaccatura

la cecità
il vescicone del garretto (7a)
lo spavenio (7b)
i gastrofili
le coronature (7c)

la bolsaggine
il cappelletto, la lupia (7d)
il cancro
la bronchite ostruttiva cronica
le coliche, i dolori
la congiuntivite (7e)
la metrite contagiosa equina
le premiture (7f)
la tosse
le ragadi (7g)
la corba (7h)
la diarrea

## ENFERMEDADES Y TARAS

el absceso
la peste equina
la anemia
los áscaris
la artritis, la inflamación de articulación
la mioglobinuria

la rozadura de montura

la ceguedad
la corvaza (7a)
el esparaván (7b)
los gastrófilos
las rodillas marcadas,
    las heridas en las rodillas (7c)
el vaho
el agrión, la bursitis (7d)
el cáncer
la bronquitis obstructiva crónica
el cólico
la conjuntivitis (7e)
la metritis contagiosa
los callos (7f)
la tos
la grieta, los talones agrietados (7g)
la corvaza (7h)
la diarrea

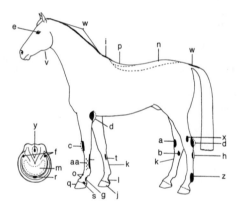

| | | |
|---|---|---|
| dust allergy | l'allergie ( *f.* ) respiratoire | die Allergie der Atemwege |
| equine influenza | la grippe equine | der seuchenhafte Husten, die Influenza |
| false curb | °la tête de métatarsien prononcée, appelée à tort 'courbe' | °Griffelbeinkopf, irrtümlicherweise als verletzte Linie angesprochen |
| fever | la fièvre | das Fieber |
| fistulous withers (7i) | la fistule du garrot (7i) | die Widerristfistel (7i) |
| fungal infection | la mycose | die Pilzerkrankung |
| glanders | la morve | der Rotz |
| grass sickness | la maladie de l'herbe | die Graskrankheit (des Pferdes) |
| heart diseases | la cardiopathie | die Herzerkrankung |
| hepatitis | l'hépatite ( *f.* ) | die Leberentzündung |
| hernia | l'hernie ( *f.* ) | der Bruch |
| insect bite | la piqûre d'insecte | der Insektenstich |
| jaundice | la jaunisse | die Gelbsucht |
| joint disease | la pathologie articulaire | die Erkrankung der Gelenke |
| lameness | la boiterie | die Lahmheit |
| laminitis (7j) | la fourbure (7j) | die Rehe, der Hufverschlag, die Hufrehe (7j) |
| lice | les poux ( *m.pl.* ), la phtiriase | die Haarlinge |
| liver fluke | la douve | der Leberegelbefall |
| lungworm infection | l'infection par strongles ( *m.pl.* ) pulmonaires | die Lungenwurm-Infektion |
| lymphangitis | la lymphangite | die Lymphangitis |
| malnutrition | la dénutrition | die Unterernährung |
| mange | la gale | die Räude |
| mites | les acariens ( *m.pl.* ) | die Milben ( *f.pl.* ) |
| mud fever (7k) | les crevasses ( *f.pl.* ) (7k) | das Ekzem (7k) |
| navicular disease | la maladie naviculaire | die chronische Hufrollenentzündung |
| obesity | l'obésité ( *f.* ) | die Fettleibigkeit |
| overreach injury (7l) | l'atteinte ( *f.* ) (7l) | der Ballentritt (7l) |
| paralysis | la paralysie | die Lähmung |
| peritonitis | la péritonite | die Peritonitis, Bauchfellentzündung |
| pneumonia | la pneumonie | die Lungenentzündung |
| poisoning | l'empoisonnement ( *m.* ) | die Vergiftung |
| puncture wound (7m) | la piqûre, le clou de rue, la plaie pénétrante (7m) | die Stichwunde, der Nageltritt (7m) |
| rain scald, dermatophilosis (7n) | l'eczéma ( *m.* ) du dos (7n) | das Ekzem (7n) |
| redworms, strongyles | les strongles ( *m.pl.* ) | die Blutwürmer ( *m.pl.* ) |
| ringbone (7o) | les formes ( *f.pl.* ) de la couronne, les formes ( *f.pl.* ) du paturon (7o) | die Schale, das Ringbein (7o) |

| | |
|---|---|
| l'allergia (*f.*) alla polvere | la alergia respiratoria |
| l'influenza (*f.*) equina | la influenza, la gripe equina |
| la falsa corva | la 'falsa corvaza' |
| | |
| la febbre | la fiebre |
| il mal del garrese (7i) | la fístula de la cruz (7i) |
| la micosi | el muermo, el moquillo |
| la morva | los ganglios |
| la malattia da erba | la enfermedad de la hierba |
| la cardiopatia | la cardiopatía |
| l'epatite (*f.*) | la hepatitis |
| l'ernia (*f.*) | la hernia |
| la puntura d'insetti | la picadura |
| l'itterizia (*f.*) | la ictericia |
| la patologia articolare | la enfermedad articular |
| la zoppia, la claudicazione | la cojera |
| la podoflemmatite, la laminite (7j) | la infosura, la laminitis (7j) |
| i pidocchi | los piojos |
| la distomatosi | la fasciola hepática |
| l'infestazione (*f.*) da | las lesiones pulmonares por larvas de |
|    strongili polmonari |    estróngilos |
| la limfangite | la limfangitis |
| la denutrizione | la desnutrición |
| la rogna | la sarna |
| gli acari | los ácaros |
| le ragadi (7k) | el arestín (7k) |
| la sindrome navicolare | la enfermedad del navicular |
| l'obesità | la obesidad |
| il raggiungersi (7l) | el alcance (7l) |
| la paralisi | la parálisis |
| la peritonite | la peritonitis |
| la polmonite | la neumonía |
| l'avvelenamento | el envenenamiento |
| la puntura, il chiodo da strada (7m) | la herida punzante, el punzamiento (7m) |
| l'eczema del dorso (7n) | la eczema del dorso (7n) |
| gli strongili | los estróngilos |
| le formelle (7o) | el sobremano, el sobrepie (7o) |

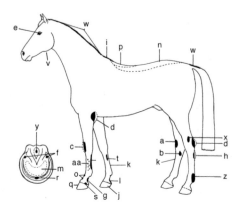

| | | |
|---|---|---|
| ringworm | la teigne | die Ringelflechte |
| roundworms, nematodes | les nematodes (*m.pl.*) | die Rundwürmer (*m.pl.*) |
| saddle sores (7p) | les plaies (*f.pl.*) dues au harnachement (7p) | der Satteldruck (7p) |
| sandcrack (7q) | la seime (7q) | die (durchgehende) Hornspalte (7q) |
| sarcoptic mange | la gale sarcoptique, l'ascabiose (*f.*) | die Kopfräude |
| seedy toe (7r) | la fourmillière (7r) | die lose Wand (7r) |
| sidebone (7s) | la forme cartilagineuse (7s) | die Hufknorpelverknöcherung (7s) |
| splint (7t) | le suros (7t) | das Überbein (7t) |
| strained tendons (7u) | les tendons chauffés, — claqués, la tendinite (7u) | die Sehnenentzündung, — klapp (7u) |
| strangles (7v) | la gourme (7v) | die Druse (7v) |
| stringhalt | l'éparvin sec, le pas de coq, harper | der Hahnentritt |
| sweet itch, allergic pruritic dermatitis (7w) | la dermite estivale récidivante (7w) | das Sommerekzem (7w) |
| tapeworms | les ténias (*m.pl.*) | die Bandwürmer (*m.pl.*) |
| tetanus | le tétanos | der Wundstarrkrampf |
| thoroughpin (7x) | le vessignon tendineux (au jarret) (7x) | die Schleimbeutelentzündung des Sprunggelenks (7x) |
| threadworms (oxyuris) | les oxyures (*m.pl.*) | die Madenwürmer (*m.pl.*), die Pfriemenschwänze (*m.pl.*) |
| thrush (7y) | la pourriture de fourchette (7y) | die Strahlfäule (7y) |
| ticks | les tiques (*f.pl.*) | die Zecken (*f.pl.*) |
| tumour | la tumeur | die Geschwulst |
| twisted gut, torsion | le volvulus | der Darmverschlingung |
| ulcer | l'ulcère | das Geschwür |
| urticaria | l'urticaire (*f.*) | der Nesselausschlag, der Quaddelausschlag |
| venereal disease | la maladie vénérienne | die Geschlechtskrankheit |
| warts | les verrues (*f.pl.*) | die Warzen (*f.pl.*) |
| whistling | le cornage | das Rohren, das Kehlkopfpfeifen |
| windgall (7z) | la molette (7z) | die Galle (7z) |
| worms | les vers (*m.pl.*) | die Würmer (*m.pl.*) |

## GENERAL VETERINARY TERMS

## TERMES VÉTÉRINAIRES GÉNÉRAUX

## ALLGEMEINE TIERÄRZTLICHE WÖRTER

| | | |
|---|---|---|
| injury | la blessure | die Verletzung |
| weakness | la faiblesse | die Schwäche |
| disease | la maladie | die Krankheit |

l'erpete (*m.*) tonsurante, la tigna
i nematodi
la fiaccatura (7p)
la setola (7q)
la rogna sarcóptica
il tarlo dello zoccolo (7r)
l'ossificazione (*f.*) della cartilagine alare (7s)
la schinella (7t)
la tendinite (7u)

l'adenite equina (7v)
l'arpeggio
la dermatite estiva (7w)
le tenie
il tetano
il vescicone trafitto, — del garretto (7x)

gli ossiuri

l'imputridimento (*m.*) del fettone (7y)
le zecche
il tumore
il volvolo
l'ulcera (*f.*)
l'urticaria (*f.*)
la malattia venerea
le verruche
il corneggio laringeo
la molletta (7z)
i vermi

la tiña
los nemátodos
las rozaduras de la silla (7p)
la grieta en el casco (comenzando en la corona), el cuarto (7q)
la sarna sarcóptica
el hormiguillo (7r)
el fibrocartilago lateral (7s)
el sobrehueso (7t)
la distensión de tendones (7u)

las paperas (7v)
el arpeo
la dermatitis estival (7w)
las tenias
el tétanos
la vejiga debajo del tendón de Aquiles (7x)

los oxiuros

la ranilla podrida (7y)
las garrapatas
el tumor
el vólvulo intestinal
la úlcera
la urticaria
la enfermedad venérea
las verrugas
el silbido laríngeo
la vejiga (7z)
las lombrices

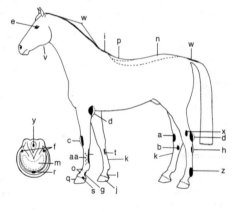

## TERMINI VETERINARI GENERALI

la ferita
la debolezza
la malattia, la condizione patologica

## TÉRMINOS VETERINARIOS GENERALES

la herida
la debilidad
la enfermedad, la dolencia, el mal

| | | |
|---|---|---|
| contagious | contagieux | ansteckend |
| soundness | la santé | die Gesundheit |
| vice | le vice (d'écurie) | die Untugend |
| bodily defects and injuries, blemishes | tares ( *f.pl.*) et maux (*m.pl.*) | Fehler und Mängel (*m.pl.*) |
| castration | la castration | die Kastration |
| to geld, to castrate | castrer | Kastrieren |
| to destroy a horse | abattre un cheval, euthanasier — | ein Pferd töten, — schlachten, — euthanasieren |
| analgesic | les analgésiques (*m.pl.*) | das schmerzstillendes Mittel |
| anaesthetic | les anesthésiques (*m.pl.*) | das unempfindlich machendes Mittel |
| anthelmintic, 'wormer' | le vermifuge | die Wurmkur, das Wurmmittel |
| antibiotics | l'antibiotique (*m.*) | das Antibiotikum |
| anti-inflammatory | anti-inflammatoire | entzündungshemmend |
| antiseptic | antiseptique | antiseptisch |
| bacteria | les bactéries ( *f.pl.*), les microbes ( *f.pl.*) | die Bakterien ( *f.pl.*) |
| bandages | les bandes ( *f.pl.*), le pansement | die Bandagen ( *f.pl.*), der Verband |
| bleeding | le saignement, l'hémorrhagie ( *f.*) | das Bluten, die Blutung |
| blood test | l'analyse ( *f.*) de sang | die Blutprobe |
| body temperature | la température corporelle | die Körperinnentemperatur |
| bruise | la meurtrissure, la contusion | die Prellung |
| burns | les brûlures ( *f.pl.*) | die Brandwunden ( *f.pl.*) |
| central nervous system | le système nerveux central | das Zentralnervensystem |
| digestive system | l'appareil (*m.*) digestif | das Verdauungssystem |
| respiratory system | l'appareil (*m.*) respiratoire | das Atmungssystem, die Atemwege (*m.pl.*) |
| circulatory system | l'appareil (*m.*) circulatoire | das Kreislaufsystem |
| musculoskeletal system | l'appareil (*m.*) locomoteur | das Skelett und die Muskeln (*m.pl.*) |
| urinary system | l'appareil (*m.*) urinaire | die Harnorgane (*n.pl.*) |
| cold compress | le pansement glacé | der Kühlverband |
| cold hosing | la douche | die Dusche |
| concussion | le choc, l'ébranlement (cérébral), la secousse, l'étonnement (*m.*) (du pied) | die Erschütterung |
| dehydration | la déshydratation | die Austrocknung |
| discharge | le jetage, l'écoulement | der Ausfluss, der Auswurf |
| dressings | les pansements (*m.pl.*) | das Verbandmaterial, die Verbände (*m.pl.*) |
| drug [1] (medicinal) | le médicament | das Medikament |
| drug [2] (prohibited substance) | le produit dopant | die Dopingmittel (*n.pl.*) |
| eczema | l'eczéma (*m.*) | das Ekzem |
| electrolytes | les électrolytes ( *f.pl.*) | die Elektrolyte (*m.pl.*) |
| faradism | la stimulation musculaire électrique | die elektrische Muskelstimulierung |

| | |
|---|---|
| contagioso | contagioso |
| la salute | la salud |
| il vizio | el vicio, el resabio |
| le tare ed i difetti | los defectos y las taras |
| la castrazione | la castración |
| castrare | castrar |
| abbattere un cavallo | eutanasiar un caballo |
| gli analgesici | los analgésicos |
| l'anestesia ( *f.* ) | los anestésicos |
| l'antielmintico, il vermifugo | el antiparasitario |
| gli antibiotici | el antibiótico |
| antinfiammatorio | antiinflamatorio |
| l'antisettico ( *m.* ) | el antiséptico |
| i batteri ( *m.pl.* ) | la bacteria |
| le bende, le fascie | las vendas |
| l'emorragia ( *f.* ) | la hemorragia |
| l'esame del sangue, — ematologico | el test sanguíneo, el análisis sanguíneo |
| la temperatura corporea | la temperatura corporal |
| la contusione | la contusión |
| le ustioni | la quemadura |
| il sistema nervoso centrale | el sistema nervioso central |
| l'apparato digerente | el aparato digestivo |
| l'apparato respiratorio | el aparato respiratorio |
| l'apparato circolatorio | el sistema circulatorio |
| l'apparato locomotore, — muscolo-scheletrico | el sistema músculo-esquelético |
| l'apparato urinario | el aparato urinario |
| l'impacco ( *m.* ) raffreddante | la compresa fría |
| la doccia fredda | la ducha de agua fría |
| la concussione (del piede), la commozione cerebrale | la contusíon, la conmoción |
| la disidratazione | la deshidratación |
| lo scolo nasale, il gemizio | la secreción |
| le medicazioni | las curas, los apósitos |
| la medicina, il farmaco | el medicamento |
| le droghe, il doping | la droga |
| l'eczema | la eczema |
| gli elettroliti | los electrolitos |
| la stimolazione elettrica della muscolatura | la estimulación eléctrica de los músculos |

| first aid | les premiers secours (*m.pl.*) | die Erste Hilfe |
| first-aid kit | la trousse de secours | die Notfallapotheke |
| flexion test | le test de fléxion | die Beugeprobe |
| fracture | la fracture | der Bruch, die Fraktur |
| hormones | les hormones (*f.pl.*) | die Hormone (*n.pl.*) |
| inflammation | l'inflammation (*f.*) | die Entzündung |
| itchiness | la démangeaison, le prurit | das Jucken, der Juckreiz |
| laser therapy | le traitement au laser | die Lasertherapie |
| lotion | la lotion | die Lotion, die Mixtur |
| microscopic examination | l'examen microscopique | die mikroskopische Untersuchung |
| muscle-relaxant drug | le myorelaxant | das muskelrelaxierende Medikament |
| nerve | le nerf | der Nerv |
| nerve-blocking | l'anesthésie (*f.*) diagnostique | die Nervenblockade, die Schmerzausschaltung am Nerv |
| numbness | l'engourdissement (*m.*) | die Empfindungslosigkeit |
| to nurse | soigner | pflegen |
| ointment | la pommade, l'onguent (*m.*) | die Salbe |
| nutrition | la nutrition | die Ernährung |
| open wound | la plaie | die offene Verletzung |
| pain | la douleur | der Schmerz |
| parasites | les parasites (*m.pl.*), le parasitisme | die Parasiten (*m.pl.*), der Parasitenbefall |
| to perform surgery | faire une intervention chirurgicale | eine chirurgische Behandlung vornehmen |
| pin firing (7aa) | les feux (*m.pl.*) en pointe (7aa) | das Punktbrennen (7aa) |
| poultice | le cataplasme | der Breiumschlag |
| powder | la poudre | das Pulver |
| pressure bandage | le pansement compressif | der Druckverband |
| pus | le pus | der Eiter |
| soreness | l'endolorissement (*m.*) | die Empfindlichkeit |
| swab | le tampon | der Tupfer |
| swelling | la tuméfaction, l'engorgement (*m.*) | die Geschwulst, das Anschwellen |
| syringe | la seringue | die Spritze |
| tranquillizer | le tranquillisant | das Beruhigungsmittel |
| ultrasound scanning | le doppler | die Ultraschalluntersuchung |
| vaccination | la vaccination | die Impfung |
| virus | le virus | das Virus |
| X-ray | l'examen (*m.*) radiographique | die Röntgenuntersuchung |

| | |
|---|---|
| il pronto soccorso | la primera cura, — ayuda |
| la cassetta del pronto intervento | el botiquín de urgencia |
| la prova di flessione | la prueba de la flexión |
| la frattura | la fractura |
| gli ormoni | las hormonas |
| l'infiammazione ( *f.*), la flogosi | la inflamación |
| il prurito | el prurito |
| la laserterapia | la terapia por laser |
| la lozione | la loción |
| l'esame microscopico | el examen microscópico |
| il miorilassante | el miorelajante |
| il nervo | el nervio |
| l'anestesia diagnostica | el bloqueo nervioso |
| | |
| l'intorpidimento (*m.*), l'insensibilità ( *f.*) | el entumecimiento, la insensibilidad |
| curare | cuidar |
| la pomata, l'unguento (*m*) | la pomada, el ungüento |
| la nutrizione | la nutrición |
| la ferita aperta | la herida |
| il dolore | el dolor |
| i parassiti | los parásitos |
| intervenire chirurgicamente | operar |
| la focatura, l'ignipuntura ( *f.*) (7aa) | los puntos de fuego (7aa) |
| l'impacco (*m.*), il cataplasma | el apósito, el emplasto |
| la polvere | el polvo |
| il bendaggio compressivo | el vendaje compresivo |
| il pus | el pus |
| l'indolenzimento | el dolor, la sensibilidad |
| il tampone | el algodón, el tampón |
| la tumefazione | la tumefacción |
| la siringa | la jeringa |
| il tranquillante | el tranquilizante |
| l'ecografia | la ecografía |
| la vaccinazione | la vacunación |
| il virus | el virus |
| l'esame (*m.*) radiografico | la radiografía |

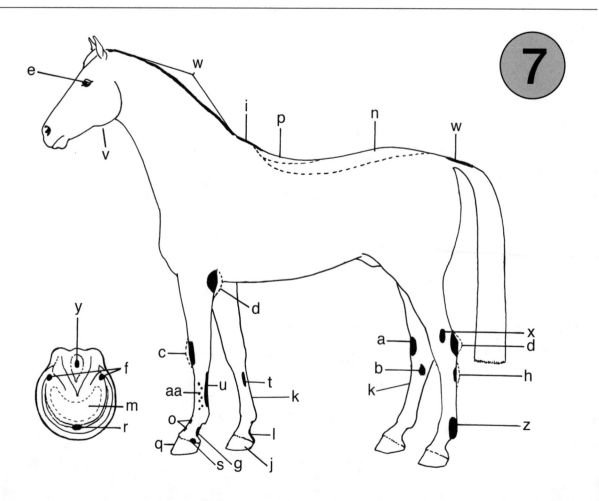

**Horse and Rider**

**Cheval et Cavalier**

**Pferd und Reiter**

**Cavallo e Cavaliere**

**Caballo y Jinete**

## SCHOOLING/DRESSAGE: BASIC NOTIONS

## DRESSAGE: NOTIONS DE BASE

## DRESSUR: GRUNDBEGRIFFE

| | | |
|---|---|---|
| forehand (8a) | l'avant-main (*m.*) (8a) | die Vorhand (8a) |
| barrel, body (8b) | le milieu (8b) | die Mittelhand (8b) |
| hindquarters, haunches (8c) | l'arrière-main (*m.*) (8c) | die Hinterhand (8c) |
| off-side | le côté hors-montoir (droit) | die rechte Seite |
| near-side | le côté montoir (gauche) | die linke Seite |
| inside | le côté intérieur | die innere Seite |
| outside | le côté extérieur | die äussere Seite |
| legs | les membres (*m.pl.*) (jambes) | die Beine (*n.pl.*) |
| forelegs (9a, 9b) | les antérieurs (*m.pl.*) (9a, 9b) | die Vorderbeine (9a, 9b) |
| hind legs (9c, 9d) | les postérieurs (*m.pl.*) (9c, 9d) | die Hinterbeine (9c, 9d) |
| pairs of legs | les bipèdes (*m.pl.*) | die Beinpaare (*n.pl.*) |
| lateral pairs (9a/d, 9b/c) | les bipèdes latéraux (9a/d, 9b/c) | die seitlichen Beinpaare (9a/d, 9b/c) |
| diagonal pairs (9a/c, 9b/d) | les bipèdes diagonaux (9a/c, 9b/d) | die diagonalen Beinpaare (9a/c, 9b/d) |
| leg on the ground (9b, 9d) | le membre à l'appui (9b, 9d) | das Standbein (9b, 9d) |
| leg in the air (9a, 9c) | le membre au soutien, au lever (9a, 9c) | das Spielbein (9a, 9c) |
| one beat, one step | une battue, un poser | ein Takt (*m.*) |
| one stride | une foulée, un pas | ein Tritt (*m.*), ein (Galopp-) Sprung (*m.*) |
| a ride, performance, test | une reprise | eine Reprise, Tour |
| track | la piste | der Hufschlag |
| halt, immobility | l'immobilité (*f.*), l'arrêt (*m.*), la station | das Stillstehen, Halten, die ganze Parade |
| impulsion | l'impulsion (*f.*) | der Schwung |
| action | l'action (*f.*) | die Aktion |
| movement | le mouvement | die Bewegung |
| direction of movement | la direction du mouvement | die Richtung der Bewegung |
| change of direction | le changement de direction | der Richtungswechsel |
| pace, gait | l'allure (*f.*) | die Gangart, der Gang |
| tempo | le temps | das Tempo |
| rhythm, cadence | le rythme, la cadence | der Rhythmus, die Kadenz, die Balance |
| straightness, straight | la rectitude, droit | das Geradegerichtetsein, gerade |
| straighten | redresser | geraderichten |
| regularity | la régularité | die Regelmässigkeit |
| suppleness | la souplesse, le moelleux | die Biegsamkeit, die Losgelassenheit, die Durchlässigkeit |
| carriage | la prestance, l'attitude (*f.*) soutenue | die Haltung |

## ADDESTRAMENTO: NOZIONI DI BASE

l'anteriore (8a)
il tronco (8b)
il posteriore (8c)
il lato destro
il lato sinistro
il lato interno
il lato esterno
gli arti
gli anteriori (9a, 9b)
i posteriori (9c, 9d)
i bipedi
i bipedi laterali (9a/d, 9b/c)
i bipedi diagonali (9a/c, 9b/d)
l'arto (*m.*) in appoggio (9b, 9d)
l'arto (*m.*) in sostegno (9a, 9c)
una battuta, una posata
una falcata, un passo
una ripresa
la pista
la fermata, l'immobilità (*f.*), la stazione
l'impulso (*m.*)
l'azione (*f.*)
il movimento
la direzione del movimento
il cambiamento di direzione
l'andatura (*f.*)
il tempo
il ritmo, la cadenza
il cavallo diritto
mettere dritto,
la regolarità
la flessibilità, la morbidezza

il portamento

## DOMA: CONCEPTOS FUNDAMENTALES

la mano delantera, el tercio anterior (8a)
el tronco (8b)
las caderas, el tercio posterior (8c)
el lado derecho
el lado izquierdo
el lado interior
el lado exterior
los miembros
los miembros anteriores (9a, 9b)
los miembros posteriores (9c, 9d)
los bípedos
los bípedos laterales (9a/d, 9b/c)
los bípedos diagonales (9a/c, 9b/d)
el miembro apoyado (9b, 9d)
el miembro elevado (9a, 9c)
un tiempo, una pisada, un tranco
un tranco, una pisada
una reprise
la pista
la parada, la inmovilidad
la impulsión
la acción
el movimiento
la dirección del movimiento
el cambio de dirección
el aire
el tiempo
el ritmo, la cadencia
la rectitud, recto/derecho
enderezar
la regularidad
la elasticidad

la prestancia

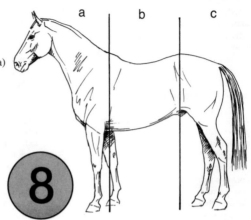

| | | |
|---|---|---|
| freedom | la franchise | die Freiheit |
| harmony | l'harmonie ( *f.* ) | die Harmonie |
| °freedom from constraint | °la décontraction, le manque de tension | •die Zwanglosigkeit, die Entspannung |
| °looseness, suppleness | °la décontraction, la souplesse | •die Losgelassenheit, locker |
| mobility | la mobilité | die Beweglichkeit, die Tätigkeit |
| inactivity | le manque d'activité | die Untätigkeit |
| base of support | la base de sustentation | die Basis |
| moment of suspension | le temps de suspension | die Schwebephase, der Moment der freien Schwebe |
| | | |
| ease | l'aisance ( *f.* ) | die Ungezwungenheit |
| purposeful, keen, sharp | perçant | schwungvoll |
| transition | la transition | der Übergang |
| longitudinal axis | l'axe longitudinal (le rachis) | die Längsachse (Wirbelsäule) |
| one-sided | l'asymétrie | die Schiefe der Achse |
| concave side | le côté concave | die hohle (schwierige) Seite |
| convex side | le côté convexe | die gewölbte (steife) Seite |
| the straight horse | le cheval droit | das geradegerichtete Pferd |
| to be (work) crooked | se traverser | schief sein |
| (lateral) flexion, 'position' (10.1) | le pli, le placer, le ploiement (10.1) | die Stellung (10.1) |
| (lateral) bend, bent (10.2) | l'incurvation ( *f.* ), incurvé (10.2) | die Biegung, gebogen (seitwärts) (10.2) |
| position | la position, le placer | die Haltung, die Stellung |
| contact with mouth | le contact | der Kontakt, die Verbindung zwischen Hand und Maul |
| | | |
| contact with bit (11.1) | l'appui ( *m.* ) (11.1) | die Anlehnung (11.1) |
| soft/confident contact | l'appui moelleux/franc, le contact — | die federnde/vertrauende Anlehnung |
| submission | la soumission | der Gehorsam |
| to accept the bit | accepter l'action de la main | anlehnen |
| yielding the mouth | la décontraction de la mâchoire | das Nachgeben des Unterkiefers |
| yielding at the poll | la flexion de la nuque | die Biegung im Genick |
| on the bit (13.1) | sur la main (13.1) | am Zügel, am Gebiss (13.1) |
| top line | la ligne du dessus | die Oberlinie |
| °bent/flexed (longitudinally) at the poll with head raised (11.2) | •le ramener, ramené (11.2) | die Beizäumung, beigezäumt (11.2) |
| °in the hand (11.3) | •la mise en main (11.3) | das An (In)-die-Hand-Stellen (11.3) |
| direct (longitudinal) flexion | la flexion directe, la mise en main | die Biegung in der Längsachse, die Beizäumung |
| | | |
| to engage the haunches/hind legs | engager les postérieurs | die Hinterhand heranstellen |
| to collect, gather, the horse | asseoir, rassembler | auf die Hanken setzen, versammeln |

| | |
|---|---|
| la franchezza | la franqueza |
| l'armonia ( *f.* ) | la armonía |
| °non contratto, la decontrazione | °la descontracción, estar sin tensión |
| °la morbidezza, la flessibilità | °la descontracción, la elasticidad |
| la mobilità | la movilidad |
| l'inattività ( *f.* ) | la pereza, la falta de actividad |
| la base d'appoggio | la base de sustentación |
| il tempo di sospensione | la suspensión, el tiempo de suspensión |
| | |
| la disinvoltura, la facilità | la soltura |
| la perspicacia, (l'azione) penetrante | decidido |
| la transizione | la transición |
| l'asse ( *m.* ) longitudinale, il rachide | el eje longitudinal |
| l'assimetria | asimétrico, torcido |
| il lato concavo | el lado cóncavo |
| il lato convesso | el lado convexo |
| il cavallo diritto | el caballo recto, el caballo derecho |
| traversarsi | tener la grupa desplazada |
| il piego laterale (10.1) | el pliegue lateral (10.1) |
| l'incurvamento, incurvato (10.2) | la incurvación, incurvado (10.2) |
| la posizione | la posición, la colocación |
| il contatto | el contacto |
| | |
| l'appoggio ( *m.* ) (11.1) | el contacto con la mano, el apoyo de la boca (11.1) |
| l'appoggio morbido, — franco, — fiducioso | el contacto muelle/franco |
| la sottomissione | la sumisión |
| accettare l'azione della mano | aceptar la embocadura |
| la decontrazione della mascella | la descontracción de la boca |
| la flessione della nuca | la flexión de la nuca |
| sulla mano (13.1) | en la mano (13.1) |
| la linea superiore | la línea superior (dorso-cuello) |
| °la posizione della testa con il piego verticale (11.2) | °el 'recoger' (11.2) |
| la messa in mano (11.3) | °la puesta en mano del caballo avanzado (11.3) |
| il piego diretto, — verticale | la flexión directa |
| | |
| impegnare le anche | remeter los posteriores |
| riunire | reunir el caballo |

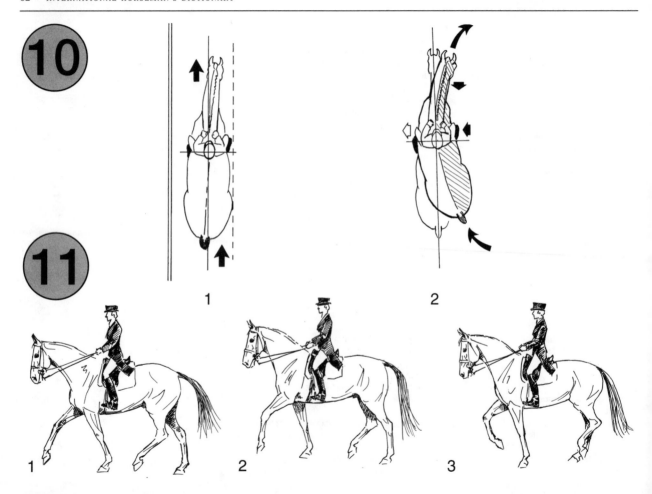

1

2

1

2

3

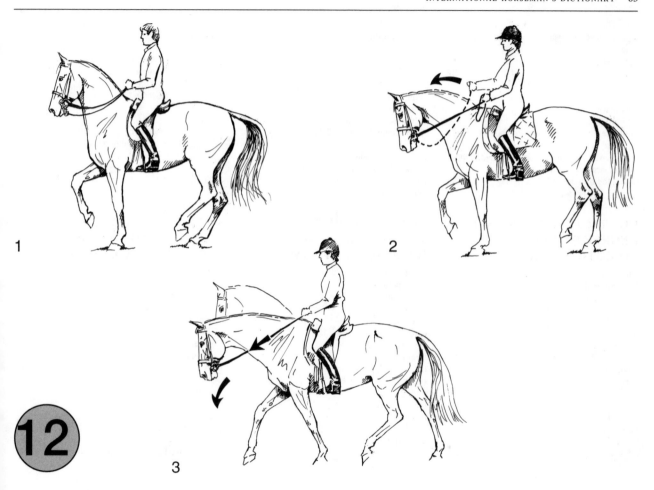

1

2

3

12

| | | |
|---|---|---|
| collection | le rassembler | die Versammlung |
| 'coming through', suppleness, permeability to the aids | la permeabilité aux aides | die Durchlässigkeit |
| lightness | la légèreté | °vollkommenes Eingehen des Pferdes auf sehr fein abgestimmte Zügel- und Schenkelhilfen, die Leichtigkeit |
| balance | l'équilibre (*m.*) | das Gleichgewicht |
| obedience | la soumission, l'obéissance | der Gehorsam |
| forward thrust | la poussée des postérieurs | der Schub |
| °releasing the contact, relaxing the rein aids (horse in self-carriage) (12.1) | •la descente de main (12.1) | °das Nachgeben der Hand, Pferd am langen Zügel (im Selbsthaltung) (12.1) |
| giving away the rein, giving and retaking the rein, stroking the neck (12.2) | céder et reprendre le contact (en caressant le cheval le long de la crinière) (12.2) | das Überstreichen (12.2) |
| taking the rein down (12.3) | l'extension (*f.*) de l'encolure, la descente de l'encolure (12.3) | Zügel-aus-der Hand-kauen-lassen (12.3) |

## CHARACTER, TEMPERAMENT, DEGREE OF TRAINING, CONDITION, FORM

## LE CARACTÈRE, LE TEMPÉRAMENT, DEGRÉ DE DRESSAGE, LA FORME

## DER CHARAKTER, DAS TEMPERAMENT, DER DRESSURGRAD, DIE FORM

| | | |
|---|---|---|
| character | le caractère | der Charakter |
| temperament | le tempérament | das Temperament |
| confidence | la confiance | das Vertrauen |
| fiery, highly strung, hot, fresh | chaud | heftig, feurig, munter |
| difficult, problem horse | difficile | schwierig |
| quiet, calm | calme, tranquille | ruhig |
| shy, nervous | peureux | scheu |
| sluggish, phlegmatic | flegmatique | phlegmatisch, schläfrig |
| cold, lazy | froid, lourd, paresseux | faul |
| tired | fatigué | müde |
| stiff | raide | steif |
| tense | tendu | gespannt |
| relaxed | détendu | entspannt |
| green, unbroken | vert | roh, ungeritten |
| to break in | débourrer | anreiten |
| a horse broken in | un cheval débourré | eine junge Remonte, angerittenes Pferd |

| | |
|---|---|
| la riunione | la reunión |
| la permeabilità agli aiuti | la permeabilidad a las ayudas |
| | |
| la leggerezza | la ligereza |
| | |
| | |
| l'equilibrio (*m.*) | el equilibrio |
| la sottomissione, l'ubbidienza (*f.*) | la obediencia |
| la spinta dei posteriori | empujar con los posteriores |
| la discesa della mano (12.1) | el descenso de mano, la 'cesión' (12.1) |
| | |
| cedere e riprendere il contatto (12.2) | soltar y coger (12.2) |
| l'estensione (*f.*) dell'incollatura (*f.*), | |
|    la discesa dell'incollatura (*f.*) (12.3) | el descenso del cuello (12.3) |

## IL CARATTERE, IL TEMPERAMENTO, LA FORMA

## EL CARÁCTER, EL TEMPERAMENTO, EL NIVEL DE DOMA, LA FORMA

| | |
|---|---|
| il carattere | el carácter |
| il temperamento | el temperamento |
| la fiducia | la confianza |
| caldo | fuerte |
| difficile | difícil |
| tranquillo | dócil, tranquilo |
| pauroso | nervioso |
| flemmatico | abúlico |
| freddo, pesante, pigro | frío, perezoso |
| affaticato | cansado |
| rigido | rígido |
| teso | tenso |
| disteso | relajado |
| verde | verde |
| iniziare l'addestramento (*m.*), domare | iniciar |
| un cavallo all'inizio (*m.*) dell'addestramento,— | un caballo echado hacia delante |
|    domato | |

| | | |
|---|---|---|
| made, well-schooled horse | cheval dressé, mis, confirmé | ein gerittenes Pferd |
| youngster, novice horse | le poulain | die Remonte, das Nachwuchspferd, das Jungpferd |
| dressage, schooling | le dressage | die Dressur |
| fitness, form, condition | la forme, la condition, l'état (*m.*) | die Form, Kondition, der Zustand |
| unfit, out of condition | bas d'état, hors de forme | schlechter Zustand, nicht fit sein |
| fit | haut d'état, en état | guter Zustand, fit sein |
| exhausted, overridden | surmené, épuisé | erschöpft |
| a delicate feeder, a shy feeder | cheval difficile à nourrir, petit mangeur | ein schlechter Fresser, — Futterverwerter |
| a good feeder | cheval sobre, facile à nourrir; gros mangeur | leichtfütterig |
| a 'good doer' | frugal | ein guter Futterverwerter |
| lungeing | le travail à la longe | das Longieren |
| long-reining | le travail aux longues rênes, — en guides, — dans les guides | die Arbeit mit der Doppellonge |

## REACTIONS OF THE RIDDEN HORSE, EVASIONS, DISOBEDIENCE

## RÉACTIONS DU CHEVAL MONTÉ, LES DÉFENSES, DÉSOBÉISSANCES

## DIE REAKTION DES REITPFERDES, DER UNGEHORSAM, WIDERSETZLICHKEIT, UNARTEN

| | | |
|---|---|---|
| mouth | la bouche | das Maul |
| green mouth | bouche qui n'est pas faite | rohes Maul |
| sensitive mouth | bouche souple, moelleuse | empfindliches Maul, weiches — |
| 'mouthy', unsteady contact | bouche bavarde | unstetes Maul, unruhiges —, 'geschwätziges' — |
| fine mouth, sensitive — | bouche fine, — aimable | durchlässiges Maul, angenehmes — |
| light mouth | bouche légère, — aimable | fein gestimmtes Maul |
| dead mouth | bouche muette | 'stummes' Maul, flaues — |
| hard mouth | bouche contractée, — dure | gespanntes Maul, hartes — |
| spoiled mouth, ruined — | bouche abimée | verdorbenes Maul |
| fresh mouth, wet — | bouche fraîche | frisches Maul |
| mouth/champ the bit | mâcher le mors | abkauen (am Gebiss) |
| foam | la bave | der Schaum |

| | |
|---|---|
| un cavallo addestrato,—messo,—confirmato | un caballo domado |
| il puledro, il cavallo debuttante | el potro |
| | |
| l'addestramento | la doma, el adiestramiento |
| la forma, la condizione, lo stato | la forma |
| fuori forma, passato di forma, in cattiva condizione | no en forma, fuera de forma |
| in forma, in condizione, in buona condizione | en forma |
| sovrallenato, finito | agotado, cansado |
| cavallo difficile da alimentare | delicado para la comida |
| cavallo sobrio/facile da nutrire, gran mangiatore | fácil para la comida |
| frugale | frugal |
| il lavoro alla corda | el trabajo a la cuerda |
| il lavoro alle redini lunghe | el trabajo a riendas largas |

## LE REAZIONI DEL CAVALLO MONTATO, LE DIFESE, LE DISUBBIDIENZE

## REACCIONES DEL CABALLO MONTADO, LAS DEFENSAS, LAS DESOBEDIENCIAS

| | |
|---|---|
| la bocca | la boca |
| la bocca non fatta | la boca poco hecha |
| la bocca sensibile, morbida | la boca blanda |
| la bocca chiacchierona, — sempre in movimento | la boca demasiado móvil |
| la bocca fine, — sensibile | la boca fina, sensible |
| la bocca leggera, — amabile | la boca blanda |
| la bocca muta | la boca insensible |
| la bocca contratta, — dura | la boca dura |
| la bocca rovinata | la boca destruída |
| la bocca fresca | la boca fresca |
| masticare il morso | tascar |
| la schiume | la espuma |

| | | |
|---|---|---|
| swallow the tongue, draw up — behind the bit | la langue serpentine | das Hochziehen der Zunge |
| stick/hang out the tongue | sortir la langue | die Zunge herausstrecken |
| put the tongue over the bit | passer la langue au-dessus du mors | die Zunge über das Mundstück legen |
| grind the teeth | grincer des dents | knirschen |
| take the bit in the teeth | prendre le mors aux dents | die Stange greifen |
| in front of the bit (hand), to pull, bore (13.2) | en avant de la main, tirer à la main, bourrer (13.2) | vor dem Zügel, schwer auf der Hand liegen, pullen (13.2) |
| above the bit, to star-gaze, above the contact (13.3) | au-dessus de la main, porter au vent (13.3) | über der Hand, mit dem Kopf nach oben ausweichen (13.3) |
| behind the bit, overbent (13.4) | acculé, derrière la main, en dedans de la main, encapuchonné (13.4) | verhalten, hinter der Hand, überzäumt (13.4) |
| to lower head abruptly and with force, to plunge | plonger | auf die Hand stossen |
| to toss the head, head-shaking | encenser | mit dem Kopf schlagen |
| in front of the legs, sensitive to — | en avant des jambes, dans les jambes, léger à jambe | leicht an dem Schenkel stehen, schenkelgehorsam, fein gestimmt |
| behind the legs, insensitive to the leg, not going forward from — | en arrière des jambes; lourd, froid aux jambes | hinter den Schenkeln, schenkelfaul |
| between legs and hands, on the aids | entre main et jambes, bien encadré | zwischen Hand und Schenkeln, an den Hilfen |
| horse with supple back | cheval assoupli du dos | Pferd mit schwingendem Rücken |
| stiff back | le gros dos | gespannter Rücken, harter — |
| hollow back | le dos creux | hohler Rücken |
| swish the tail, tail going round | fouailler de la queue | mit dem Schweif wedeln |
| to jog instead of walk | trottiner | zackeln (in Schritt) |
| disunited canter | se désunir au galop | kreuzen (im Galopp) |
| to shy | faire un écart | erschrecken, scheuen |
| to kick, lash out | ruer | ausschlagen, streichen |
| to snap, bite, nip | happer, mordre | schnappen, beissen |
| stubborn, disobedient | rétif | störrisch |
| nappy, behind the bit | rétif, acculé | stätisch, klebend |
| bucking | le saut de mouton, le bond | das Bocken, die Bocksprünge (*m.pl.*) |
| to rear | pointer, se cabrer | steigen |
| to run away, bolt | s'emballer | durchgehen |
| to throw, unseat the rider | désarçonner le cavalier | den Reiter abwerfen |

| | |
|---|---|
| la lingua serpentina | tragarse la lengua |
| far uscire la lingua | sacar la lengua |
| passare la lingua sopra il morso | pasar la lengua por encima del hierro |
| digrignare i denti | rechinar los dientes |
| prendere il morso fra i denti | morder el hierro |
| davanti alla mano, tirare la mano, puntare sulla mano (13.2) | delante de la mano, apoyarse en las riendas (13.2) |
| sopra la mano, testa al vento (13.3) | despapado (13.3) |
| seduto, dietro la mano, incappucciato (13.4) | detrás de la mano (13.4) |
| tuffarsi sulla mano | cabecear |
| incensare | sacudir la cabeza |
| davanti alle gambe, leggero alla gamba, tra le gambe | delante de la pierna |
| dietro le gambe, pesante alle gambe, freddo — | detrás de la pierna |
| tra mani e gambe, ben inquadrato | obediente a las ayudas |
| cavallo con il dorso morbido | el caballo con dorso flexible |
| cavallo che monta con il dorso | el caballo con dorso rígido |
| il dorso concavo | el dorso cóncavo |
| agitare la coda | protestar con la cola |
| trottignare | retrotar |
| disunirsi al galoppo | el galope desunido |
| fare uno scarto (di spavento) | hacer un quiebro |
| scalciare | cocear, patear |
| fare il gesto di mordere, mordere | morder, mordisquear |
| disubbidiente | desobediente |
| restio, che si difende alle gambe | pegarse |
| la smontonata | botar |
| impennarsi | encabritarse |
| scappare | desbocarse, irse de caña |
| disarcionare il cavaliere | tirar al jinete, voltear — |

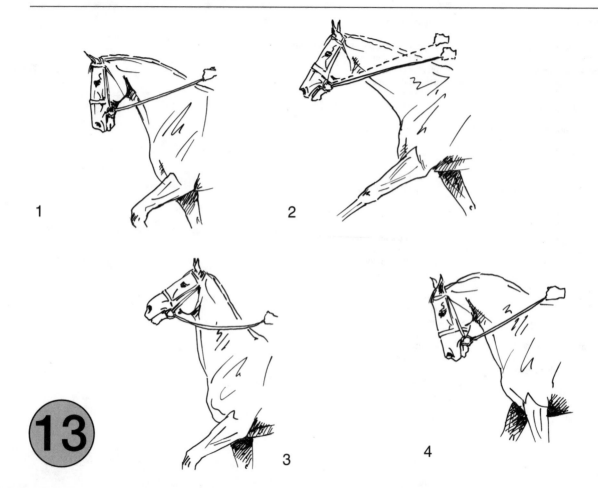

1

2

13

3

4

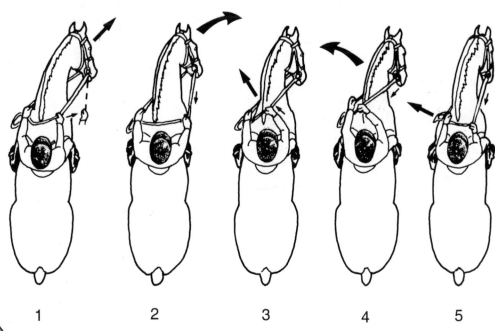

1    2    3    4    5

14

| RIDING TECHNIQUE | TECHNIQUE DE L'ÉQUITATION | REITTECHNIK |
|---|---|---|
| to mount | se mettre en selle, monter — , enfourcher le cheval | aufsitzen |
| to dismount | mettre pied à terre, descendre | absitzen |
| seat, position | l'assiette ( *f.*) (du cavalier), la position à cheval | der Sitz, die Haltung |
| normal seat, dressage — | position normale, — assis | der Dressursitz |
| forward seat, jumping — | position sportive, — en avant, — en équilibre | der leichter Sitz, Entlastungsitz, Springsitz, Vorwärtssitz |
| jockey seat | position du jockey | der Rennsitz |
| sitting too far back, backward seat, chair seat | position assis sur le  trousseqin | der Stuhlsitz |
| sitting on the fork, fork seat | position sur l'enfourchure | der Gabelsitz |
| stiff seat | assiette crispée | steifer Sitz |
| supple seat | assiette souple | weicher Sitz |
| aids | les aides ( *f.pl.*) | die Hilfen ( *f.pl.*) |
| legs, leg aids | les jambes ( *f.pl.*) | Schenkelhilfen |
| hands, rein aids | la main | (Hand), Zügelhilfen |
| the rider's weight, seat (weight) aids | le poids du cavalier, la pesée de l'assiette, le poids du corps | Gewichtshilfen |
| the back muscles, seat (pushing) aids | la poussée d'assiette | das Kreuz |
| voice, tongue clicking | la voix, l'appel de langue | die Stimme, der Zungenschlag |
| reward, to reward | la récompense, récompenser | die Belohnung, belohnen |
| caress, to caress | la caresse, caresser | das Streicheln, loben |
| to pat | tapoter | abklopfen |
| to calm | calmer | beruhigen |
| to animate | animer, réveiller | aufmuntern, wecken |
| active, passive | actif, passif | aktiv, passiv |
| (sitting) square | d'aplomb | symmetrisch |
| upper body | le buste | der Oberkörper |
| hips | les hanches ( *f.pl.*) | die  Hanken ( *f.pl.*) |
| thighs | les cuisses ( *f.pl.*) | die Oberschenkel ( *m. pl.*) |
| calves, lower legs | les mollets ( *m. pl.*) | die Unterschenkel ( *m. pl.*) |
| heels | les talons ( *m. pl.*) | die Absätze ( *m. pl.*), die Fersen ( *f.pl.*) |
| seat bones | les ischions ( *m. pl.*) | die Gesässknochen ( *m. pl.*) |
| touch with the whip | toucher avec la cravache | berühren, 'tuschieren' |
| punishment; to punish | la punition; punir, corriger | die Strafe; strafen, korrigieren |
| to hit | frapper | einen Hieb versetzen |

# TECNICA EQUESTRE

montare in sella, montare a cavallo

smontare, far piede a terra
l'assetto del cavaliere, la posizione a cavallo
la posizione accademica
la posizione sportiva

la posizione da fantino
il cavaliere seduto sulla paletta, — sfilato
    indietro
la posizione sull' inforcatura
l'assetto contratto, — rigido
l'assetto morbido, — flessibile
gli aiuti
le gambe
le mani
il peso del cavaliere, l'effetto del peso
    del corpo
la spinta dell'assetto
la voce, lo schiocco della lingua
la ricompensa, ricompensare
la carezza, accarezzare
dare leggeri colpi a mo' di carezza
calmare
animare, risvegliare
attivo, passivo
(seduto) in appiombo
il busto
le anche
le cosce
i polpacci
i talloni
gli ischi
toccare con la frusta
la punizione; punire, correggere
colpire

# TÉCNICAS DE EQUITACIÓN

montar

desmontar
el asiento, la posición
el asiento de doma
el asiento de salto, — de Caprilli

el asiento de carreras
el asiento atrasado

el asiento adelantado
el asiento rígido
el asiento flexible
las ayudas
(la acción de) las piernas
(la acción de) las manos
la acción del peso

la acción de la espalda
la voz, el chasquido de la lengua
recompensar
acariciar
palmear, dar una palmada
calmar, tranquilizar
animar
activo, pasivo
aplomado
el busto
las caderas
las muslos
las pantorrillas
los talones
los isquiones
tocar con la fusta
el castigo; castigar
pegar

| | | |
|---|---|---|
| stroke of the whip | un coup de cravache | ein Stockhieb (*m.*) |
| jab of the spurs | une attaque d'éperons | ein Spornstich (*m.*) |
| passive, inactive, leg | la jambe passive | passiver Schenkel |
| active leg | la jambe active | aktiver Schenkel, treibender — |
| action of one leg only, the leg behind the girth | l'action d'une jambe isolée | einseitiger Schenkeldruck |
| simultaneous action of the legs | l'action simultanée des jambes | beidseitige, gleichzeitige Schenkelwirkung |
| °stop the action of the legs, relax the leg aids (the horse continues the exercise with the aids relaxed) | la descente de jambes | Ausschalten der Schenkel |
| | | |
| manner of handling reins, of holding reins | la tenue des rênes, le maniement des rênes | die Zügelhaltung, Zügelführung |
| to adjust the reins | ajuster les rênes | die Zügel verpassen, aufnehmen |
| to lengthen the reins | allonger les rênes | Zügel verlängern |
| to shorten the reins | raccourcir les rênes | Zügel verkürzern |
| to give, yield | rendre, céder | nachgeben |
| active rein | la rêne tendue, — active, — résistante | tätiger, aktiver Zügel |
| passive rein | rêne passive | passiver Zügel |
| completely loose rein | rêne abandonnée sur l'encolure | hingegebener Zügel |
| inner rein | rêne intérieure | innerer Zügel |
| outer rein | rêne extérieure | äusserer Zügel |
| to separate the reins | partager les rênes | die Zügel teilen |
| reins in both hands | conduire à deux mains | beidhändig führen |
| reins in one hand | les rênes dans une seule main | Zügel in einer Hand |
| on the curb only | sur la bride seule | auf blanker Kandare |
| vibration | la vibration | °der schwingende/lockende Zügelanzug |
| half-halt | le demi-arrêt | die halbe Parade |
| jerk, jag of reins | la saccade | die Sakkade, brutaler Zügelanzug |
| opening rein (14.1) | •rêne d'ouverture (14.1) | °der offnende, richtungsweisende Zügel (14.1) |
| counter-rein (14.3) | •rêne contraire, — d'appui (14.3) | °der Gegenzügel (14.3), der gegenhaltende Zügel |
| | | |
| direct rein of opposition (14.2) | •rêne directe d'opposition (14.2) | °der 'direkte' Zügel, verwahrende Zügel (14.2) |
| indirect rein of opposition in front of the withers (14.4) | •rêne contraire d'opposition, en avant du garrot (14.4) | °der 'indirekt verwahrende' Zügel (diagonal vor dem Widerrist) (14.4) |
| indirect rein of opposition behind the withers (14.5) | •rêne contraire d'opposition, en arrière du garrot (14.5) | °der 'indirekt verwahrende' Zügel (diagonal hinter dem Widerrist) (14.5) |
| lateral aids | les aides latérales (*f.pl.*) | einseitige Hilfen (*f.pl.*) |
| diagonal aids | les aides diagonales (*f.pl.*) | diagonale Hilfen (*f.pl.*) |

| | |
|---|---|
| un colpo di frusta | el golpe de la fusta |
| un attacco con lo sperone | el golpe con las espuelas |
| la gamba passiva | la pierna passiva, inactiva |
| la gamba attiva | la pierna activa |
| l'azione di una gamba isolata | la acción de una sola pierna |
| l'azione simultanea delle gambe | la acción simultánea de las piernas |
| la discesa delle gambe | cesar la acción de las piernas |
| | |
| la tenuta delle redini, il modo di usare le redini | el modo de sostener las riendas |
| aggiustare le redini | ajustar las riendas |
| allungare le redini | alargar las riendas |
| accorciare le redini | acortar las riendas |
| cedere | ceder |
| la redine attiva, — che resiste | la rienda activa |
| la redine passiva | la rienda passiva |
| la redine abbandonata | la rienda suelta |
| la redine interna | la rienda interior |
| la redine esterna | la rienda exterior |
| separare le redini | abrir las riendas |
| condurre con due mani | sostener las riendas con las dos manos |
| le redini in una mano | las riendas en una mano |
| sulla sola redine del morso | coger/sostener sólo las riendas del bocado |
| la vibrazione | la tensión |
| la mezza fermata | la media parada |
| lo strattone | el tirón |
| la redine d'apertura (14.1) | la rienda de abertura (14.1) |
| la redine contraria, — d'appoggio (14.3) | la rienda de apoyo (14.3) |
| | |
| la redine diretta d'opposizione (14.2) | la rienda de oposición (14.2) |
| la redine contraria d'opposizione davanti al garrese, — alle spalle (14.4) | la rienda indirecta de oposición delante de las espaldas (14.4) |
| la redine contraria d'opposizione dietro al garrese, — le spalle (14.5) | la rienda indirecta de oposición detrás de las espaldas (14.5) |
| gli aiuti laterali | las ayudas laterales |
| gli aiuti diagonali | las ayudas diagonales |

| | | |
|---|---|---|
| °'combined effect', simultaneous action of hand and leg, riding into a resisting hand | •effet d'ensemble (m.), — sur l'éperon | °'Einstellung am Sporn' (Zusammenfassen der vortreibenden und verhaltenden Hilfen zu einem bestimmten Zweck), die durchhaltende Zügelhilfe |
| equestrian feel, — tact | le tact équestre | das Gefühl des Reiters, die Einfühlung, der Reitertakt |
| walk on, trot on, canter on; move off at a walk, — trot; strike off at the canter (from the halt) | partir au pas, — au trot, — au galop (de pied ferme) | anreiten im Schrift, antraben, angaloppieren (aus dem Halten) |
| to walk, trot, canter | marcher au pas, — au trot, — au galop | Schritt reiten, Trab —, Galopp — |
| to trot, canter, gallop | trotter, galoper | traben, galoppieren |
| sitting trot | le trot assis, trotter à la française | aussitzen im Trabe, werfenlassen, 'deutsch' traben |
| rising trot | le trot enlevé, trotter à l'anglaise | zum leichten Trab übergehen, leichttraben, 'englisch' traben |
| to trot on the left (right) diagonal | trotter avec le diagonal gauche (droit) | auf der linken (rechten) Diagonale traben |
| to change the diagonal | changer de diagonal au trot enlevé | die Diagonale (den Fuss) wechseln |
| left/right canter | le galop à gauche/ — à droite | der Galopp links/— rechts |
| change of leg | changer de pied | den Fuss wechseln |
| to change in the air | changer de pied en l'air | den Fuss fliegend wechseln |
| change of leg at every stride | changer de pied au temps, — du tact au tact | fliegend wechseln von Sprung zu Sprung, — à Tempo |
| counter canter | le galop à faux | der Kontergalopp |
| to change the rein | changer de direction, — de main | die Richtung wechseln, die Hand — |
| to change gait | changer d'allure | die Gangart wechseln |
| to change speed, — tempo | changer de vitesse | das Tempo wechseln |
| to extend | allonger | zulegen, verlängern, verstärken |
| to slow down, shorten | ralentir, raccourcir | abkürzen |
| the halt | l'arrêt (m.) | das Halten, die Parade, das Stillstehen |
| to halt, stop, pull up | arrêter | anhalten, parieren |
| rein back | reculer, le reculer | zurücktreten, das Rückwärtsrichten |
| immobility | l'immobilité (f.) | das Stillstehen |
| simple change | le changement de pied de 'ferme à ferme' | der einfache Galoppwechsel |

# CLASSICAL EQUITATION / ÉQUITATION CLASSIQUE / KLASSISCHE REITKUNST

| | | |
|---|---|---|
| equitation | l'équitation (f.) | das Reiten, dei Reiterei, Reitkunst |

| | |
|---|---|
| l'effetto d'insieme sullo sperone | °el efecto de conjunto (acción simultánea de piernas y manos) |
| la sensibilità, il tatto equestre | la sensibilidad ecuestre |
| partire al passo, — trotto, — galoppo (da fermo) | salir al paso, — al trote, — al galope (de la parada) |
| camminare al passo, — trotto, — galoppo | ir al paso, — trote, — galope |
| trottare, galoppare | trotar, galopar |
| il trotto seduto | el trote sentado |
| il trotto sollevato, — all'inglese | el trote levantado |
| trottare con il diagonale sinistro (destro) | trotar sobre la diagonal izquierda (derecha) |
| cambiare diagonale di trotto | cambiar de diagonal |
| il galoppo sinistro/destro | el galope a la izquierda/ — a la derecha |
| cambiare di piede | cambiar de pie |
| cambiare di piede in aria | cambiar de pie 'en el aire' |
| cambiare di piede a tempo | cambiar de pie al tranco |
| il galoppo rovescio | el galope en trocado |
| cambiare direzione, — mano | cambiar de dirección, — de mano |
| cambiare andatura | cambiar de aire |
| cambiare velocità | cambiar de velocidad |
| allungare | alargar |
| rallentare, raccorciare | acortar |
| l'alt (*m.*), la fermata | la parada |
| fermare | parar |
| indietreggiare, passi indietro | recular, el paso atrás |
| l'immobilità (*f.*) | la inmovilidad |
| il cambiamento di piede passando al passo/ — al trotto | el cambio de pie con pasos intermedios, el cambio de pie 'ferme a ferme' |

## L'EQUITAZIONE CLASSICA

l'equitazione (*f.*)

## LA EQUITACÍON CLÁSICA

la equitación

| | | |
|---|---|---|
| classical equitation | l'équitation classique | die klassische Reitkunst |
| the art of riding, academic riding, school riding | l'équitation académique, — savante, — artistique | die akademische Reitkunst, Schulreiterei |
| low school | la basse école | die niedere Schule, Kampagne-Reiterei, das Dressurreiten |
| high school, 'haute école' | la haute école | die hohe Schule |

## GENERAL EQUITATION

## ÉQUITATION PRATIQUE

## ANGEWANDTE REITKUNST

| | | |
|---|---|---|
| riding for sport | l'équitation ( *f.* ) sportive, les sports ( *m.pl.* ) équestres, sports hippiques | sportliches Reiten, der Reitsport |
| competition riding | la compétition | der Turniersport, das Turnierreiten |
| competition, test | le concours, l'épreuve ( *f.* ) | das Turnier, der Wettbewerb, die Prüfung |
| riding school, equestrian centre, riding stables | l'école d'équitation, le centre équestre, le club hippique, le poney-club | der Reitverein, der Reitstall, die Reitschule, der Ponyhof |
| leisure riding | l'équitation de loisir | das Freizeitreiten |
| hacking | l'équitation de promenade | das Promenadenreiten, Reiten im Gelände |
| hunting, riding to hounds | la chasse à courre, vénerie | das Jagdreiten, Reiten zu Hunden |
| cross-country | le cross | der Geländritt, die Geländestrecke, die Geländeprüfung |
| long-distance ride, endurance ride | le raid, la randonnée | der Distanzritt |
| touring on horseback, trekking | les voyages à cheval, la randonnée | die Reisen im Sattel, der Wanderritt, das Trekking |
| race riding | les courses ( *f.pl.* ) | das Rennreiten |
| show jumping, jumping competition | les épreuves ( *f.pl.* ) d'obstacles, le concours hippique | das Springreiten, Springturnier |
| polo | le polo | das Polo |
| equestrian games | les jeux équestres ( *m.pl.* ) | die Reiterspiele ( *n.pl.* ) |
| circus riding, (circus) high school | l'équitation de fantaisie, — de cirque | die Kunst-, Zirkus-Reiterei |
| eventing, horse trials | le concours complet | die Vielseitigkeitsprüfung, die Military |
| vaulting, voltige | la voltige équestre | das Voltigieren |
| western riding | l'équitation ( *f.* ) western | das Western-Reiten |
| hunter trial | le concours de cross | die Geländeprüfung |
| combined training | les épreuves ( *f.pl.* ) combinées | die Kombinierte Prüfung |
| point to point | le 'point-to-point' | das 'Point-to-Point' |
| gymkhana | le gymkana | das Gymkhana |
| horse ball | le Horse ball | der Horse Ball |
| carriage driving | l'attelage ( *m.* ) | das Fahren |

l'equitazione ( *f.* ) classica
l'equitazione accademica, — sapiente, — artistica
la bassa scuola

la alta scuola

la doma clásica
la equitación académica, — de alta escuela
la escuela básica, — de iniciación

la alta escuela

## L'EQUITAZIONE PRATICA

## LA EQUITACIÓN PRÁCTICA

l'equitazione ( *f.* ) sportiva; gli sport equestri, — ippici
montare in concorsi
il concorso, la gara
il club ippico, il centro ippico, il centro equestre, la scuola di equitazione, il maneggio, il pony club
l'equitazione ( *f.* ) di svago
l'equitazione ( *f.* ) di passeggio
la caccia con i cani
il cross

il raid, l'escursione ( *f.* ) equestre
il raid, il trekking, il turismo equestre, il viaggio a cavallo
le corse
il salto, il concorso di salto ostacoli

il polo
i giochi a cavallo
l'equitazione ( *f.* ) di fantasia, — di circo
il concorso completo
il volteggio
la monta americana, — Western
il concorso con la sola prova di campagna
la gara combinata
la corsa al campanile, — da punto a punto
la gincana
il gioco di palla a cavallo
gli attacchi

los deportes hípicos

montar en concursos
el concurso, la prueba
el club hípico, la escuela de equitación, la sociedad hípica, el poni club

la equitación de recreo
el paseo
la caza, la cacería a caballo
el cross

el raid
el turismo ecuestre

la carrera
el salto, la prueba de salto

el polo
los juegos ecuestres
la equitación de fantasía
el concurso completo
el volteo
la equitación 'Western'
la prueba de cross
la prueba combinada
la carrera 'point to point'
la gymkhana
el horse ball
los enganches

| | | |
|---|---|---|
| to ride astride | monter à califourchon | reiten im Herrensitz |
| — side-saddle | — en amazone | — im Damensattel |
| — bareback | — à poil | reiten ohne Sattel |
| quadrille | le quadrille | die Reiter-Quadrille |
| 'carrousel' (French equestrian display) | le carrousel | das Reiter-Karussell |
| performance test | l'épreuve ( *f.* ) de performance pour jeunes chevaux | die Leistungsprüfung |
| show class | le concours de modèles | die Materialprüfung |
| course | le stage | der Lehrgang |

| THE SCHOOL, THE MANÈGE, SCHOOL FIGURES | LE MANÈGE, LES FIGURES DE MANÈGE | DIE REITBAHN, DIE HUFSCHLAGFIGUREN |
|---|---|---|
| (indoor) school, manège | le manège, manège couvert | die Reitbahn, -schule, -halle |
| (outdoor) school | la carrière, le rectangle | der Reitplatz |
| wall | le mur | die Wand, die Mauer |
| corner | le coin | die Ecke |
| surface | le sol, la surface | der Boden |
| sand | le sable | der Sand |
| track | la piste | der Hufschlag |
| ride, bridleway | l'allée cavalière | der Reitweg, der Reiterpfad |
| to turn across the school/— down the centre line (15.1) | doubler (15.1) | halbe Reitschule, -bahn (15.1) |
| to change the rein (direction) (15.2–3) | changer de main, de direction (15.2–3) | die Hand wechseln, Richtung — (15.2–3) |
| counter-change of hand (15.4) | le contre-changement de main (15.4) | der Konter-Wechsel (15.4) |
| to change the rein through the middle of the school | doubler et changer de main | durch die halbe Bahn wechseln |
| to change the rein down the centre line | doubler dans la longueur et changer de main | durch die Länge wechseln |
| diagonal change of hand (15.2) | le changement en diagonale, changer de main en prenant la diagonale (15.2) | der Diagonalwechsel (15.2) |
| half-volte (16.2b) | la demi-volte (16.2b) | die halbe Volte (16.2b) |
| volte (16.2a, 16.2c) | la volte (16.2a, 16.2c) | die Volte (16.2a, 16.2c) |
| circle (16.3) | le cercle (16.3) | der Zirkel (16.3) |
| turn | tourner | wenden |
| centre line | la ligne du milieu | die Mittellinie |
| straight line | la ligne droite | die gerade Linie |

| | |
|---|---|
| montare a cavalcioni | montar a la jineta |
| montare da amazzone | montar a la amazona |
| montare a pelo | montar a pelo |
| la quadriglia | el conjunto, el grupo |
| il carosello | el carrusel |
| la prova di attitudine | la prueba funcional |
| | |
| la prova di modello | el concurso morfológico |
| il corso | el cursillo |

## IL MANEGGIO, LE FIGURE, GLI ESERCIZI

## EL PICADERO, LAS FIGURAS

| | |
|---|---|
| il maneggio (coperto), la cavallerizza | el picadero (cubierto) |
| il maneggio (all'aperto/scoperto), il rettangolo | la pista |
| la parete | el muro |
| l'angolo (*m.*) | el rincón, la esquina |
| il suolo | el suelo |
| la sabbia | la arena |
| la pista | la pista |
| la pista riservata ai cavalieri | el circuito |
| tagliare (15.1) | doblar (15.1) |
| | |
| cambiare di mano, — direzione (15.2–3) | el cambio de mano, el cambio de dirección (15.2–3) |
| | |
| il contro-cambiamento di mano (15.4) | el contracambio de mano (15.4) |
| il cambiamento traversale | cambiar de mano a lo ancho |
| | |
| il cambiamento longitudinale | cambiar de mano a lo largo, doblar y cambiar de mano |
| | |
| il cambiamento diagonale (15.2) | el cambio de mano por diagonal (15.2) |
| | |
| la mezza volta (16.2b) | la media vuelta (16.2b) |
| la volta (16.2a, 16.2c) | la vuelta (16.2a, 16.2c) |
| il circolo (16.3) | el círculo (16.3) |
| girare | girar, hacer una variación |
| la linea di centro | la línea de centro |
| la linea retta | la línea recta |

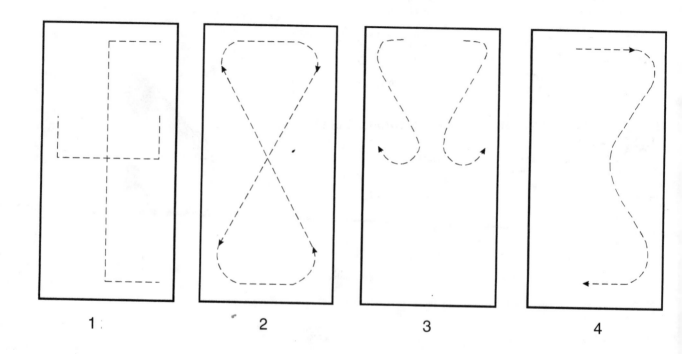

1    2    3    4

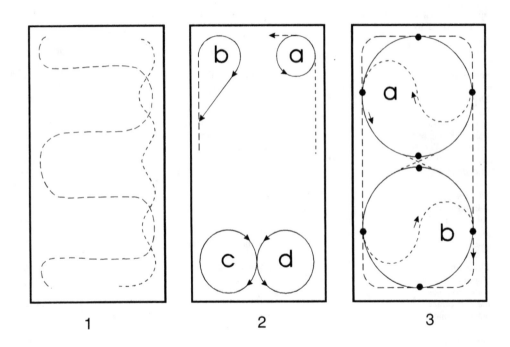

1     2     3

| | | |
|---|---|---|
| serpentine (16.1) | la serpentine (16.1) | die Schlangenlinie (16.1) |
| figure of eight | le huit de chiffre | die Acht |
| change of rein in the circle, — through the circle (16.3a, b) | changer de main sur le cercle (16.3a, b) | durch den Zirkel wechseln (16.3a, b) |
| halt | l'arrêt (*m.*) | die Parade, das Stillstehen, das Halten |
| loop | la boucle | der Bogen |

| **School paces** | **Les allures de l'école basse** | **Die Gangarten der Kampagneschule** |
|---|---|---|
| ***The walk*** | ***Le pas*** | ***Der Schritt*** |
| free walk | pas libre | freier Schritt, langer — |
| walk on a loose rein | pas, les rênes abandonnées | Schritt am hingegebenen Zügel |
| walk on a long rein | pas, les rênes longues | Schritt am langen Zügel |
| collected walk | pas rassemblé | versammelter Schritt |
| medium walk | pas moyen | Mittelschritt |
| extended walk | pas allongé | starker Schritt |
| | | |
| ***The trot*** | ***Le trot*** | ***Der Trab*** |
| working trot | trot de travail | Arbeitstrab |
| collected trot | trot rassemblé | versammelter Trab |
| medium trot | trot moyen | Mitteltrab |
| extended trot | trot allongé, — en extension | starker Trab |
| | | |
| ***The canter*** | ***Le galop*** | ***Der Galopp*** |
| working canter | galop de travail | Arbeitsgalopp |
| collected canter | galop rassemblé | versammelter Galopp |
| medium canter | galop moyen | Mittelgalopp |
| extended canter | galop allongé | starker Galopp |
| the canter | le canter, le galop | der Kanter, der Galopp |
| hand-gallop | le demi-train | Handgalopp |
| racing gallop | galop de course | Renngalopp |
| canter on the correct leg | galop juste | Innengalopp, richtiger Galopp |
| canter, off fore leading; right canter | galop sur le pied droit, — à droite | Rechtsgalopp |
| canter, near fore leading; left canter | galop sur le pied gauche, — à gauche | Linksgalopp |
| counter canter, canter counter-lead | galop à faux (c.à.d. demandé), 'contre-galop' | Aussengalopp, Konter- |
| canter on the wrong leg | galop sur le mauvais pied | falscher Galopp |
| disunited canter | galop désuni | Kreuzgalopp |

la serpentina (16.1)
l'otto (*m.*)
cambiare di mano all'interno del circolo
   (16.3a, b)
l'alt, la fermata
la curva della serpentina

la serpentina (16.1)
el ocho de cifra
el cambio de mano dentro del círculo
   (16.3a, b)
la parada
el bucle

## Le andature della bassa scuola

## Los aires básicos de escuela

### *Il passo*
il passo libero
il passo con le redini abbandonate
il passo con le redini lunghe
il passo riunito
il passo medio
il passo allungato

### *El paso*
el paso libre
el paso con riendas sueltas
el paso con riendas largas
el paso reunido
el paso medio
el paso largo

### *Il trotto*
il trotto di lavoro
il trotto riunito
il trotto medio
il trotto allungato

### *El trote*
el trote de trabajo
el trote reunido
el trote medio
el trote largo, — en extensión

### *Il galoppo*
il galoppo di lavoro
il galoppo riunito
il galoppo medio
il galoppo allungato
il galoppo lento, il galoppo
il galoppo a una velocità media
il galoppo da corsa
il galoppo giusto
il galoppo sul piede destro, — a destra
il galoppo sul piede sinistro, — a sinistra
il galoppo rovescio
il galoppo falso
il galoppo disunito

### *El galope*
el galope de trabajo
el galope reunido
el galope medio
el galope largo
el galope lento, el galope
el galope refrenado
el galope de carrera
el galope a la mano
el galope a la derecha
el galope a la izquierda
el galope en trocado
el galope cambiado
el galope desunido

## Work on two tracks, lateral work
inside leg (horse's)
leg-yielding
shoulder-in (17.1)
quarters in, head to the wall, *travers* (17.2)
half-pass (across the arena) (18.2)

quarters out, tail to the wall, *renvers* (18.1)

## Pirouettes and turns
half-turn on the haunches, half-pirouette (19)

turn on the forehand, reversed pirouette
turn on the haunches, pirouette (20)

## High school airs

### *Airs on the ground*

school walk
school trot
passage
piaffe

### *Airs above the ground*
mezair
levade
pesade
'courbette' of the French school

### *School jumps*
courbette
croupade
ballotade
capriole

## Travail de deux pistes, pas de côté
le pied de dedans
la cession à la jambe
l'épaule ( *f.*) en dedans (17.1)
la croupe en dedans, la tête au mur (17.2)
l'appuyer (*m.*)(sur la diagonale) (18.2)

la croupe en dehors, la tête en dedans (18.1)

## Les pirouettes
la demi-pirouette (19)

la pirouette renversée
la pirouette ordinaire (20)

## Les airs d'école

### *Airs près de terre*

le pas d'école
le trot d'école
le passage
le piaffer

### *Airs relevés*
le mezair
la levade
la pesade
la courbette

### *Sauts d'école*
la courbette classique
la croupade
la ballotade
la cabriole

## Arbeit auf zwei Hufschlägen, Seitengänge
der innere Fuss
das Schenkelweichen
das Schulterherein (17.1)
traversieren, der Travers, das Kruppeherein (17.2)
die Traversalverschiebung, die Traversale, der Halbtravers (18.2)

der Renvers (18.1)

## Pirouetten und Wendungen
die Kurzkehrtwendung, die Hinterhandwendung (19)
die Wendung auf der Vorhand
die Wendung auf der Hinterhand, die Hinterhandwendung, die Pirouette, die Wendung um die Hinterhand (20)

## Schulgänge

### *Schulen auf der Erde*

der Schulschritt
der Schultrab
die Passage, der spanische Tritt
die Piaffe

### *Schulen über der Erde*
der Mezair
die Levade
die Pesade
die 'französische' Kurbette

### *Schulsprünge*
die Kurbette
die Kruppade
die Ballotade
die Kapriole

| | |
|---|---|
| **Il lavoro su due piste, i passi laterali** | **El trabajo en dos pistas, los pasos de costado** |
| il piede interno | el pie interior |
| la cessione alla gamba | la cesión a la pierna |
| la spalla in dentro (17.1) | la espalda adentro (17.1) |
| la groppa in dentro, la testa al muro (17.2) | la cabeza al muro, el 'travers' (17.2) |
| appoggiare (sulla diagonale) (18.2) | el apoyo (sobre la diagonal) (18.2) |
| la groppa in fuori, la testa in dentro (18.1) | la grupa al muro, el 'renvers' (18.1) |
| **Le piroette** | **Piruetas** |
| la mezza piroetta (19) | la media pirueta (19) |
| la piroetta rovesciata | la pirueta inversa |
| girare intorno alle anche, la piroetta (20) | la pirueta directa (20) |
| **Le arie di scuola** | **Los aires de alta escuela** |
| *Le arie basse, — vicino a terra* | *Los aires fundamentales de alta escuela* |
| il passo di scuola | el paso de escuela |
| il trotto di scuola | el trote de escuela |
| il passeggio | el 'passage' |
| il piaffo, far ciambella | el 'piaffer', el piafe |
| *Le arie alte* | *°Los aires de media elevación* |
| la mezzaria | °el 'mezair' |
| la levata | la elevada, la 'levade' |
| la pesata | la posada |
| la corvetta | la corveta a la francesa |
| *I salti di scuola* | *Los saltos de escuela* |
| la corvetta classica | la corveta clásica |
| la sgroppata | la grupada |
| la ballotata | la balotada |
| la capriola | la cabriola |

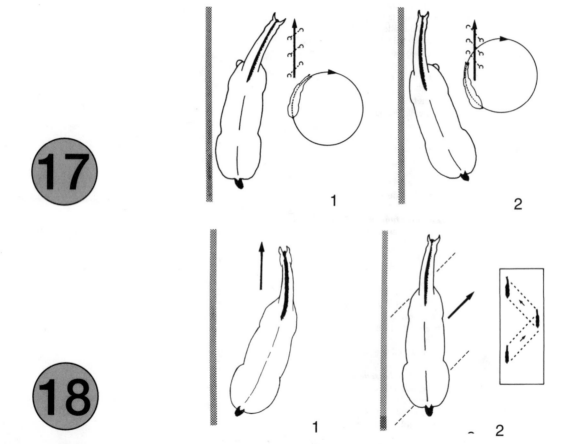

17

1

2

18

1

2

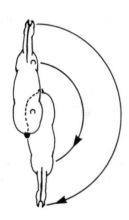

| | | |
|---|---|---|
| high school horse | le cheval d'école | das Schulpferd |
| ° 'sauteur' (a horse which performs the school jumps) | •le sauteur (cheval exécutant les sauts d'école) | °der 'Springer' (Schulpferd, das Schulsprünge ausführt) |
| work in hand | le travail à la main | die Arbeit an der Hand |
| work in long reins | le travail aux longues rênes | die Arbeit am langen Zügel |
| work in the pillars | le travail aux piliers | die Arbeit in den Pilaren |

## RIDERS

## CAVALIERS, ÉCUYERS

## REITER, BEREITER

| | | |
|---|---|---|
| rider, equestrian | le cavalier | der Reiter |
| lady rider, equestrienne, horsewoman | la cavalière, l'amazone | die Reiterin, die Amazone |
| high school rider, circus rider | l'écuyer (de cirque) | der Schulreiter, Zirkusreiter, die Schulreiterin, Zirkusreiterin |
| a true horseman | un homme de cheval, un maître | ein Pferdemann, -kenner, -freund, ein Meister |
| jockey | le jockey | der Jockey |
| trainer | l'entraîneur | der Trainer |
| pupil, student | l'élève | der Reitschüler, die -in |
| advanced rider/trainer/instructor; school rider | l'écuyer (m.), professeur | der Reitmeister, -künstler, Schulreiter, Bereiter |
| riding instructor | l'instructeur (m.) d'équitation | der Reitlehrer |
| assistant riding instructor | le moniteur | der Hilfs-Reitlehrer, der Reitwart |
| °under 'écuyer'[1] | •le sous-écuyer[1] | •der Bereiter[1] |
| °'écuyer'[1] | •l'écuyer[1] | •der Oberbereiter[1] |
| °chief 'écuyer'[1] | •l'écuyer en chef[1] | •der Chef-Bereiter, Reitmeister[1] |
| Master of the Horse | le Grand Ecuyer[1] | der Hofstallmeister[1] |
| Equerry | l'Ecuyer-Cavalcadour[1] | der Leibstallmeister[1] |
| beginner, novice | le débutant | der Anfänger |
| skilled rider | le cavalier confirmé | der geschulte Reiter |

## THE DRESSAGE TEST

## LE CONCOURS DE DRESSAGE

## DIE DRESSURPRÜFUNG

| | | |
|---|---|---|
| preliminary/novice | élémentaire | die Klasse 'A' |
| elementary | élémentaire | leicht (L) |

---

[1]Officers of the Saumur Cavalry School and officials of the Spanish Riding School in Vienna.

[1]Membres du Cadre Noir de Saumur et de l'école espagnole de Vienne.

[1]Personal des 'Cadre Noir' in Saumur und der spanischen Reitschule Wien.

| | |
|---|---|
| il cavallo di scuola | el caballo de alta escuela |
| ° il saltatore (il cavallo che esegue i salti di scuola) | ° el 'saltador' (caballo que ejecuta, los saltos de escuela) |
| il lavoro alla mano | el trabajo a la mano |
| il lavoro alle redini lunghe | el trabajo a riendas largas |
| il lavoro ai pilieri | el trabajo en los pilares |

## CAVALIERI

## JINETES

| | |
|---|---|
| il cavaliere | el jinete |
| l'ammazone ( f.) | la amazona |
| il cavaliere (di circo) | °el 'écuyer' (jinete de circo) |
| | |
| un uomo di cavalli | °el verdadero professional del caballo |
| il fantino | el jockey |
| l'allenatore (m.) | el adiestrador |
| l'allievo (m.) | el alumno |
| il cavaliere professore, il cavallerizzo | el jinete, el instructor de alta escuela |
| l'insegnante (m.) di equitazione, l'istruttore (m.) | el instructor |
| l'aiuto-istruttore (m.) | el monitor |
| °l'aiuto-scudiero[1] | °el 'sous-ecuyer', el 'Bereiter'[1] |
| °lo scudiero[1] | °el 'ecuyer', el 'Oberbereiter'[1] |
| °lo scudiero capo[1] | °el 'ecuyer en chef', el 'Chef Bereiter', el 'Reitmeister'[1] |
| °il Grande Scudiero[1] | °el 'Grand Ecuyer', el 'Hofstallmeister'[1] |
| °lo Scudiero Cavaliere[1] | °el 'Ecuyer Cavalcadour', el 'Leibstallmeister'[1] |
| il novizio | el principiante |
| il cavaliere esperto | el jinete experimentado |

## IL CONCORSO DI ADDESTRAMENTO

## LA PRUEBA DE DOMA

| | |
|---|---|
| il concorso per cavalli debuttanti elementare | la reprise nivel 1 la reprise nivel 2, 3 |

---

[1]Membra del 'Cadre Noir' di Saumur e della Scuola Spagnuola di Vienna.

[1]Los componentes del 'Cadre Noir' de Saumur y de la Escuela Española de Viena.

| | | |
|---|---|---|
| medium | de difficulté moyenne | mittel (M) |
| advanced | difficile | schwer (S) |
| | | |
| Intermediaire | la Reprise Intermédiaire | die Intermédiaire |
| free-style | la reprise libre | die Kür |
| dressage to music | la reprise libre musicale | die Kür mit Musik |
| Prix St Georges | le Prix St-Georges | der St Georg Preis (M) |
| Grand Prix | la Reprise Olympique, le Grand Prix | die Olympia-Dressurprüfung (S) |
| arena, school | la piste | der Reitplatz |
| markers | les points de repère | die Markiertafeln ( f.pl.) |
| exercises to be carried out, the test | le texte de la reprise | die Dressuraufgabe |
| execution of the test | l'exécution ( f.) | die Ausführung |
| dressage test | la reprise | die Prüfung |
| salute | le salut | der Gruss |
| error of course | l'erreur ( f.) de parcours | das Verreiten |
| error of test | l'erreur ( f.) de reprise | der Fehler bei der Aufgabe |
| sounding the bell | le coup de cloche | das Glockenzeichen |

| *Scale of marks* | *L'échelle ( f.) des notes* | *Notenschlüssel* |
|---|---|---|
| 10. excellent | 10. excellent | 10. ausgezeichnet |
| 9. very good | 9. très bien | 9. sehr gut |
| 8. good | 8. bien | 8. gut |
| 7. fairly good | 7. assez bien | 7. ziemlich gut |
| 6. satisfactory | 6. satisfaisant | 6. befriedigend |
| 5. sufficient | 5. suffisant | 5. ausreichend |
| 4. insufficient | 4. insuffisant | 4. mangelhaft |
| 3. fairly bad | 3. assez mal | 3. ziemlich schlecht |
| 2. bad | 2. mal | 2. schlecht |
| 1. very bad | 1. très mal | 1. sehr schlecht |
| 0. not executed | 0. non executé | 0. nicht ausgeführt |

# JUMPING

# SAUTS D'OBSTACLES

# SPRINGEN

| | | |
|---|---|---|
| jumper (horse) | le sauteur | das Springpferd |
| rider | le cavalier (d'obstacle) | der Springreiter |
| fence, jump, obstacle | l'obstacle (m.) | das Hindernis |
| jumping ability | l'aptitude au saut ( f.) | das Springvermögen |
| style of jumping (of horse) | le geste (du cheval) à l'obstacle | die Springtechnik (des Pferdes) |

| | |
|---|---|
| di media difficoltà | la reprise nivel 4 |
| difficile | los concursos de categoría A, B; la doma clásica |
| | |
| la ripresa intermedia | la Intermedia |
| la ripresa libera | la reprise libre (Kür) |
| la ripresa libera con musica | la reprise libre con música |
| il Premio San Giorgio | la reprise San Jorge |
| la Ripresa Olimpica, il Gran Premio | el Gran Premio |
| la pista | la pista de doma, el picadero |
| i punti di riferimento | las letras |
| il testo della ripresa | las movimientos, las figuras, el texto |
| l'esecuzione ( *f.*) | la ejecución |
| la ripresa | la reprise, la prueba de doma |
| il saluto | el saludo |
| l'errore (*m.*) di percorso | el error de recorrido |
| l'errore (*m.*) di ripresa | el error de reprise |
| il suono della campana | el toque de campana, el toque de timbre |

| *La scala dei voti* | *La escala de nota* |
|---|---|
| 10. eccelente | 10. excelente |
| 9. molto bene | 9. muy bien |
| 8. bene | 8. bien |
| 7. abbastanza bene | 7. bastante bien |
| 6. soddisfacente | 6. satisfactorio |
| 5. sufficiente | 5. suficiente |
| 4. insufficiente | 4. insuficiente |
| 3. abbastanza male | 3. bastante mal |
| 2. male | 2. mal |
| 1. molto male | 1. muy mal |
| 0. non eseguito | 0. no ejecutado |

# IL SALTO OSTACOLI

# OBSTÁCULOS

| | |
|---|---|
| il saltatore | el caballo de salto de obstáculos |
| il cavaliere da ostacoli | el jinete de salto |
| l'ostacolo (*m.*) | el obstáculo |
| l'attitudine ( *f.*) | la aptitud |
| il gesto (del cavallo), lo stile all'ostacolo | el gesto del caballo |

| | | |
|---|---|---|
| seat of rider, style of rider | le style du cavalier | der Springstil (des Reiters) |
| to school a jumper | entraîner à l'obstacle | einspringen |
| to supple, ride in | détendre, assouplir | abreiten, lösen |
| to approach | aborder, attaquer | gegenreiten, anreiten |
| to jump | sauter, franchir | springen, überwinden |
| to take off | s'enlever | abspringen, sich aufnehmen |
| to bascule | basculer | mit Basküle springen |
| to land | se recevoir | fussen, landen |
| to turn | tourner | wenden |
| to turn short, sharply | tourner court | scharf, kurz wenden |
| to take a wide turn | tourner large | im grossen Bogen wenden |
| loose jumping, — along a jumping lane | exercice en liberté, — dans un couloir | Springübung im Couloir, — Springgarten, über die Gymnastikreihe |
| | | |
| solid fence | l'obstacle (*m.*) fixe | festes, starres Hindernis |
| attractive-looking fence, inviting — | l'obstacle (*m.*) sautant | anziehendes Hindernis |
| to respect | respecter | respektieren, achten |
| to neglect, be careless | négliger | nachlässig springen, unachtsam — |
| to assess, judge, size up | taxer | taxieren, abschätzen |
| distance | la distance | der Abstand, die Distanz |
| to clear | sauter juste, — sans faute | sauber springen |
| to graze, brush | effleurer l'obstacle | das Hindernis streifen |
| to rap | toucher | anschlagen |
| to knock down | déplacer | abwerfen |
| to knock over | renverser | umwerfen |
| to run out | se dérober | ausbrechen |
| to stop | s'arrêter | stehen-bleiben |
| to refuse | refuser | verweigern |
| to fall | tomber | stürzen, fallen |
| fall | la chute | der Sturz |
| accident | l'accident (*m.*) | der Unfall |
| course, track | le parcours, la piste | die Sprungfolge, die Springbahn |
| jumping competition, show jumping | le concours hippique, concours de sauts d'obstacles | das Springturnier |
| | | |
| course designer | le chef de piste | der Parcourschef |
| to walk the course | reconnaître le parcours | die Parcoursbesichtigung |
| to ride against the clock | monter au chronomètre | gegen die Uhr reiten |
| method of judging, table — | le barème | das Richtverfahren |
| bonus points | la bonification | die Gutpunkte (*m.pl.*) |

| | |
|---|---|
| l'assetto del cavaliere | el estilo del jinete |
| l'addestramento all'ostacolo | el entrenamiento del caballo de salto |
| distendere, ammorbidire | poner flexible |
| avvicinare, affrontare | acercar, aproximar |
| saltare, superare, passare | saltar |
| alzarsi | batir |
| basculare | bascular |
| riceversi | recibirse |
| girare | girar |
| girare stretto | el giro cerrado |
| girare largo | el giro abierto |
| saltare in libertà, — nel corridoio | los ejercicios en libertad, — el callejón |
| | |
| l'ostacolo fisso | el obstáculo fijo |
| l'ostacolo invitante | el obstáculo sin difficultades |
| rispettare | respectar |
| non rispettare | no respectar |
| stimare l'ostacolo | medir |
| la distanza | la distancia |
| saltare giusto, — netto | saltar ajustado |
| sfiorare l'ostacolo (m.) | rozar |
| toccare | tocar |
| spostare | derribar |
| rovesciare | derribar |
| scartare | escaparse |
| fermarsi, piantarsi | pararse |
| rifiutare | rehusar |
| cadere | caer |
| la caduta | la caída |
| l'incidente (m.) | el accidente |
| il percorso, il campo | el recorrido |
| il concorso ippico, — di salto ostacoli | la prueba de salto de obstáculos |
| | |
| il direttore di campo | el jefe de pista |
| la ricognizione del percorso | inspeccionar el recorrido |
| far un percorso a tempo | la prueba contra reloj, montar — |
| la tabella | el baremo, el metodo de enjuiciamiento |
| i punti di bonifico | las bonificaciones |

| | | |
|---|---|---|
| penalty points | la pénalisation ( *f.pl.*) | die Strafpunkte (*m.pl.*) |
| jumping faults | les pénalités ( *f.pl.*) pour fautes aux obstacles | die Springfehler (*m.pl.*) |
| time faults | les pénalités ( *f.pl.*) de temps | die Zeitfehler (*m.pl.*) |
| jump off | le barrage | das Stechen |
| placing | le classement | die Placierung |
| to eliminate | éliminer | ausscheiden |
| prize | le prix | der Preis |
| rosette | le flot | die Rosette |
| (fences, *see* p. 154) | (obstacles: *V.* p. 154) | (Hindernisse: *siehe* Seite 154) |

| ***Competitions*** | ***Épreuves d'obstacles*** ( *f.pl.*) | ***Springkonkurrenzen*** |
|---|---|---|
| scurry jumping (with time factor) | épreuve au chronomètre | Zeitspringen |
| double accumulator | épreuve de précision, — avec barrage | Zeitspringen mit Stechen |
| 'puissance' | — de puissance | Puissance, Kanonenspringen, Mächtigkeitsspringen |
| open jumping | — nationale | die Springprüfung Klasse 'S', — ohne Teilnahmebeschränkungen |
| six bars | — des six barres | Barrierenspringen |
| fault and out | — à l'américaine | amerikanisches Jagdspringen |
| team jumping (Nations Cup) | la coupe des Nations | Mannschaftsspringen (der Preis der Nationen) |
| top score | épreuve 'choisissez vos points' | die Prüfung 'Jagd um Punkte' |

# HORSE TRIALS/EVENTING

# LE CONCOURS COMPLET

# VIELSEITIGKEITSPRÜFUNGEN

| | | |
|---|---|---|
| one-day event | le concours complet d'une journée | die Vielseitigkeitsprüfung |
| three-day event | le concours complet (de trois jours) | die Grosse Vielseitigkeitsprüfung |
| event rider | le cavalier de concours complet | der Vielseitigkeitsreiter |
| eventer (horse) | le cheval de concours complet | das Vielseitigkeitspferd, das Militarypferd |
| dressage phase | l'épreuve ( *f.*) de dressage | die Dressurprüfung |
| roads and tracks | le routier, le parcours sur routes et sentiers | die Wegestrecke |
| steeplechase | le steeple, le parcours de steeple-chase | die Rennbahn |
| cross-country phase | le cross, le parcours de cross-country | die Geländestrecke, die Querfeldeinstrecke |
| speed and endurance | l'épreuve ( *f.*) de fond | die Geländeprüfung |
| show-jumping phase | l'épreuve ( *f.*) de saut d'obstacles | die Springprüfung |
| horse inspection | l'inspection ( *f.*) vétérinaire | die Verfassungsprüfung |
| competitors' briefing | le dossard, la réunion des concurrents | die Teilnehmer-Besprechung |
| to walk the course | reconnaître le parcours | den Parcours besichtigen |
| cross-country obstacles | les obstacles (*m.pl.*) de cross | die Geländehindernisse (*n.pl.*) |

la penalizzazione

la penalización, los puntos de penalidad

le penalità agli ostacoli

la penalidad por obstáculo

le penalità per il tempo

la penalidad por tiempo

lo spareggio

el desempate

la classifica

la clasificación

eliminare

eliminar

il premio

el premio

la coccarda

la escarapela, el lazo

(ostacoli: *vedi* pagina 155)

(obstáculos: *mirar en* p. 155)

*Le categorie di salto*

*Las pruebas de salto*

la categoria al cronometro

la prueba de salto contra reloj

la categoria di precisione, — con spareggio

la prueba en dos mangas/— fases

la categoria di potenza

la prueba de potencia

la categoria nazionale

la prueba abierta, — nacional

la categoria delle sei barriere

la prueba de seis barras

la categoria all'americana

la prueba a la americana

la coppa delle nazioni

la prueba por equipos (Copa Naciones)

la categoria a punti

la prueba 'elija sus puntos'

# IL CONCORSO COMPLETO

# EL CONCURSO COMPLETO

il concorso completo di una giornata

el concurso completo de un día

il concorso completo

el concurso completo (de tres días)

il cavaliere da concorso completo

el jinete de concurso completo

il cavallo di concorso completo

el caballo de concurso completo

la prova di addestramento

la prueba de doma

la marcia, il percorso su strade e sentieri

el recorrido de campo

lo steeplechase

el steeple chase

il cross country

la prueba de cross

la prova di fondo

la prueba de fondo

la prova di salto ostacoli

la prueba de salto de obstáculos

la visita veterinaria

la inspección y examen de los caballos

la riunione dei concorrenti

la reunión de información

fare la ricognizione del percorso

inspeccionar el recorrido

gli ostacoli di cross country

los obstáculos de cross

| | | |
|---|---|---|
| start box | l'enclos de départ, la boîte de départ | die Startbox |
| ten-minute halt box | l'arrêt de dix minutes | die Zwangspause |
| optimum time | le temps optimum | die Bestzeit |
| time faults | les pénalités (*f.pl.*) (de dépassement) de temps | die Zeitfehler (*m.pl.*) |
| penalty points | les points (*m.pl.*) de pénalité | die Strafpunkte (*m.pl.*) |
| penalty zone | la zone de pénalité | die Strafzone |
| to retire | abandonner | aufgeben |
| to fall | tomber | stürzen |
| fall | la chute | der Sturz |
| elimination | l'élimination (*f.*) | der Ausschluss |
| disqualification | la disqualification | die Disqualifikation |
| ground jury | le jury de terrain | die Richtergruppe |
| interval training | l'entraînement (*m.*) fractionné | der Intervalltraining |
| outside assistance | les aides (*f.pl.*) de complaisance | die fremde Hilfe |
| starting signal | le signal de départ | das Startzeichen |
| (cross-country fences, *see* p. 154) | (les obstacles de cross: *voir* p. 154) | (feste Hindernisse: *siehe* S. 154) |

## DRIVING

## L'ATTELAGE

## DAS FAHREN

| | | |
|---|---|---|
| to drive | atteler | fahren |
| driver (whip) | le meneur | der Fahrer |
| vehicle | la voiture | der Wagen |
| carriage | la voiture | der Wagen, die Kutsche |
| dog cart | le dog-cart | der Dogcart |
| gig | le gig | der Gig |
| phaeton | le phaëton | der Phaeton |
| brake (vehicle) | le break | der Break |
| turnout | l'attelage (*m.*) | das Gespann |
| single turnout | l'attelage (*m.*) simple | der Einspänner |
| pair | l'attelage (*m.*) à deux | der Zweispänner |
| tandem | l'attelage (*m.*) en tandem | das Tandem |
| unicorn, spike | l'attelage (*m.*) en arbalète | das Einhorn |
| randem | l'attelage (*m.*) en tridem | das Random |
| team, four-in-hand | l'attelage (*m.*) à quatre | der Vierspänner, der Viererzug |
| six-in-hand | l'attelage (*m.*) à six | der Sechsspänner, der Sechserzug |
| harness | le harnais | das Geschirr |

| | |
|---|---|
| il recinto di partenza | el recinto de salida |
| l'intervallo di dieci minuti | la parada de diez minutos |
| il tempo ottimo | el tiempo óptimo |
| le penalità per il tempo | los puntos de penalidad por tiempo |
| le penalità | los puntos de penalidad |
| la zona di penalità | la zona de penalización |
| ritirarsi | retirar |
| cadere | caer |
| la caduta | la caída |
| l'eliminazione ( *f.* ) | la eliminación |
| la squalifica | la descalificación |
| la giuria | el jurado de campo |
| l'allenamento intervallato | el entrenamiento por fases |
| gli aiuti di compiacenza | las ayudas exteriores |
| il segnale di partenza | la señal de partida |
| (gli ostacoli di cross country: *vedi* pag. 155) | (los obstáculos de cross: *ver* p. 155) |

## GLI ATTACCHI, LA GUIDA

## LOS ENGANCHES

| | |
|---|---|
| attaccare, guidare | guiar |
| il guidatore, il conduttore | el cochero |
| la carrozza | el carruaje |
| la carrozza | el carruaje |
| il dog-cart | el dog-cart |
| il gig, la charrette inglese | el gig |
| il phaeton | el faeton |
| il break | el break |
| l'attacco | el enganche |
| l'attacco del singolo | la limonera |
| l'attacco in pariglia, la pariglia | el tronco |
| il tandem | el tándem |
| l'unicorn ( *m.* ), la pariglia di cavalli con cavallo davanti | el tresillo |
| tre cavalli in fila, il randem | el tiro de tres a la larga |
| il tiro a quattro | el enganche de cuatro caballos, el tiro de cuatro, el doble tronco |
| il tiro a sei | el enganche de seis caballos |
| i finimenti | las guarniciones |

| | | |
|---|---|---|
| collar (21a) | le collier (21a) | das Kumt (21a) |
| breastcollar harness | le harnais avec une bricole | das Brustblattgeschirr, das Sielengeschirr |
| full collar harness | le harnais avec un collier | das Kumtgeschirr |
| driving bridle | la bride | das Kopfstück, der Fahrzaum |
| blinkers (21b) | les oeillères ( *f.pl.* ) (21b) | die Blendklappen, die Sheuklappen ( *f.pl.* ) (21b) |
| terret (21c) | la clef de sellette (21c) | der Leinenschlüssel (21c) |
| pad (21d) | la sellette, le mantelet (21d) | das Sellett, der Kammdeckel (21d) |
| trace (21e) | le trait (21e) | der Zugstrang (21e) |
| crupper (21f) | la croupière (21f) | der Schweifriemen (21f) |
| buckle | la boucle | die Schnalle |
| shaft (21g) | le brancard (21g) | die Schere (21g) |
| pole | le timon | die Deichsel |
| tug (21h) | le porte-brancard, le bracelet de brancard (21h) | der Scherenträger, die Trageöse (21h) |
| belly band (21i) | la sous-ventrière (21i) | der kleine Bauchgurt (21i) |
| breeching (21j) | l'avaloire (21j) | das Hintergeschirr (21j) |
| breeching strap (21k) | la courroie ( *f.* ) de reculement (21k) | der Scherenriemen (21k) |
| hame (21l) | l'attelle ( *f.* ) (21l) | der Kumtbügel (21l) |
| wheels | les roues ( *f.pl.* ) | die Räder ( *n. pl.* ) |
| vehicle body | la caisse de la voiture | der Wagenkasten |
| springs | les ressorts ( *m.pl.* ) | die Federn ( *f.pl.* ) |
| swingle tree | le palonnier | das Ortscheit |
| splinter bar | la volée | die Bracke |
| seat | le siège | der Sitz, der Bock |
| footboard | la coquille | der Bockbrett |
| dashboard | le garde-crotte | das Spritzbrett |
| upholstery | le capitonnage, la sellerie | die Polsterung |
| brake | le frein | die Bremse |
| carriage lamp | la lanterne | die Wagenlampe |
| to harness up | garnir | aufschirren |
| to unharness | dégarnir | abschirren |
| to put to | atteler | anspannen |
| driving whip | le fouet | die Fahrpeitsche, die Fahrgerte |
| apron | le tablier | die Bockdecke |
| scurry driving | le parcours de maniabilité contre la montre | das Hindernisfahren nach Zeit |
| marathon driving | le marathon, l'épreuve ( *f.* ) de fond | das Geländefahren, das Streckenfahren |
| obstacle driving | la maniabilité | das Hindernisfahren |

la collana (21a)
il finimento a petto
il finimento a collana
la briglia
i paraocchi (21b)

la chiave passaredini, l'anello (*m.*) 'reggi-
    guide' (21c)
il sellino (21d)
il tirante (21e)
la groppiera e la sottocoda (21f )
la fibbia
la stanga (21g)
il timone
il bracciale portastanga (21h)
il sottopancia della dorsiera (21i)
la braga, la braca (21j)
la cinghia della braga (21k)
la maglia dei ferri (21l)
le ruote
la cassa
le molle
il bilancino
la volata (fissa)
la cassetta, il sedile
la pedana
il parafango anteriore
l'imbottitura ( *f.*)
il freno
la lanterna
vestire
svestire
attaccare
la frusta
la copertina
il percorso di velocità
la prova di fondo, la maratona
la maneggevolezza

el collerón (21a)
la guarnición con petral
la guarnición inglesa
el bridón
las anteojeras (21b)

la anilla, la llave (21c)

el sillín, el sobreaguja (21d)
el tirante (21e)
el baticola (21f )
la hebilla
el brazo, la bara, la limonera (21g)
la lanza
el porta-baras (21h)
la cincha (21i)
el reculante (21j)
la correa del reculante (21k)
la costilla del collar (21l)
las ruedas
la caja del carruaje
las ballestras
la giratoria, el juego delantero
el palo de guardia, la vara de guardia
el asiento, el pescante
la concha, la pechina
el salpicadero, el guardabarro delantero
el tapizado
el freno
el farol
aparejar, atalajar
desatalajar
enganchar
la tralla, el látigo, la fusta (inglesa)
el mandil
la prueba de obstáculos al tiempo
el marathón, la prueba de campo
el recorrido de obstáculos, la manejabilidad

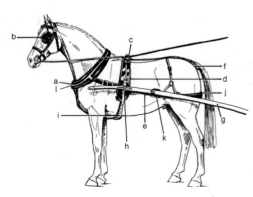

| | | |
|---|---|---|
| long-distance driving | le concours d'endurance attelé | das Distanzfahren |
| driving trials | le concours complet d'attelage (*m.*) | die Vielseitigkeitsprüfung (für Wagenpferde) |
| combined driving | le combiné attelé | die Kombinierte Prüfung (für Wagenpferde) |
| driven dressage | le dressage attelé, le test de dressage d'attelage | die Dressurprüfung für Wagenpferde |
| harness horse | le cheval d'attelage (*m.*) | das Wagenpferd, das Fahrpferd |
| carriage horse | le carrossier | das Wagenpferd, das Kutschpferd |
| hackney | le hackney | der Hackney |
| cones | les quilles ( *f.pl.*) | die Kegel (*m.pl.*) |
| groom | le groom | der Beifahrer |

## HUNTING

## CHASSE À COURRE, VÉNERIE

## REITJAGD

| | | |
|---|---|---|
| fox-hunting | la chasse au renard | die Fuchsjagd |
| cub-hunting, cubbing | la chasse au renardeau | die Jungfuchsjagd |
| stag-hunting | courir le cerf | reiten zu Hirschhunden |
| drag-hunting | chasse sur une piste odorante artificielle, drag (*m.*) | die Schleppjagd |
| quarry | le gibier, l'animal (*m.*) | das Wild, das jagdbare Tier |
| scent | la trace, l'empreinte ( *f.*) | die Witterung, die Spur |
| kennel | le chenil | der Zwinger |
| pack | la meute | die Meute |
| couple | le couple | die Koppel |
| hound | le chien | der Hund |
| master of hounds | le maître d'équipage | der Jagdherr, der Master |
| huntsman | le piqueur | der Hundsmann |
| whipper-in, whip | la valet-de-chiens | der Pikör |
| field | le peloton | das Feld |
| follower of the hunt | le veneur | der Jagdreiter |
| hunter | le cheval de chasse | das Jagdpferd |
| second horse | le cheval de rechange, de relais | das Ersatzpferd |
| meet | le rendez-vous | das Stelldichein, Rendez-vous |
| the 'gone away' | le lancer | freie Jagd |
| run | la poursuite | die Folge |
| at bay | forcer l'animal | das Stellen (des Wildes) |
| to kill | servir l'animal | Abfangen des Wildes |
| the kill | le hallali | das Halali, der Tod |
| 'curée' (parts of quarry given to the hounds) | la curée | das Küree |
| trophy | le trophée | die Trophäe |

il concorso di fondo attaccato
il concorso completo di attacchi
la gara combinata di attacchi
la prova di addestramento degli attacchi
il cavallo d'attacco, — da carrozza
il carrozziere
il hackney
i birilli
il groom

°el marathón, la prueba de campo
el concurso completo de enganches
el concurso combinado de enganches
la reprise de enganches
el caballo de enganche
el caballo de enganche
el hackney
los 'conos', los señales
el lacayo

## LA CACCIA A CAVALLO

la caccia alla volpe
la caccia ai piccoli della volpe
la caccia al cervo
la caccia alla strusa
il selvatico
la traccia, l'usta ( *f.* )
il canile
la muta
la coppia
il cane da seguito
il mastro
il cacciatore
il whipper-in
il seguito, il field
gli spettatori
il cavallo da caccia
il cavallo di ricambio, — riserva
l'appuntamento ( *m.* )
l'attacco ( *m.* ), l'inizio ( *m.* ) dell'inseguimento ( *m.* )
l'inseguimento ( *m.* )
l'abbaiare (della muta), forzare l'animale ( *m.* )
uccidere l'animale ( *m.* )
la morte
la distribuzione della carne ai cani
il trofeo

## LA CACERÍA A CABALLO

la cacería de zorro
la cacería de iniciación
la cacería de venado
la cacería por pista falsa
la cacería, la pieza
el rastreo
la perrera
la juaría
la traílla
el perro
el master
el director de cacería, el huntsman
el mozo de perros
la comitiva, el pelotón
el cazador
el caballo de caza
el segundo caballo, et caballo de repuesto
la reunión
zorro a vista
la partida
la persecución
abatir
el cobro de la pieza
la carnaza
el trofeo

| | | |
|---|---|---|
| presentation of stag's foot (end of French hunt ceremony) | les 'honneurs du pied' (France) | zeremonielle Überreichung eines Hirschlaufs (Frankreich) |
| 'green branch' (German and Polish ceremony) | le 'rameau vert' (Allemagne, Pologne) | der grüne Bruch (Deutschland, Polen) |
| brush | la queue de renard | die Fuchslunte |
| dagger | la dague, le coutelas | das Waidmesser, der Hirschfänger |
| hunting-horn (French type) | la trompe, le cor de chasse | das (frz.) Jagdhorn |
| hunting-horn (English type, carried on the saddle) | la cornette à l'anglaise (fixée à la selle) | das kurze (englische) Jagdhorn am Sattel geschnallt |
| hunting-whip | le fouet de chasse | die Hetzpeitsche |
| hunt uniform | la tenue de l'équipage (*m.*) | die Jagduniform, -dress |
| scarlet coat, pink — | l'habit rouge (*m.*) | der rote Rock |

| | |
|---|---|
| gli onori del piede | la ceremonia de presentación francesa |
| | |
| l'ultimo boccone (Germania, Polonia) | el brote de roble (uso alemán y polaco) |
| la coda della volpe | la cola del zorro |
| la daga | el machete |
| la tromba da caccia (Francia) | la trompa de caza |
| il corno da caccia (Inghilterra) | el cuerno de caza |
| | |
| la frusta da caccia | la fusta de caza |
| la livre | el traje de caza |
| la giacca rossa | la levita roja, la chaqueta roja |

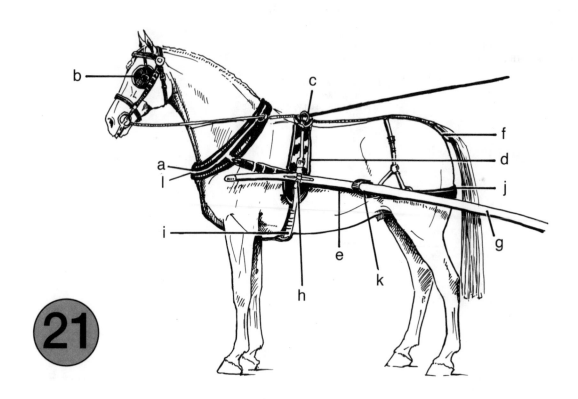

21

**Racing**

**Les Courses**

**Das Rennen**

**La Corsa**

**La Carrera**

| RACING PERSONNEL | LE PERSONNEL DE L'ÉCURIE DE COURSES | DER RENNVEREIN |
|---|---|---|
| the apprentice | l'apprenti (*m.*) | der Lehrling, der Azubi |
| lady jockey | la femme jockey | der Jockey |
| auctioneer | le commissaire-priseur | der Auktionator, der Versteigerer |
| stewards | les commissaires (*m.pl.*) | die Rennleitung |
| breeder | l'éleveur (*m.*) | der Züchter |
| connections of the horse | l'entourage du cheval (*m.*) | die Interessenten (*m.pl* ), die am Pferd Beteiligten (*m.pl*) |
| trainer | l'entraîner (*m.*) | der Trainer |
| stallion man | l'étalonnier (*m.*) | der Hengstwärter |
| handicapper | le handicapeur | der Ausgleicher |
| lad | le lad | der Pfleger |
| jockey | le jockey | der Jockey |
| judge | le juge | der Richter |
| clerk of the scales | le juge responsable de la pesée | der Auswieger |
| owner | le propriétaire | der Besitzer |
| lady owner | la propriétaire | die Besitzerin |
| owner-breeder | l'éleveur propriétaire | der Besitzer gleich Züchter |
| owner-trainer | le propriétaire-entraîneur | der Besitzer gleich Trainer |
| clerk of the course | le secrétaire de l'hippodrome | der Manager der Rennbahn |
| the starter | le starter | der Starter |
| punter | le turfiste | der Wetter |
| veterinary officer, veterinary surgeon | le vétérinaire | der Bahntierarzt |

| RACING ADMINISTRATION | L'ADMINISTRATION DES COURSES | DIE VERWALTUNG, DIE RENNBEHÖRDE |
|---|---|---|
| purses | les allocations ( *f.pl.* ) | die Rennpreise (*m.pl.*) |
| appeal | l'appel (*m.*) | der Widerspruch |
| partnership | l'association ( *f.* ) | die Teilhaberschaft |
| syndication | le syndicat | das Syndikat |
| transfer of entries | la cession d'engagements | die Veröffentlichung der Nennungen |
| age specifications | les dénominations ( *f.pl.* ) | das Altersgewichtsrennen |
| colts | les poulains entiers (*m.pl.*) | die zwei-/dreijähringen Hengste (*n.pl.*) |
| geldings | les hongres (*m.pl.*) | die Wallache (*m.pl.*) |

# IL PERSONALE DELLA SCUDERIA DA CORSA

l'allievo fantino (*m.*)
la fantina, l'amazzone (amateur) (*f.*)
il banditore
i commissari
l'allevatore (*m.*)
il mondo del cavallo

l'allenatore (*m.*), il trainer
l'uomo dello stallone
l'handicapper
l'uomo (*m.*) di scuderia
il fantino
il giudice all'arrivo
il commissario al peso
il proprietario
la proprietaria
l'allevatore (*m.*) proprietario
l'allenatore (*m.*) proprietario
il segretario della società di corse
lo starter
il giocatore
il veterinario di servizio

# L'AMMINISTRAZIONE

i premi
il reclamo
il comproprietà
il sindacato
la cessione delle iscrizioni
l'età (*f.*)
i maschi, i cavalli
i castroni

# GENTE DEL TURF

el aprendíz
la amazona
el subastador
los comisarios
el criador
el alrededor del caballo, la cuadra

el entrenador, el preparador
el paradista
el handicapper
el groom, el palafrenero
el jockey
el juez
el juez de peso
el proprietario
la proprietaria
el criador-proprietario
el proprietario-entrenador
el secretario de hipódromo
el juez de salida
el apostador
el veterinario oficial

# LA ADMINISTRACIÓN

los premios
la llamada
los copropietarios
el sindicato
la cesión de entradas
las especificaciones de la edad
los potros
los castrados

| fillies | les pouliches (*f.pl.*) | die zwei-/dreijährigen Stuten (*f.pl.*) |
| not eligible to race | pas qualifié | unqualifiziert für Rennen |
| disqualified from final placings | distancé | disqualifiziert für eine Placierung |
| entry | l'engagement (*m.*) | die Nennung |
| to lodge an objection | déposer une réclamation | Protest einlegen |
| jockey's licence | la licence de jockey | die Jockey-Lizenz |
| apprentice's licence | la licence d'apprenti | die Auszubildende-Lizenz, Lehrlings-Lizenz |
| trainer's licence | la licence d'entraîner | die Trainer-Lizenz |
| passport | le passeport | der Pferdepass |
| registration certificate | le certificat d'origine | der Abstammungsnachweis |
| vaccination certificate | le feuillet de vaccination | der Impfpass |
| trainer's permit | le permis d'entraîner | der Trainerausweis/- erlaubnis |
| private sale | la vente à l'amiable | der Privatverkauf |
| auction | la vente aux enchères | die Auktion |
| sale with a reserve price | la vente avec réserve | der Verkauf mit Mindestpreis, — Reservepreis |
| sale without a reserve price | la vente sans réserve | der Verkauf ohne Mindestpreis, — Reservepreis |

## RACE CATEGORIES

## LES CATÉGORIES (*f.pl.*)

## ART (*f.pl.*) DER RENNEN

| condition race | la course à conditions | das eingeschränkte Rennen |
| weight for age event | la course à poids pour âge | das Altersgewichtsrennen |
| classic race | la course classique | das klassische Rennen |
| category race | la course de catégorie | das Handicaprennen |
| jumping race | la course à obstacles | das Hindernisrennen |
| hurdle race | la course de haies | das Hürdenrennen |
| steeplechase | le steeple-chase | das Jagdrennen |
| maiden race | la course de maiden | das Sieglosenrennen in Flachrennen |
| novices' race | la course d'inédits | das Sieglosenrennen in Hürdenrennen |
| flat race | la course plate | das Flachrennen |
| series race | la course en partie liée | die Serie in Rennen |
| pattern race | la course principale | das Gruppenrennen |
| open race | la course publique | das Öffenerennen, das Öffentliche-Rennen |
| selling race | la course à réclamer | das Verkaufsrennen |
| handicap | le handicap | das Handicap, Ausgleichsrennen |
| match | le match | das Vergleichsrennen |

| | |
|---|---|
| le femmine | las potras |
| non qualificato | no útil para carreras |
| distanziato | distanciado |
| l'iscrizione ( *f.*) | las matrículas, las inscripciones |
| presentare un reclamo | poner una reclamación |
| la patente da fantino | la licencia de jockey, — jinete |
| la patente da allievo fantino | la licencia de aprendíz |
| la patente da allenatore | la licencia de entrenador |
| il passaporto | el pasaporte |
| il certificato d'origine | la carta de orígen |
| il certificato di vaccinazione | el certificado de vacunación |
| il permesso di allenare | la licencia de entrenador |
| la vendita all'amichevole | la venta privada |
| la vendita all'asta | la subasta |
| la vendita con riserva sui premi | la venta con precio de reserva |
| la vendita senza riserva sui premi | la venta sin precio de reserva |

## LE CATEGORIE

## LAS CATEGORÍAS

| | |
|---|---|
| la condizionata | la carrera con condiciones |
| la corsa a peso per età | el peso según la edad |
| la corsa classica | la distancia clásica |
| la corsa di categoria | las carreras con handicaps |
| la corsa ostacoli | la carrera de obstáculos |
| la corsa di siepi | la carrera de vallas |
| lo steeplechase | la carrera de obstáculos, el steeplechase |
| la maiden | la primera carrera, el debut |
| la debuttanti | la carrera de debutantes |
| la corsa in piano | la carrera lisa |
| la corsa di serie | las carreras en serie |
| la corsa di gruppo | la carrera principal |
| la corsa pubblica | la carrera pública/abierta |
| la corsa a vendere | la carrera de venta |
| l'handicap (*m.*) | el handicap |
| il match | el partido |

| RACE ORGANISATION | L'ORGANISATION DES COURSES | DIE RENNORGANISATION |
|---|---|---|
| the field | le lot | das Feld, das Starterfeld |
| crossing | le changement de ligne | das Kreuzen |
| rails | la corde | die Bande, das Geländer |
| barrier draw | le tirage des places à la corde | die Starterauslosung |
| to declare forfeit | déclarer forfait pour un cheval | Strafe anzeigen |
| the parade | le défilé | die Parade |
| elimination, balloting out | l'élimination ( f.) | die Auslosung |
| to enter a horse | engager un cheval | ein Pferd nennen |
| winnings | les gains | die Gewinne (m.pl.) |
| mounts | la monte | die Ritte (m.pl.) |
| change of rider | le changement de monte | der Reiterwechsel |
| declaration of riders | la déclaration de monte | die Reitererklärung |
| riding fee | le tarif de monte | das Reitgeld |
| scratched | non partant | gestrichen |
| unplaced | non placé | unplaziert |
| trophies | les objects d'art (m.pl.) | die Ehrenpreise (m.pl.) |
| the race | la course | das Rennen |
| preliminary canter to the starting post | le galop d'essai, le canter | der Aufgalopp |
| the start | le départ | der Start |
| starting gate | le départ à l'australienne | die Startboxe |
| tape start | de départ aux élastiques | der Bänderstart |
| flag start | le départ au drapeau | der Flaggenstart |
| start from the stalls | le départ en stalles | der Start von der Startmaschine |
| to be under the starter's orders | être sous les ordres du juge du départ | unter Starterskommando |
| false start | le faux départ | der Fehlstart |
| the back straight | la ligne d'en face | die Gegenseite |
| at the half-way mark | à mi-parcours | auf halbem Wege |
| the descent | la descente | abwärts |
| the rise | la montée | aufwärts |
| turn | le tournant | die Wendung, die Kurve |
| last corner | le dernier tournant | die letzte Ecke |
| the distance | la distance | die Entfernung |
| in the straight | dans la ligne d'arrivée | in der Geraden |
| the finish | l'arrivée ( f.) | der Endkampf, das Finish |
| winning post | le poteau d'arrivée | das Ziel |

## L'ORGANIZZAZIONE DELLE CORSE

il campo dei partenti
appoggiare, cambiare direzione
lo steccato, la corda
l'estrazione ( *f.*) del numero di partenza
dichiarare forfeit
la sfilata
l'eliminazione ( *f.*), il ballottagio
iscrivere un cavallo
i premi
le monte
il cambiamento di monta
la dichiarazione della monta
il prezzo della monta
non partente
non piazzato
i trofei
la corsa
andare in partenza, il canter
la partenza, lo start
le gabbie di partenza
la partenza con i nastri
la partenza con la bandiera
la partenza dalle gabbie
essere agli ordini dello starter
la falsa partenza
la dirittura di fronte
a metà corsa
la discesa
la salita
la curva
l'ultima curva ( *f.*)
la distanza
nella retta d'arrivo
l'arrivo (*m.*), il finish
il traguardo

## LA ORGANIZACIÓN DE LAS CARRERAS

el lote
el cambio de línea
los palos, la cuerda
el número de sorteo
la declaración de forfait
el desfile
la eliminación
matricular un caballo, inscribir —
los premios
la monta
el cambio de monta
la declaración de monta
los derechos de monta
no participante
no colocado
los trofeos
la carrera
el canter preliminar
la salida
el poste de salida
la salida con gomas
la salida con bandera
la salida con cajones
estar a las ordenes del juez de salida
la salida falsa
la recta de enfrente
la mitad de carrera
el descenso
la salida
la curva
la última curva
la distancia
la línea de llegada, la meta
la llegada, la meta
los postes de llegada

| | | |
|---|---|---|
| dead-heat | le dead-heat | totes Rennen |
| a nose | un nez | eine Nase |
| a short head | une courte tête | ein kurzer Kopf |
| a head | une tête | ein Kopf |
| a short neck | une courte encolure | ein kurzer Hals |
| a neck | une encolure | ein Hals |
| half a length | une demi-longueur | eine halbe Länge |
| a length | une longueur | eine Pferdelänge |
| distant | loin | entfernt |
| win bet | le pari simple gagnant | die Siegwette |
| place bet | le pari simple placé | die Platzewette |
| circuit of the track | le tour | die Bahnrunde |
| the starters, runners | les partants (*m.pl.*) | die Starter (*m.pl.*) |
| the list of runners | la déclaration des partants | die Startliste, die Starterliste |
| the track | la piste | die Rennbahn |
| right-handed track | la piste à main droite | die Rechtsbahn |
| left-handed track | la piste à main gauche | die Linksbahn |
| straight course | la ligne droite | die Geradebahn |
| training track | la piste d'entraînement | die Trainierbahn |
| grass track | la piste de gazon | die Grasbahn |
| sand track | la piste en sable | die Sandbahn |
| public enclosure | la pelouse | der Öffentlichkeitsring |
| photo-finish | la photo-finish | das Zielfoto |
| the weight | le poids | das Gewicht |
| weight allowance | la décharge, la remise de poids | das Erlaubnisgewicht |
| weight penalty | la surcharge | das Zusätzlichegewicht, das Mehrgewicht |
| to carry less | recevoir du poids | weniger tragen |
| to carry over | rendre du poids | mehr tragen |
| weighing room | la salle de balances | der Auswiegeraum |
| the weigh-in | la pesée avant la course | das Auswiegen |
| the weigh-out | la pesée après la course | das Zurückwiegen |
| race card | le programme | das Rennprogramm |

## THE GOING

| | | |
|---|---|---|
| hard | sec | trocken |
| firm | ferme | fest |
| good | bon | gut |

## LE TERRAIN

## DAS GELÄUF

| | |
|---|---|
| la parità | el empate |
| una narice | una nariz |
| una corta testa | una corta cabeza |
| la testa | una cabeza |
| corta incollatura | un medio cuello |
| l'incollatura ( *f.* ) | un cuello |
| mezza lunghezza | un medio cuerpo |
| una lunghezza | un cuerpo |
| molte lunghezze | lejos, distanciado |
| la vincente | el ganador |
| la piazzato | los colocados |
| il tracciato della pista | la vuelta de la pista |
| i partenti | los participantes, los partants |
| la dichiarazione dei partenti | la declaración de partants |
| la pista | la pista |
| la pista a mano destra | la pista a mano derecha |
| la pista a mano sinistra | la pista a mano izquierda |
| la dirittura | la recta |
| la pista d'allenamento | la pista de entrenamiento |
| la pista d'erba | la pista de hierba, — verde |
| la pista di sabbia | la pista de arena |
| il recinto del pubblico | el recinto del público, la pelouse |
| il foto-finish | la foto-finish |
| il peso | el peso |
| il discarico | el descargo de peso |
| il sovraccarico | el sobrecargo de peso |
| portare meno peso | dar peso, — kilos |
| portare più peso | dar más peso |
| la sala bilance | la sala de balanzas |
| il peso prima della corsa | el peso antes de la carrera |
| il peso dopo la corsa | el peso después de la carrera |
| il programma | el programa |

## IL TERRENO

| | |
|---|---|
| duro | duro |
| consistente | firme |
| buono | bueno |

## EL TERRENO, EL PISO

| | | |
|---|---|---|
| dead | assez souple | tief |
| yielding | souple | elastisch |
| soft | collant | weich |
| holding | très souple | sehr weich |
| heavy | lourd | schwer |

## RACING COLOURS AND DESIGNS

## LES COULEURS (*f.pl.*) D'ÉCURIE ET LES DISPOSITIFS (*m.pl.*)

## DAS RENNDRESS UND ABZEICHEN (*n.pl.*)

| | | |
|---|---|---|
| cream | beige | beige |
| white | blanc | weiss |
| blue | bleu | blau |
| light blue | bleu-clair | hellblau |
| dark blue | bleu foncé | dunkelblau |
| maroon | grenat | rotbraun |
| yellow | jaune | gelb |
| brown | marron | braun |
| mauve | mauve | malvenfarbig |
| black | noir | schwarz |
| orange | orange | orange |
| pink | rose | rosè |
| green | vert | grün |
| light green | vert-clair | hellgrün |
| dark green | vert foncé | dunkelgrün |
| purple | violet | violett |
| plain | unie | ohne Abzeichen (*n.pl.*) |
| strip | la bande | der Streifen |
| braces | les bretelles (*f.pl.*) | zwei Streifen |
| belt | la ceinture | der Gürtel |
| hooped | cerclée | geringelt |
| chevron | le chevron | 'V' |
| chevrons | les chevrons | mehrere 'V' |
| seams | les coutures (*f.pl.*) | die Nähte (*f.pl.*) |
| cross belts | la croix de St-André | Schärpen (*f.pl.*) Überkreuz |
| Lorraine cross | la croix de Lorraine | Lothringer Kreuz |
| check squares | les damiers (*m.pl.*) | kariert |
| diamond | le losange | die Raute |

buono-morbido
morbido
attaccaticcio
leggermente pesante
pesante

ligeramente pesado
flexible
blando
pesado
muy pesado

## I COLORI DI SCUDERIA, I COLORI DELLE GIUBBE

## LOS COLORES DE CUADRA Y LOS DIBUJOS

| | |
|---|---|
| beige | beige |
| bianco | blanco |
| blu | azul |
| azzurro | azul claro |
| blu scuro | azul oscuro, — marino |
| granata | granate |
| giallo | amarillo |
| marrone | marrón |
| viola | malva |
| nero | negro |
| arrancione | naranja |
| rosa | rosa |
| verde | verde |
| verde chiaro | verde claro |
| verde scuro | verde oscuro |
| porpora | púrpura, violeta |
| di un solo colore | liso |
| la striscia | la banda |
| le bretelle | las mangas |
| la fascia | la franja |
| cerchiata | los círculos |
| a V | el chevron |
| a più V | los chevrons |
| le cucciture | las costuras |
| la croce di St Andrea | la cruz de S. Andrés |
| la croce di Lorena | la cruz de Lorena |
| gli scacchi | los cuadros |
| la losanga | el rombo |

| | | |
|---|---|---|
| diamonds | les losanges | rautiert |
| quartered | ecartelée | gevierteilt |
| shoulders | les epaulettes (*f.pl.*) | Schultern (*f.pl.*) |
| star | l'étoile (*f.*) | der Stern |
| stars | les étoiles | Sterne |
| spots | les pois (*m.pl.*) | Punkte (*m.pl.*) |
| stripes | rayée | Streifen |
| disc | le disque | der Punkt |

**Racing colour schemes**

*Key to illustration 22*

1. plain
2. strip
3. braces
4. belt
5. hooped
6. chevron
7. chevrons
8. seams
9. cross belts
10. Lorraine cross
11. check squares
12. diamond
13. diamonds
14. quartered
15. shoulders
16. star
17. stars
18. spots
19. stripes
20. disc

**Dispositifs de couleurs**

*Légende d'illustration 22*

1. unie
2. la bande
3. les bretelles (*f.pl.*)
4. la ceinture
5. cerclée
6. le chevron
7. les chevrons
8. les coutures (*f.pl.*)
9. la croix de St-André
10. la croix de Lorraine
11. les damiers (*m.pl.*)
12. le losange
13. les losanges
14. écartelée
15. les épaulettes (*f.pl.*)
16. l'étoile (*f.*)
17. les étoiles
18. les pois (*m.pl.*)
19. rayée
20. le disque

**Abzeichen/Rennfarben**

*Legende des Bild 22*

1. ohne Abzeichen (*n.pl.*)
2. der Streifen
3. zwei Streifen
4. der Gürtel
5. geringelt
6. 'V'
7. mehrere 'V'
8. Nähte (*f.pl.*)
9. Schärpen (*f.pl.*) Überkreuz
10. Lothringer Kreuz
11. kariert
12. die Raute
13. rautiert
14. gevierteilt
15. Schultern (*f.pl.*)
16. der Stern
17. Sterne
18. Punkte (*m.pl.*)
19. Streifen (*m.pl.*)
20. der Punkt

# TRAINING TERMS

sprinter
stayer

# VOCABULAIRE D'ENTRAÎNEMENT

le flyer, le sprinter
le cheval de course ayant du fond, stayer

# TRAININGSVOKABELN

der Flieger, der Sprinter
der Steher

le losanghe
a quarti
le spalline
la stella
le stelle
le palle
le striscie
la palla

en losange
en cuadros
las hombreras
la estrella
las estrellas
los lunares
las barras
los puntos

**Disegni dei colori**

*Leggenda dell' illustrazione 22*

1. di un colore
2. la striscia
3. le bretelle
4. la fascia
5. circhiata
6. il V
7. più V
8. le cucciture
9. la croce di St Andrea
10. la croce di Lorena
11. gli scacchi
12. la losanga
13. le losanghe
14. a quarti
15. le spalline
16. la stella
17. le stelle
18. le palle
19. le striscie
20. la palla

**Dibujos de los colores**

*Leyenda de la descripción 22*

1. liso
2. la banda
3. las mangas
4. la franja
5. los círculos
6. el chevron
7. los chevrons
8. las costuras
9. la cruz de S. Andrés
10. la cruz de Lorena
11. los cuadros
12. el rombo
13. en losange
14. en cuadros
15. las hombreras
16. la estrella
17. las estrellas
18. los lunares
19. las barras
20. los puntos

# VOCABOLARIO DI ALLENAMENTO

il velocista
il cavallo che fa la distanza

# TERMINOLOGÍA DE ENTRENADORES

el velocista, el flyer
el fondista, el stayer

| quality, class | la classe | die Klasse |
| novice | l'inédit (*m.*) | das sieglose Hindernispferd |
| mile specialist | le miler | der Meiler |
| middle-distance horse | le cheval de distance moyenne | das Mitteldistanzpferd |
| to have racing ability | avoir l'aptitude à la course | Renneigenschaft besitzen |
| to like the going | avoir l'aptitude au terrain | das Geläuf mögen |
| to let down | arrêter l'entraînement | das Pferd in die Ecke stellen |
| to retire | sortir de l'entraînement | aus dem Rennstall nehmen; pensionieren |
| form | l'état (*m.*), la forme | die Rennform |
| loss of form | la baisse de forme | das Verlieren von Rennform |
| to be unfit | être hors de forme, être passé de forme | nicht fit sein |
| to be fit | être en état | fit sein |
| to be of limited ability | être limité | von begrenzter Renneigenschaft |
| stamina | la résistance, la trempe | der Ausdauer |
| to take to training | résister au travail | in Training nehmen |
| to be short of work | être à court de travail | nicht ausreichend trainiert |
| breaking-in | le débourrage | das Einbrechen, das Anreiten |
| to be broken-in | être débourré | eingeritten sein |

## RACING PERFORMANCE

## LA PERFORMANCE

## DIE RENNLEISTUNG

| win record | le palmarès des victoires | die Gewinnstatistik |
| the pace | l'allure (*f.*) | die Geschwindigkeit |
| to force the pace | mener à grande allure, forcer l'allure | die Geschwindigkeit erhöhen |
| to set the pace | faire le train, assurer le train | die Fahrt machen, das Rennen — |
| to be under pressure | être à l'ouvrage | unter Druck sein |
| to pull up | s'arrêter | aufpullen, aufgeben |
| to have a narrow lead | prendre une légère avance | eine knappe Führung haben |
| to take the lead | s'assurer l'avantage | die Führung übernehmen |
| to be well beaten | être bien battu | glatt geschlagen sein |
| to receive interference | être bousculé | behindert worden |
| to disappoint | causer des déceptions | enttäuschen |
| to give up | céder | aufgeben |
| pacemaker | le cheval de jeu | der die Führarbeit leistet |
| stable companion | le compagnon de box | der Stallgefährte |
| to run well | courir bien | gut gelaufen |
| to run poorly | courir mal | schlecht gelaufen |
| to be disqualified | être distancé | disqualifiziert werden |

| | |
|---|---|
| la qualità, la classe | la clase |
| il debuttante | el debutante |
| il miler | el millero |
| il cavallo da milleotto a due mila | el caballo de media distancia, — media milla |
| avere attitudine ( *f.* ) alla corsa | tener condiciones |
| avere attitudine ( *f.* ) al terreno | el especialista del terreno |
| mettere a riposo, interrompere l'allenamento | parar el entrenamiento, el caballo parado |
| ritirare dall'allenamento | retirar el caballo del entrenamiento |
| la forma | la forma |
| la perdita di forma, poca forma | la pérdida de forma |
| fuori forma, passato di forma | fuera de forma |
| essere in condizione | estar en forma |
| essere limitato | limitado en forma |
| la stamina | hacer la distancia |
| prendere bene il lavoro | aguantar el trabajo |
| a corto di lavoro | el falto de preparación |
| la domatura | la doma |
| essere domato | estar domado, — puesto |

## LA PRESTAZIONE

## LOS RESULTADOS

| | |
|---|---|
| l'elenco delle vittorie | las victorias |
| l'andatura ( *f.* ) | el paso, la velocidad |
| forzare l'andatura ( *f.* ) | forzar el paso |
| far l'andatura ( *f.* ) | asegurarse la plaza |
| essere incalzato | estar bajo presión |
| fermare | pararse |
| avere un piccolo vantaggio | tomar distancia |
| andare in testa | escaparse, ir en cabeza |
| battuto da lontano | batido de lejos |
| essere danneggiato | estar cerrado |
| deludente | causar decepción |
| cedere | ceder |
| il battistrada | el pacemaker |
| il compagno di scuderia | el compañero de cuadra |
| correre bene | correr bien |
| correre male | correr mal |
| essere squalificato | estar distanciado |

| | | |
|---|---|---|
| to quicken | s'étendre | beschläunigen |
| to weaken | faiblir | einbrechen |
| close finish | une arrivée disputée | kurzes Ende |
| to fail to respond | être froid | keinen Widerstand leisten |
| winner | le gagnant, le lauréat, le vainqueur | der Sieger |
| the field | le lot | das Starterfeld |
| the outsider | l'outsider (*m.*) | der Aussenseiter |
| to race on the rails | serrer la corde | an den Rails laufen |

| | |
|---|---|
| distendersi | acelerar |
| calare | aminorar |
| l'arrivo (*m.*) combattuto | la llegada en un pañuelo |
| non reagire | estar frío |
| il vincitore | el ganado |
| il campo dei partenti | el lote |
| l'outsider (*m.*) | el outsider, la sorpresa |
| stare allo steccato | coger los palos |

**Equipment**

**Le Matériel**

**Das Material**

**Gli Attrezzi**

**El Equipo,**

**Los Utensilios**

---

## THE STABLE AND EQUIPMENT

| | |
|---|---|
| loose-box | |
| stall | |
| manger | |
| hay-rack, hay-net | |
| water-bowl, trough | |
| automatic drinking bowl | |
| forage, feed stuff | |
| tack room | |
| wheelbarrow | |
| bedding, bed | |
| pitchfork | |
| broom, yard broom | |
| bucket | |
| halter, head collar (23.1, 23.2) | |
| head-rope, tether | |
| chain | |
| rug (23.3) | |
| New Zealand rug | |
| sweat rug | |
| hood (23.4) | |
| roller, surcingle (23.3a) | |
| bandages (23.3b) | |
| boots (23.5) | |
| knee-caps (23.6) | |
| over-reach boots (23.7) | |
| body brush (23.8) | |
| hoof pick | |
| dandy brush (23.9) | |
| water brush | |
| curry comb | |
| sweat scraper | |
| sponge | |
| chamois leather | |

## L'ÉCURIE (*f.*), LES ACCESSOIRES

le box
la stalle
la mangeoire
le râtelier, le filet
l'abreuvoir (*m.*)
l'abreuvoir (*m.*) automatique
le fourrage
la sellerie
la brouette
la litière
la fourche
le balai
le seau
le licol (23.1, 23.2)
la longe d'attache
la chaîne
la couverture (23.3)
la couverture Nouvelle Zélande
la couverture nid d'abeilles
le camail, le béguin (23.4)
le surfaix (23.3a)
les bandes (*f.pl.*) (23.3b)
les guêtres (*f.pl.*) (23.5)
les genouillères (*f.pl.*) (23.6)
les cloches (*f.pl.*) (23.7)
la brosse douce (23.8)
le cure-pied
le bouchon de chiendent (23.9)
° le bouchon de chiendent
l'étrille (*f.*)
le couteau de chaleur
l'éponge (*f.*)
la peau de chamois

## STALL (*m.*), STALLGERÄT (*n.*)

die Box
der Stand
die Krippe
die Heuraufe, das Netz
die Tränke
die Selbsttränke
das Futter
die Sattelkammer
der Karren
die Streu
die Gabel
der Besen
der Eimer
die Stallhalfter (23.1, 23.2)
der Anbinderiemen
die Kette
die Decke (23.3)
die Neuseeland-Decke
die Abschwitzdecke
das Kopfstück (23.4)
der Deckengurt (23.3a)
die Bandagen (*f.pl.*) (23.3b)
die Streichkappen (*f.pl.*) (23.5)
die Kniekappen (*f.pl.*) (23.6)
die Gummiglocken (*f.pl.*) (23.7)
die Kardätsche (23.8)
der Hufkratzer
die Wurzelbürste (23.9)
die Waschbürste; die Mähnenbürste
der Striegel
das Schweissmesser
der Schwamm
das Waschleder

## LA SCUDERIA, GLI UTENSILI

il box
la posta
la mangiatoia
la rastrelliera, la rete
l'abbeveratoio (*m.*)
l'abbeveratoio automatico
il foraggio
la selleria
la carriola
la lettiera
la forca
la ramazza
il secchio
la capezza (23.1, 23.2)
la corda
la catena
la coperta (23.3)
la coperta da paddock
la coperta per asciugare, il sudore
il capuccio (23.4)
il sopraffascia (23.3a)
le fasce (23.3b)
le stinchiere (23.5)
le ginocchiere (23.6)
i paraglomi (23.7)
°la brusca di setola (23.8)
il curasnetta
il bruscone di saggina (23.9)
la brusca (di setola)
la striglia
il coltello da sudore, il raschiatoio
la spugna
la pelle di camoscio

## LA CABALLERIZA Y EL EQUIPO

el box
la plaza
el pesebre (comedero)
el pesebre del heno, la red del heno
el abrevadero
el abrevadero automático
el foraje
el guadarnés
la carretilla del estiércol
la cama de paja
la horquilla, la forca, el biergo
la escoba
el cubo
el ronzal, la cabezada de cuadra (23.1, 23.2)
la cuerda, el ronzal
la cadena
la manta (23.3)
la manta de Nueva Zelandia, — impermeable
la manta para desudar
la careta (23.4)
el cinchuelo, la sobrecincha (23.3a)
las vendas (23.3b)
los protectores (23.5)
las rodilleras (23.6)
las campanas (23.7)
la bruza, el cepillo suave (23.8)
el limpiacascos
el cepillo de raíces (23.9)
°el cepillo de agua
la almohaza, la rasqueta
el cuchillo de sudor
la esponja
la gamuza

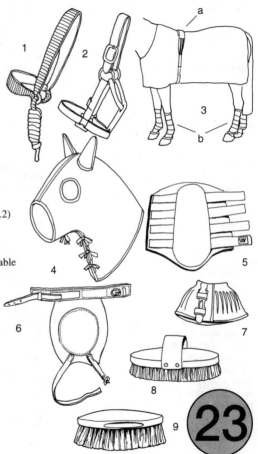

| | | |
|---|---|---|
| stable rubber | le torchon | das Wischtuch, der Lappen |
| saddle soap | le savon glycérine | die Sattelseife |
| hoof grease, oil | la graisse à pied | das Huffett |
| twitch | le tort-nez | die Nasenbremse |
| mane comb | le peigne | der Mähnenkamm |
| plaiting thread | le fil (à natter) | der Faden |
| plaiting band | les bandes ( *f.pl.* ) à natter | der Gummiband, der Leinenklebeband, die Mähnenflechtringe (*m.pl.*) |

## HORSE TRANSPORT | ## LE TRANSPORT DE CHEVAUX | ## DER PFERDETRANSPORT

| | | |
|---|---|---|
| horsebox, lorry | le van | der Pferdetransporter, der Pferdetransportwagen |
| | | |
| trailer | la remorque | der (Pferdetransport-) Anhänger |
| to tow | tracter | ziehen |
| load, unload | embarquer, désembarquer | verladen/abladen, entladen |
| | | |
| ramp | le pont | die Verladerampe, die Verladeklappe |
| groom's door | la petite porte | die Servicetür, die Personentür |
| tow hitch | la flèche, la boule | die Kupplung, die Deichsel |
| (overrun) brake | le frein ( par inertie) | die (Auflauf-) Bremse |
| partition | le bat-flanc, la séparation | die Trennwand |
| breast bar | la barre de poitrail | der Brustriegel, die Bruststütze |
| empty weight | le poids net | das Leergewicht |
| useful load | la charge utile | die Nutzlast |
| maximum (gross) weight | le poids (brut/lourd) maximum | das Hauptgewicht (Gesamtgewicht) |
| automatic reverse | la marche arrière automatique | die Rückfahrautomatik |
| (direction) indicator | le clignotant | das Blinklicht |
| number plate (light) | (l'éclairage (*m.*) de) la plaque de police | das Nummerschild (die — leuchte) |
| brake/stop light | le feu stop | das Bremslicht |
| tail/rear light | la lanterne arrière | das Rücklicht |
| spare wheel | le pneu de secours | der Reservereifen |
| nationality plate | la plaque de nationalité | das Landeskennzeichen |
| jockey wheel | la roue jockey | das Stützrad |
| tachograph | le contrôlographe | der Fahrtenschreiber |

| | |
|---|---|
| il strofinaccio | el paño, el trapo |
| il sapone di glicerina | el jaboncillo |
| il grasso per i piedi | la grasa para cascos |
| il torcinaso | el serretón |
| il pettine | el peine |
| il filo per le treccine | el hilo para trenzar |
| gli estastici per le treccine | las gomas elásticas para trenzar |

## IL TRASPORTO DEI CAVALLI

## EL TRANSPORTE DE CABALLOS

| | |
|---|---|
| il van (trasporto) | el camión |
| | |
| il trailer, il van trailer, il rimorchio | el remolque |
| trainare | remolcar |
| far salire/scendere | poner en el remolque, embarcar; sacar del remolque, desembarcar |
| | |
| la rampa (di salita), il ponte | la rampa |
| la porta laterale, — di servizio | la puerta lateral, — de servicio |
| l'aggancio (*m.*), il timone | el enganche, el acoplamiento |
| il freno inerziale | el freno (de inercia) |
| la parete divisoria | la partición |
| la barra | la barra delantera |
| il peso a vuoto, la tara | el peso neto |
| la portata, il carico utile | la carga útil |
| il peso (omologato) massimo | el peso (bruto) máximo |
| la retromarcia automatica | la marcha atrás automática |
| il fanale di direzione | la luz intermitente |
| la targa (il fanale illuminazione targa) | (la luz de) la placa de matricula |
| il fanale di arresto | la luz de pare |
| il fanale posteriore | la luz trasera |
| la ruota di scorta | la rueda de recambio |
| la targhetta di nazionalità | el disco de nacionalidad |
| il ruotino anteriore | la rueda delantera de guía, — de timón |
| il tachigrafo | el tacógrafo |

## STABLE MANAGEMENT

to water
to feed
to exercise
to clean, muck out the box
to remove the droppings, skip out
bed, litter
deep litter
(wood) shavings
making up the bed
to clean
to brush[1]
to brush[2], to sweep
to groom
to pick out the foot
to rub, massage
to dry
to sponge
to wash
quick grooming, quartering
thorough grooming
to comb
groom, stable lad
head groom, stud —, head lad
(automatic) horse walker
livery

## TRIMMING

coat
summer coat, winter coat
changing the coat, moulting
mane, tail
fetlock tuft

mane
forelock

## SOINS (*m.pl.*) À L'ÉCURIE

abreuver, donner à boire
fourrager, donner à manger, alimenter
sortir, promener
nettoyer le box
enlever les crottins
la litière
le gâteau
les copeaux (*m.pl.*)
refaire la litière
nettoyer
brosser
balayer
panser
curer le pied (sabot)
bouchonner, frotter, masser
sécher
éponger
laver
le pansage sommaire (avant la sortie)
le pansage à fond (après le retour)
peigner
le palefrenier, garçon d'écurie
le premier garçon, le chef d'écurie
le carrousel
la pension

## LA TOILETTE

le poil
poil d'été, poil d'hiver
la mue
les crins (*m.pl.*)
le fanon

la crinière
le toupet

## STALLDIENST (*m.*)

tränken
füttern, ernähren
bewegen
den Stand ausräumen
ausmisten
das Strohbett, die Einstreu, die Matratze
das Matratzenlager
die Holzspäne (*m.pl.*)
die Streu erneuern, — richten
reinigen, säubern
bürsten
fegen
putzen
den Huf auskratzen, ausräumen
abreiben, massieren
abtrocknen
abschwammen
waschen, abspritzen
flüchtiges Überputzen (vor der Arbeit)
gründliches Putzen (nach der Arbeit)
kämmen
der Pferdewärter, Stallbursche
der Stallmeister
die Pferdeführanlage
die Pension

## FRISIEREN

die Haardecke, das Haarkleid
das Sommerhaar, Winterhaar
der Haarwechsel
die Schweif-, Mähnenhaare (*n.pl.*)
die Fesselhaare, die Kötenhaare, der
    Fesselbehang
die Mähne
der Schopf

## LE CURE IN SCUDERIA

abbeverare
dare il foraggio, alimentare
far uscire, passeggiare
pulire il box
togliere le fiande
la lettiera
la lettiera permanente
i trucioli (di legno)
rifare la lettiera
pulire
spazzolare, passare la brusca
ramazzare (la scuderia)
governare
curare il piede
passar la brusca, strofinare, masseggiare
asciugare
spugnare
lavare
ripassare il cavallo (prima di uscire)
il governo a fondo (dopo il lavoro)
pettinare
il palafreniere, il ragazzo di scuderia
il caposcuderia
la giostra sgambatura
la pensione

## EL MANTENIMIENTO, EL CUIDADO

abrevar
dar pienso, alimentar
mover
levantar la cama
sacar el estiércol
la cama de paja
la cama permanente
la viruta
echar la cama
limpiar
cepillar
barrer
limpiar el caballo
limpiar los cascos
frotar, dar masajes
secar
limpiar/lavar con esponja
lavar
el cepillado rápido
el cepillado completo
peinar
el mozo de caballos
el mozo principal
la noria
la pensión

## LA TOELETTA

il mantello
il mantello estivo, — invernale
la muta
i crini
il fiocco, la barbetta

la criniera
il ciuffo

## RECORTAR

el pelo
el pelo de verano, —invierno
el cambio de pelo
la crin, la cola
el pelo de la cuartilla

la crin
el flequillo, el copete

| | | |
|---|---|---|
| tail | la queue, le fouet | der Schweif |
| dock | le coir | die Schweifrübe |
| root of the tail | la naissance de la queue, l'attache | der Schweifansatz |
| tail carriage | le port de queue | die Tragweite des Schweifes |
| trimming | la toilette | das Frisieren |
| to thin (the tail or mane) | dégrossir, éclaircir | lichten, verlesen |
| to hog | écourter | kurzscheren |
| to trim | régulariser, égaliser | ausrichten, egalisieren |
| to pull | arracher, étirer, désépaissir | ausreissen, verziehen |
| to cut | tailler, couper | schneiden, abschneiden |
| to clip | tondre | scheren |
| to plait | tresser, natter | flechten, einflechten |
| hogged mane | la crinière rase | die geschorene Mähne |
| pulled mane (24.1) | la crinière raccourcie et désépaissie (24.1) | die gepflegte, (halblange) verzogene Mähne (24.1) |
| plaited mane (24.2) | la crinière tressée (24.2) | die geflochtene Mähne (24.2) |
| short tail, docked — | courte queue | der Stummelschweif |
| to dock | amputer, sectionner | kupieren |
| pulled tail (24.3) | la queue désépaissie (24.3) | der verzogene Schweif (24.3) |
| plaited tail (24.4) | la queue tressée (24.4) | der eingeflochtene Schweif (24.4) |
| clippers | la tondeuse | die Schermaschine |
| clipper blades | le rasoir | die Kamm-Messer (*n.pl.*) |
| clipping | la tonte | das Scheren, die Schur |
| hunter clip (24.5) | la tonte de chasse (24.5) | °eine Art des Geschorenseins (24.5) |
| blanket clip (24.6) | la tonte en couverture (24.6) | °eine Art des Geschorenseins (24.6) |
| trace clip (24.7) | la tonte d'hiver (24.7) | °eine Art des Geschorenseins (24.7) |
| full clip | la tonte totale | komplett geschoren |
| comb | le peigne | der Kamm |
| scissors | les ciseaux (*m.pl.*) | die Schere |

## TACK, SADDLERY

## LA SELLERIE

## DAS SATTELZEUG

**The saddle**
general purpose saddle (25.1)
dressage saddle (25.2)
jumping saddle (25.3)
hunting saddle

**La selle**
— mixte (25.1)
— de dressage (25.2)
— d'obstacle (25.3)
— de chasse

**Der Sattel**
der Mehrzwecksattel (25.1)
der Dressursattel (25.2)
der Springsattel (25.3)
der Jagdsattel

| | |
|---|---|
| la coda | la cola |
| il fusto, il torso | el macho |
| l'attacco della coda | el nacimiento de la cola |
| il portamento della coda | el porte de la cola |
| la toeletta | recortar |
| alleggerire (la coda o la criniera) | entresacar (la crin, la cola) |
| accorciare | rapar las crines, esquilar la crin |
| regolarizzare/uguagliare/fare i crini | recortar |
| sfoltire | entresacar |
| tagliare | cortar |
| tosare | esquilar |
| fare le treccine | trenzar |
| la criniera rasata | las crines rapadas, la crin esquilada |
| la criniera accorciata e sfoltita (24.1) | las crines entresacadas (24.1) |
| | |
| la criniera con le treccine (24.2) | las crines trenzadas (24.2) |
| la coda corta | la cola corta |
| mozzare, tagliare, sezionare | descolar, cortar la cola |
| la coda sfoltita (24.3) | la cola entresacada (24.3) |
| la coda intrecciata (24.4) | la cola trenzada (24.4) |
| la macchinetta tosatrice | el esquilador |
| le lami | las cuchillas |
| la tosatura | esquilar |
| la tosatura da caccia (24.5) | el esquilado de caza de zorro (24.5) |
| la tosatura a coperta (completa) (24.6) | el esquilado de manta (24.6) |
| la tosatura a mezza coperta; — da corsa (24.7) | el esquilado de enganches (24.7) |
| la tosatura completa | el esquilado total |
| il pettine | el peine |
| le forbici | las tijeras |

## LA SELLERIA (IL MATERIALE)

## LOS ATREOS, LA GUARNICIONERÍA

**La sella**

| | |
|---|---|
| la sella (generica) (25.1) | la montura mixta (25.1) |
| la sella di addestramento (25.2) | la montura de doma (25.2) |
| la sella da salto ostacoli (25.3) | la montura de salto (25.3) |
| la sella da caccia | la montura de cacería |

**La montura, la silla**

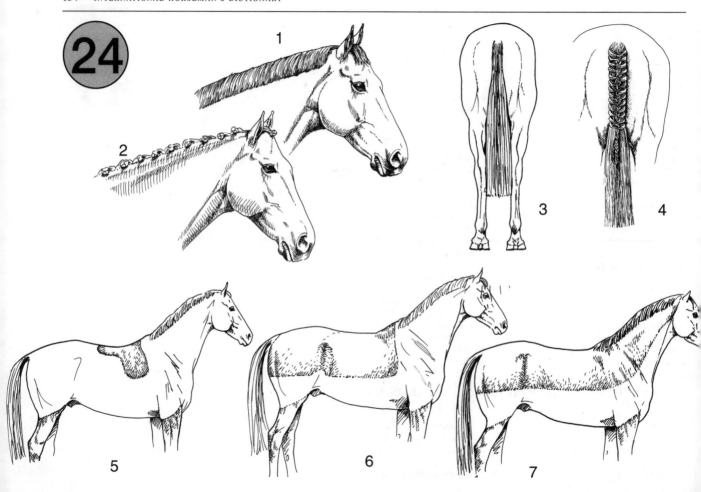

24

1

2

3

4

5

6

7

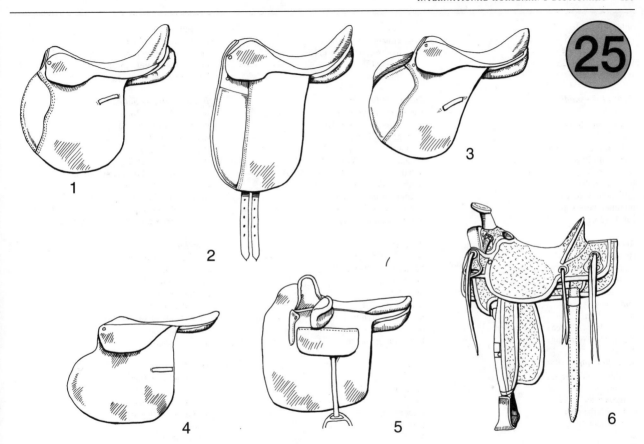

25

1

2

3

4

5

6

| | | |
|---|---|---|
| polo saddle | — de polo | der Polosattel |
| racing saddle (25.4) | — de course (25.4) | der Rennsattel (25.4) |
| side saddle (25.5) | — d'amazone, de dame (25.5) | der Damensattel (25.5) |
| Western saddle (25.6) | — cow-boy (25.6) | der Cowboysattel (25.6) |
| synthetic saddle | — synthétique | der Kunststoffsattel |

| *Parts of the saddle* | *Parties de la selle* | *Bestandteile des Sattels* |
|---|---|---|
| tree (26.1) | l'arçon (*m.*) de selle (26.1) | der Sattelbaum (26.1) |
| stirrup-bar (26.1b) | le porte-étrivière (26.1b) | die Sturzfeder (26.1b) |
| seat (26.2a) | le siège (26.2a) | der Sitz (26.2a) |
| flap, skirt (26.2b) | le quartier (26.2b) | das Blatt (26.2b) |
| knee roll (26.2c) | l'avance (*f.*) (26.2c) | der Kniewulst (26.2c) |
| panel (26.3a) | le panneau, la matelassure (26.3a) | das Kissen, die Polsterung (26.3a) |
| gullet (26.3b) | la liberté de garrot (26.3b) | die Kammer (26.3b) |
| girth strap (26.3c) | le contre-sanglon (26.3c) | die Strippe (26.3c) |
| pommel, head (26.1a) | le pommeau (26.1a) | die Sattelkammer, das Vorderzwiesel (26.1a) |
| cantle (26.1c) | le troussequin (26.1c) | das Hinterzwiesel, der Sattelkranz (26.1c) |

| *Accessories* | *Accessoires* | *Zubehör* |
|---|---|---|
| stirrup leather (26.4) | l'étrivière (*f.*) (26.4) | der Steigriemen (26.4) |
| stirrup iron (26.5) | l'étrier (*m.*) (26.5) | der Steigbügel (26.5) |
| girth (26.6) | la sangle (26.6) | der Sattelgurt (26.6) |
| surcingle | le surfaix | der Obergurt |
| numnah | le tapis de selle | die Satteldecke |
| weight cloth | le tapis de plomb | die Gewichtsdecke, der Gag |
| breast-plate (Aintree) | la bricole | das Vorderzeug |
| breast-plate (hunting) | le collier de chasse | das Jagdzeug |

| *Miscellaneous* | *Divers* | *Verschiedenes* |
|---|---|---|
| to adjust, to fit the saddle | ajuster la selle | den Sattel verpassen |
| to saddle a horse | seller un cheval | satteln |
| to tighten the girth | sangler | die Gurte anziehen |
| to loosen the girth | lâcher la sangle | die Gurte lösen, lockern |
| to unsaddle | desseller | absatteln |
| saddler | le sellier | der Sattler |
| harness-maker | le bourrelier | der Riemer, der Geschirrmacher |
| saddlery | la sellerie | das Sattelzeug |
| saddler's shop | la sellerie | die Sattlerei, das Reitsport–Fachgeschäft |
| saddle-room | la sellerie | die Sattelkammer |

la sella da polo
la sella da corsa (25.4)
la sella d'amazzone (25.5)
la sella cowboy (25.6)
la sella sintetica

*Parti della sella*
l'arcione (*m.*) (26.1)
il portastaffile (26.1b)
il seggio (26.2a)
il quartiere (26.2b)
l'appoggio (*m.*) per il ginocchio (26.2c)
l'imbottitura, il cuscinetto (26.3a)
la scanalatura tra i due cuscinetti (26.3b)
il riscontro della sella (26.3c)
il pomo, l'arco anteriore (26.1a)
la paletta (26.1c)

*Accessori*
lo staffile (26.4)
la staffa (26.5)
la cinghia (26.6)
il sopraffascia
la copertina imbottita
la copertina per i piombi
il pettorale
il pettorale da caccia

*Miscellanea*
aggiustare la sella
sellare un cavallo
stringere le cinghie
allentare le cinghie
disellare
il sellaio
il sellaio
la selleria (il materiale)
la selleria (il negozio)
la selleria (la stanza)

la montura de polo
la montura de carreras (25.4)
la montura de amazona (25.5)
la montura 'Western' (25.6)
la montura sintética

*Las partes de una montura*
el fuste (26.1)
la charnela (26.1b)
el asiento (26.2a)
el faldón (26.2b)
el apoyo-rodillas (26.2c)
el baste (26.3a)
la canal (26.3b)
la latiguilla (26.3c)
el pomo, la perilla (26.1a)
el borrén trasero (26.1c)

*Equipo adicional*
la ación, la estribera (26.4)
el estribo (26.5)
la cincha (26.6)
la sobrecincha
el sudadero
el sudadero para llevar el sobrepeso
el pecho-petral (sujeto a la cincha)
el pecho-petral (sujeto a la montura)

*Miscelánea*
adaptar la montura
ensillar
abrochar la cincha
desabrochar la cincha
quitar la montura
el guarnicionero
el guarnicionero
los atreos, la guarnicionería
la guarnicionería, la tienda de hípica
el guadarnés

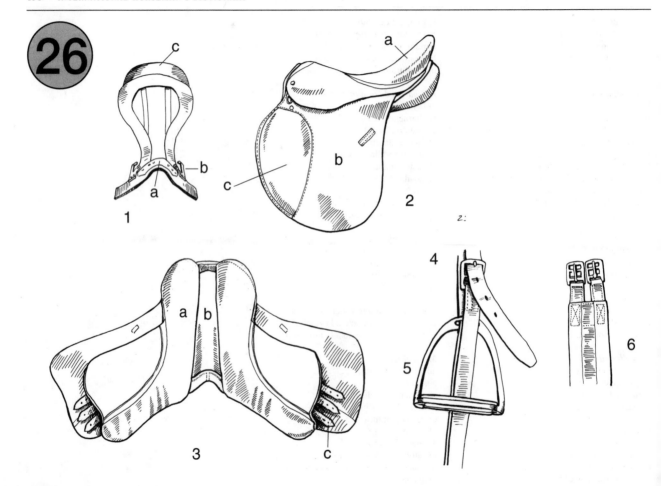

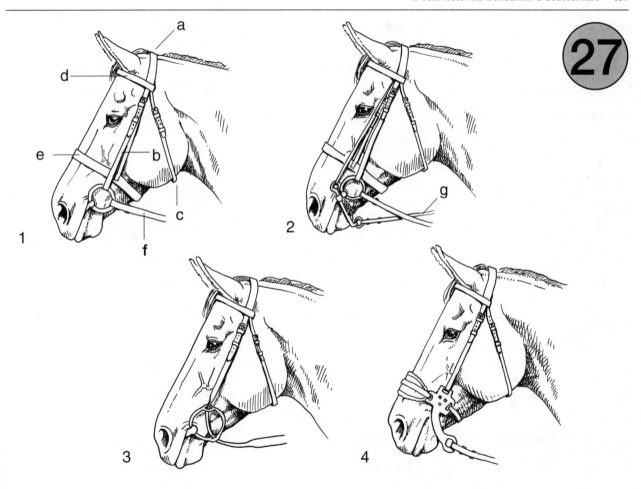

27

## The bridle

*Types*
snaffle bridle (27.1)
double bridle (27.2)
show bridle
bitless bridle, hackamore (27.4)

*Parts of the bridle*
reins
bit
headpiece (27.1a)
cheekpiece (27.1b)
throatlash (27.1c)
browband (27.1d)
noseband (27.1e)
snaffle rein (27.1f)
curb rein (27.2g)
flash noseband (28.1)
drop noseband (28.2)
grakle noseband (28.3)

*Miscellaneous*
bridle, stitched
bridle, buckled
bridle with studs
put the bridle on
take the bridle off

## Bits

snaffle bit
curb bit
gag (27.3)
bridoon (29.2)

snaffle with cheeks, cheek snaffle (29.5)
eggbutt snaffle (29.3)
loose-ring snaffle (29.1)

## La bride

*Types*
le bridon (27.1)
la bride (complète) (27.2)
la bride de présentation
le hackamore (27.4)

*Parties de la bride*
les rênes
l'embouchure (*f.*)
la têtière (27.1a)
le montant (*m.*) (27.1b)
la sous-gorge (27.1c)
le frontal (27.1d)
la muserolle (27.1e)
la rêne de filet (27.1f)
la rêne de bride (27.2g)
la muserolle combinée (28.1)
la muserolle allemande (28.2)
la muserolle à croisillon (28.3)

*Divers*
la bride cousue
— à boucles
— à crochets
brider
débrider

## Les embouchures (*f.pl.*)

le filet
le mors
le filet releveur, le gag (27.3)
le filet de mors de bride (29.2)

— à aiguilles (29.5)
— à olives, — chantilly (29.3)
— à anneaux (29.1)

## Das Zaumzeug

*Modelle*
der Trensenzaum (27.1)
der Kandarenzaum, Stangenzaum (27.2)
die Turniertrense
die gebisslose Zäumung (27.4)

*Bestandteile des Zaumzeugs*
die Zügel (*m.pl.*)
das Gebiss
das Kopfgestell (27.1a)
der Backenriemen (27.1b)
der Kehlriemen (27.1c)
der Stirnriemen (27.1d)
der Nasenriemen (27.1e)
der Trensenzügel (27.1f)
der Stangenzügel (27.2g)
das kombinierte Reithalfter (28.1)
das hannoversche Reithalfter (28.2)
das mexikanische Reithalfter (28.3)

*Verschiedenes*
der Zaum mit eingenähtem Gebiss
— Schnallen
— Knöpfen
aufzäumen
abzäumen

## Die Gebisse (*n.pl.*)

die Trense
die Stange, Kandare
die Zugtrense, Gag, das Steiggebiss (27.3)
die Unterlegtrense (29.2)

die Schenkeltrense (29.5)
die Olivenkopftrense (29.3)
die Ringtrense (29.1)

## La bardatura della testa

*Tipi*
il filetto (27.1)
la briglia (completa) (27.2)
la briglia da presentazione, il filetto —
l'hackamore, il capezzone a leva (27.4)

*Parti della briglia*
le redini
l'imboccatura ( *f.*)
la testiera, il sovaccapo (27.1a)
il montante (27.1b)
il sottogola (27.1c)
il frontale (27.1d)
la capezzina (27.1e)
la redine del filetto (27.1f)
la redine del morso (27.2g)
la capezzina con chiudibocca (28.1)
la capezzina sotto-filetto (28.2)
la capezzina incrociata (28.3)

*Miscellanea*
la briglia cucita
la briglia con la fibbia
la briglia con i ganci
mettere la briglia
togliere la briglia

## Le imboccature

il filetto
il morso
il filetto elevatore (27.3)
il filetto della briglia (29.2)

il filetto con le stanghette (29.5)
il filetto a olive, — da corsa (29.3)
il filetto ad anelli (29.1)

## La brida

*Formas*
la brida con porta-filete (27.1)
la brida con filete y bocado (27.2)
la brida de exhibición
el hackamore (27.4)

*Las partes de una brida*
las riendas
la embocadura
la testera (27.1a)
el montante (27.1b)
el ahogadero (27.1c)
la frontalera (27.1d)
la muserola (27.1e)
la rienda de filete (27.1f)
la rienda de bocado (27.2g)
la muserola 'flash', — irlandesa (28.1)
la muserola alemana (28.2)
la muserola mejicana (28.3)

*Miscelánea*
la brida cosida
la brida con hebillas
la brida con lentejas
embridar
quitar la brida

## Las embocaduras

el filete
el bocado
el filete elevador (27.3)
el filete para uso con brida, — de anillas
    pequeñas (29.2)
el filete con palillos (29.5)
el filete de olivas (29.3)
el filete de anillas (29.1)

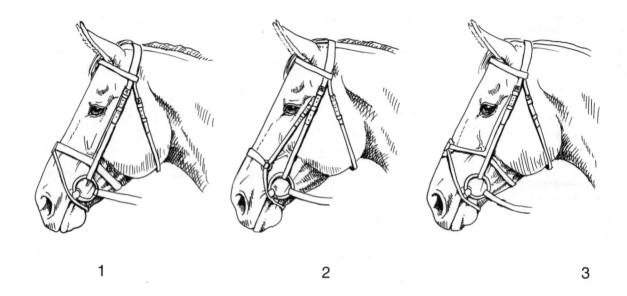

1                    2                    3

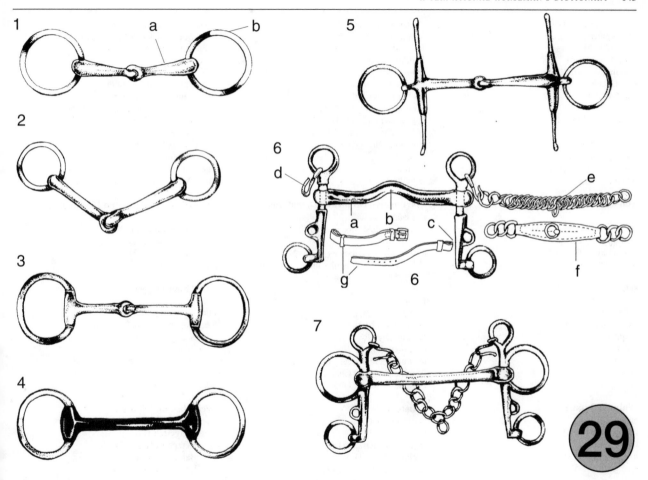

1   a   b

2

3

4

5

6   d   a   b   c   e   f   g   6

7

29

| | | |
|---|---|---|
| rubber snaffle (29.4) | — en caoutchouc (29.4) | das Gummigebiss (29.4) |
| mouthpiece (29.1a, 29.6a) | le canon (29.1a, 29.6a) | das Mundstück (29.1a, 29.6a) |
| rings (29.1b) | les anneaux (*m.pl.*) (29.1b) | die Ringe (*m.pl.*) (29.1b) |
| slide-mouth curb | le mors à pompe | das Pumpgebiss |
| Weymouth curb (29.6) | le mors de bride (29.6) | die Stange, die Kandare (29.6) |
| port (29.6b) | la liberté de langue (29.6b) | die Zungenfreiheit (29.6b) |
| cheeks (29.6c) | les branches (*f.pl.*) (29.6c) | die Bäume (*m.pl.*) (29.6c) |
| hooks (29.6d) | les crochets (*m.pl.*) (29.6d) | die Kinnkettenhaken (*m.pl.*) (29.6d) |
| curb chain (29.6e–f) | la gourmette (29.6e–f) | die Kinnkette (29.6e–f) |
| lipstrap (29.6g) | la fausse gourmette (29.6g) | der Scherriemen (29.6g) |
| plain mouthpiece | le canon d'une pièce | einteiliges Mundstück |
| jointed mouthpiece | — brisé | gebrochenes — |
| half-moon mouthpiece | — cintré | gewölbtes — |
| pelham (29.7) | le pelham (29.7) | das Pelham, die Polokandare (29.7) |

| | | |
|---|---|---|
| **Martingales and lungeing gear** | **Martingales, enrênements, matériel de dressage** | **Hilfszügel, Longier- und Dressurzeug** |
| running martingale (30.1) | la martingale à anneaux (30.1) | das Jagdmartingal (30.1) |
| standing martingale (30.2) | — fixe (30.2) | das starre Martingal (30.2) |
| Irish martingale (30.3) | — irlandaise, l'alliance (*f.*) (30.3) | das irische — (30.3) |
| draw-reins (30.5) | — les rênes (*f.pl.*) coulissantes, — allemandes (30.5) | der Schlaufzügel (30.5) |
| side-reins | — fixes | die Ausbindezügel (*m.pl.*) |
| lungeing rein | la longe | die Longe |
| roller (30.6) | le surfaix (30.6) | der Longiergurt (30.6) |
| cavesson (30.4) | le caveçon (30.4) | der Kappzaum (30.4) |
| crupper | la croupière | der Schweifriemen |
| pillars | les piliers (*m.*) | die Pilaren (*m.pl.*) |
| long reins | les longues rênes, les guides (*f.pl.*) | die Doppellonge, der lange Zügel |
| chambon | l'enrênement (*m.*) Chambon | das Chambon |
| de Gogue | l'enrênement (*m.*) Gogue | das 'de Gogue' |

| | | |
|---|---|---|
| **Whips and spurs** | **Fouets et éperons** | **Peitschen und Sporen** |
| cane (31.1) | la canne (31.1) | der Reitstock (31.1) |
| riding whip (31.4) | la cravache (31.4) | die Reitgerte (31.4) |
| hunting whip (31.6) | le fouet de chasse (31.6) | die Hetzpeitsche (31.6) |
| lungeing whip (31.2) | la chambrière (31.2) | die Bahnpeitsche (31.2) |
| race whip (31.5) | la cravache de course (31.5) | die Rennpeitsche (31.5) |

il filetto di gomma (29.4)
il cannone (29.1a, 29.6a)
gli anelli (29.1b)
il morso a pompa
il morso della briglia (29.6)
la libertà di lingua (29.6b)
le aste (29.6c)
le essi e l'uncino (*m.*) (29.6d)
il barbozzale (29.6e–f)
il falso barbozzale (29.6g)
il cannone rigido
il cannone snodato
il cannone curvo
il pelham (29.7)

el filete en caucho, — de goma, — de pasta (29.4)
la embocadura (29.1a, 29.6a)
las anillas (29.1b)
el bocado (con embadura) deslizante
el bocado de doma clásica (29.6)
el desveno (29.6b)
las palancas, las piernas (29.6c)
los alacranes (29.6d)
la cadenilla (29.6e–f)
la falsa barbada (29.6g)
la embocadura rígida
la embocadura articulada
la embocadura curva, — 'en media luna'
el pelham (29.7)

**Martingale, redini speciali**

la martingala con forchetta ad anelli (30.1)
la martingala fissa (30.2)
la falsa martingala (30.3)
la redine di ritorno (30.5)

le redine fisse
la corda
il fascione (30.6)
il capezzone (30.4)
la groppiera
i pilieri
le guide, le redini lunghe
l' abbassatesta (*f.*)
la redine gogue

**Martingalas, rendajes y equipo para
    el trabajo a la cuerda**
la martingala, las tijerillas (30.1)
la martingala fija, la gamarra (30.2)
la martingala irlandesa (30.3)
el rendaje deslizante, las riendas
    alemanas (30.5)
el rendaje lateral, las riendas de atar
la cuerda para dar cuerda
el cinchuelo, la sobrecincha (30.6)
la cabezada de dar cuerda (30.4)
la baticola
los pilares
las riendas largas
las riendas Chambon
las riendas Gogue

**Fruste e speroni**
la bacchetta (31.1)
la frusta (31.4)
la frusta da caccia (31.6)
il frustone (31.2)
la frusta da corsa (31.5)

**Fustas y espuelas**
el bastón (31.1)
la fusta (31.4)
la fusta de cacería (31.6)
la tralla (31.2)
la fusta de carreras (31.5)

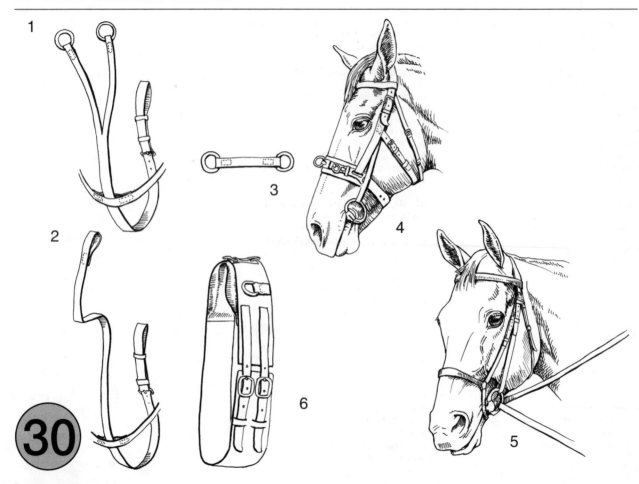

1

2

3

4

5

6

30

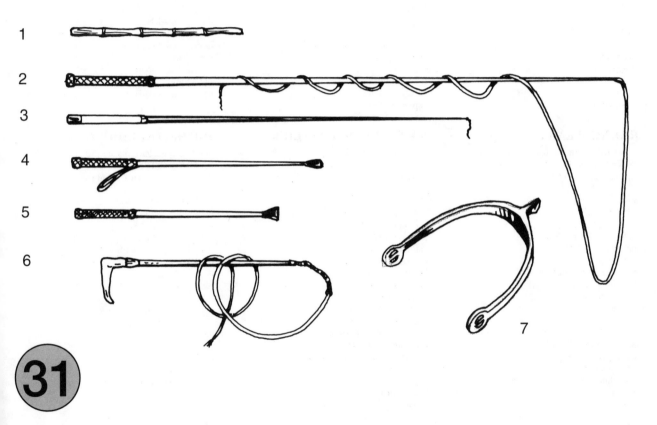

1

2

3

4

5

6

7

31

| | | |
|---|---|---|
| dressage whip (31.3) | la cravache de dressage (31.3) | die Dressurgerte (31.3) |
| thong | la monture | die Peitschenschnur |
| lash | la mèche | der Peitschenschmitz |
| spurs (31.7) | les éperons (*m.pl.*) (31.7) | die Sporen (*m.pl.*) (31.7) |
| neck | la tige | der Hals |
| rowel | la molette | das Spornrädchen |
| buckle | la boucle | die Schnalle |
| dummy spur | l'éperon (*m.*) lisse, le garde-crotte | der stumpfe Sporn |
| sharp spur | l'éperon pointu | der scharfe — |
| strapped spur | l'éperon à l'écuyère | der Anschnallsporn |
| straps | les courroies (*f.pl.*) | die Spornriemen (*m.pl.*) |
| box spur | l'éperon à boîte | der Kastensporn |
| spur-maker | l'éperonnier | der Sporer |

## RIDING WEAR

## LA TENUE DU CAVALIER

## DIE REITKLEIDUNG

| | | |
|---|---|---|
| bicorn (two-cornered hat ) (32.1) | le bicorne (32.1) | der Zweispitz, Zweimaster (32.1) |
| tricorn (three-cornered hat) (32.2) | le tricorne (32.2) | der Dreispitz, Dreimaster (32.2) |
| top hat, silk hat (32.3) | le haut-de-forme, le tube (32.3) | der Zylinderhut, der Reithut (32.3) |
| | | |
| bowler (32.4) | le melon (32.4) | die Melone (32.4) |
| riding hat (32.5) | la bombe (32.5) | die Reitkappe (32.5) |
| polo helmet (32.6) | le casque de polo (32.6) | der Polohelm (32.6) |
| jockey skull cap (32.7) | le casque (32.7) | die Sturzkappe (32.7) |
| jockey silk (32.8) | la toque (32.8) | der Überzug über der Sturzkappe (32.8) |
| chin strap | la sous-mentonnière | der Kinnriemen |
| dress (English style): | la tenue (à l'angaise): | der (englische): |
| (*a*) riding-dress | (*a*) d'équitation | (*a*) Reitfrack |
| (*b*) hunting-dress | (*b*) de chasse à courre | (*b*) Jagdfrack |
| French hunting-coat | la redingote (à la française) de chasse à courre | der (französische) Jagdrock |
| | | |
| side-saddle habit | le costume de l'amazone | das Damenreitkleid |
| racing colours (33.1) | la casaque de jockey (33.1) | die Rennjacke (33.1) |
| hacking jacket (33.2) | la veste (le veston) d'équitation (33.2) | die Reitjackett (33.2) |
| waistcoat (33.3) | le gilet (33.3) | die Weste (33.3) |
| stock, hunting tie | le plastron | der Plastron, die Jagdkrawatte |
| stock-pin | l'agrafe (*f.*) | die Agraffe |
| glove | le gant | der Handschuh |

la frusta da addestramento (31.3)
il cordone
lo sverzino, il mozzone, la punta
gli speroni (31.7)
l'asta (*f.*)
la rotella
la fibbia
lo sperone senza rotelle
lo sperone con la punta
lo sperone alla scudiera
i cinghietti
lo sperone senza cinghietti
il fabbricante di speroni

la fusta para doma (31.3)
°la guita
el latiguillo
las espuelas (31.7)
el gallo, la espiga
la rodela, la estrella
la hebilla
la espuela ciega
la espuela con gallo
la espuela de coreíllas
las correíllas
el espolín
el fabricante de espuelas

## LA TENUTA DEL CAVALIERE

il bicorno (32.1)
il tricorno (32.2)
il cilindro, la tuba (32.3)

la bombetta (32.4)
il cap (32.5)
l'elmetto da polo (32.6)
il casco (32.7)
il tocco, il copricasco (32.8)
il sottogola, la mentoniera
la tenuta (inglese):
  (*a*) da equitazione
  (*b*) da caccia
la tenuta da caccia francese

la tenuta da amazzone
la giubba del fantino (33.1)
la giacca da cavallo (33.2)
il panciotto (33.3)
il plastron, la cravatta a plastron, lo stock
la spilla da plastron
il guanto

## LOS TRAJES DE JINETE

el bicornio (32.1)
el tricornio (32.2)
el sombrero de copa, el sombrero
   forrado de seda (32.3)
el sombrero hongo, el bombín (32.4)
el casco equitación (32.5)
el casco de polo (32.6)
el casco protector, el casco de cross (32.7)
los colores de la cuadra (32.8)
la correa de la barbilla
el traje (a la inglesa):
  (*a*) el traje a la inglesa
  (*b*) el traje de caza
la levita de caza (francesa), la chaqueta —

el traje de amazona
los colores de cuadra (de carrera) (33.1)
la chaqueta de sport (33.2)
la chaleco (33.3)
el plastrón
el alfiler (de adorno y sujeción)
el guante

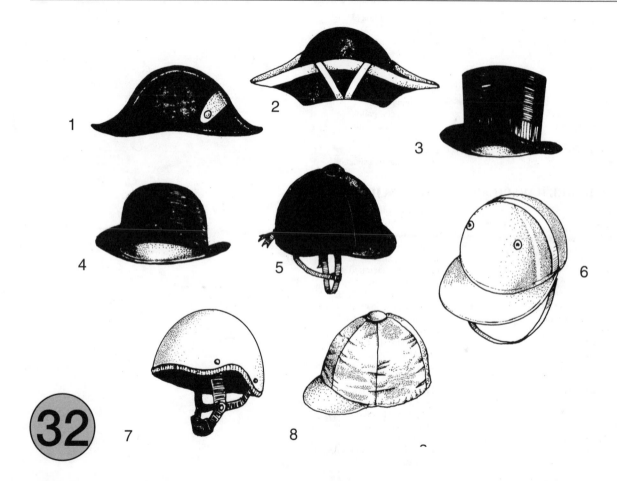

1

2

3

4

5

6

32

7

8

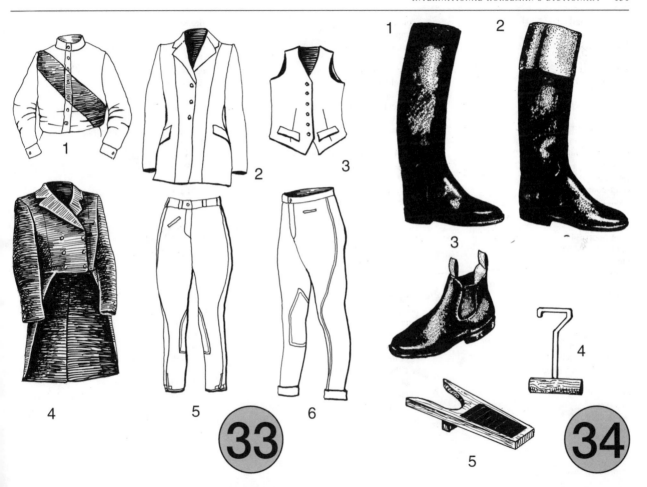

| | | |
|---|---|---|
| (dressage) tail coat (33.4) | l'habit (*m.*) (33.4) | der Reitfrack (33.4) |
| raincoat | l'imperméable (*m.*) | der Regenmantel |
| breeches (33.5) | la culotte (*f.*) (33.5) | die Reithose, die Breeches |
| | | (*f.pl.*) (33.5) |
| waxed jacket | la veste huilée, le barbour | der Wachsmantel |
| jodhpurs (33.6) | le jodhpur (33.6) | die lange Reithose (33.6) |
| chaps | les chaps (*m.pl.*) | die Chaps |
| back protector | le gilet de protection | die Schutzweste |
| boots | les bottes (*f.pl.*) | die Stiefel (*m.pl.*) |
| riding boot (34.1) | la botte d'équitation (34.1) | der Reitstiefel, hohe Stiefel (34.1) |
| rubber riding boot | — en caoutchouc | der Gummistiefel |
| top-boot, hunting boot (34.2) | — (à revers) de vénerie (34.2) | der Stulpen-, Jagdstiefel (34.2) |
| jockey boot, racing boot | — à revers de jockey | der Renn-, Jockeystiefel |
| polo boot | — de polo | der Polostiefel |
| field-boot | — de campagne | der Feldstiefel |
| jodhpur boot (34.3) | le boot 'jodhpur' (34.3) | der Jodhpurstiefel, die Stiefelette (34.3) |
| tree | l'embauchoir (*m.*) | der Stiefelblock, die Stiefelleiste |
| boot-hook (34.4) | le crochet (34.4) | der Stiefelhaken (34.4) |
| boot-jack (34.5) | le tire-botte (34.5) | der Stiefelknecht (34.5) |
| cleaning kit | la trousse de nettoyage | das Putzzeug |
| brush | la brosse | die Bürste |
| polish, cream | le cirage | die Wichse, die Paste |
| polishing bone | l'os polissoir | der Polierknochen |
| to clean the boots | nettoyer les bottes | die Stiefel reinigen, — putzen |
| to polish | cirer | schmieren |
| to brush | brosser | bürsten |
| to bone, polish | astiquer | polieren, wienern |
| to pull on one's boots | se botter, se chausser | die Stiefel anziehen |
| to take off one's boots | se débotter, se déchausser | — ausziehen |
| to dress | s'habiller | sich ankleiden, — anziehen |
| to change | se changer | sich umankleiden, — umanziehen |
| to undress | se déshabiller | sich entkleiden |
| bootmaker | le bottier | der Stiefelmacher |
| tailor | le tailleur | der Schneider |

| | |
|---|---|
| la marsina (33.4) | el frac (33.4) |
| l'impermeabile (*m.*) | el abrigo impermeable |
| i pantaloni da cavallo (33.5) | el calzón de montar, tipo inglés, los breeches (33.5) |
| la cerata | el barbour |
| i pantaloni da cavallo lunghi (all'indiana) (33.6) | el jodhpur (33.6) |
| i copripantaloni in pelle | los chaps |
| il giubbotto protettivo | el protegedorso |
| gli stivali | las botas |
| gli stivali da cavallo (34.1) | la bota equitación, — de montar (34.1) |
| gli stivali di gomma | — de goma |
| gli stivali con risvolto, — da caccia (34.2) | — de cacería con campana (34.2) |
| gli stivali con risvolto da fantino | — de carreras con campana |
| gli stivali da polo | — de polo |
| gli stivali da campagna | — de campo |
| la scarpa alta per i pantaloni lunghi (all'indiana) (34.3) | el botín (34.3) |
| il gambale | la horma |
| il gancio (34.4) | el gancho (34.4) |
| il cava-stivali (34.5) | el saca-botas, la tablilla (34.5) |
| il servizio per la pulizia degli stivali | la caja de útiles de limpieza |
| la spazzola | el cepillo |
| il lucido | el betún |
| l'osso per pulire e lisciare gli stivali | el hueso saca-brillo |
| pulire gli stivali | limpiar las botas |
| lucidare | dar brillo (a) |
| spazzolare | cepillar |
| passare l'osso | pasar el hueso saca-brillo, dar brillo |
| mettersi gli stivali, calzare — | ponerse las botas |
| togliersi gli stivali | quitarse las botas |
| vestirsi | vestirse |
| cambiarsi | mudarse |
| spogliarsi | desnudarse |
| lo stivalaio | el zapatero |
| il sarto | el sastre |

## OBSTACLES, JUMPS

stand, post
pole
ground line
wing
cavaletti (35.1)
upright obstacle
ascending parallel
oxer, square parallel (35.4)
simple obstacle
double obstacle, combination
treble obstacle, combination
course, track
hedge, brush (35.2)
post and rails (35.3)
water jump
triple bars, staircase jump (35.5)
gate (35.6)
brick wall (35.7)
stone wall (35.8)
road crossing (in and out)
bank
Irish bank
woodpile
open ditch
brook, water
bounce fence

drop fence
spread fence
bullfinch (36.4)
steps (36.2)
ski jump (36.3)
coffin (36.1)
trakehner (36.5)
table

## LES OBSTACLES (*m.pl.*)

le chandelier
la perche, la barre
le pied, la barre d'appel
l'encadrement (*m.*)
le cavaletti (35.1)
l'obstacle (*m.*) vertical, droit
l'oxer (*m.*) montant
l'oxer (*m.*) au carré (35.4)
l'obstacle simple
l'obstacle double, la combinaison
l'obstacle triple, la combinaison
le parcours, la piste
la haie (35.2)
la stationata (35.3)
la rivière
les barres (*f.pl.*) de spa (35.5)
la barrière (35.6)
le mur de brique (35.7)
le mur de pierre (35.8)
le passage de route
le talus
la butte, banquette, irlandaise
le stère de bois
le fossé
la rivière
le saut de puce

la descente, le contre-bas
le saut en largeur
le bullfinch, la haie vive (36.4)
le piano (36.2)
l'obstacle de volée (36.3)
les fossés (*m.pl.*) (36.1)
le trakehnen (36.5)
la table

## DIE HINDERNISSE

der Ständer
die Stange
den Absprung markierende Stange
der Fang
das Bodenrick, das Cavaletti (35.1)
steiles Hindernis
das aufsteigende Hindernis
der Oxer (35.4)
einfaches Hindernis
zweifaches Hindernis, die Kombination
dreifaches Hindernis, die Kombination
die Sprungfolge, die Springbahn
die Hürde (35.2)
die Staccionata, das Rick (35.3)
der Wassergraben
die Trippelbarre (35.5)
das Tor, das Gatter (35.6)
die Mauer, Backsteinmauer (35.7)
die Steinmauer (35.8)
der Wegübergang
der Wall, der Erdwall
die irische Bank
der Holzscheit
der Graben
der Wassergraben, der Bach
die Hindernisse (*n.pl.*) ohne
    Galoppzwischensprung
der Tiefsprung
der Weitsprung
der Bullfinch (36.4)
die Stufen (*f.pl.*) (36.2)
die Schanze (36.3)
der Coffin (36.1)
der Trakehner (36.5)
der Tisch

# GLI OSTACOLI

il piliere
la barriera
il piede, la barriera di richiamo
l'inquadramento
il cavalletto (35.1)
il verticale, il dritto
l'oxer in salita
l'oxer pari (35.4)
l'ostacolo (*m.*) semplice
la gabbia, la combinazione
la doppia gabbia, la combinazione
il percorso, la pista
la siepe (35.2)
la staccionata (35.3)
la riviera
la triplice (35.5)
il cancello sbarrato (35.6)
il muro (35.7)
la maceria (35.8)
il passaggio di strada
il talus
la banchina
l'abattuta (*f.*) di tronchi
il fosso
la riviera
il salto da pulce

la discesa
il largo
il bull-fence (36.4)
il pianoforte (36.2)
l'ostacolo (*m.*) di volata (36.3)
il coffin, il fosso tra ostacoli (36.1)
la staccionata sul fosso, il travone — (36.5)
il tavolo

# LOS OBSTÁCULOS

el pie
la barra
la barra de llamada
el reparo
el caballete (35.1)
el obstáculo vertical
el oxer de barras desiguales
el oxer quadrado (35.4)
el obstáculo simple
el obstáculo doble, la combinación
el obstáculo triple, la combinación
el recorrido
el seto (35.2)
el vertical de barras (35.3)
la ría
la volea, la triple barra (35.5)
la barrera (35.6)
el muro de ladrillos (35.7)
el muro de piedras (35.8)
el paso de caminos
la banqueta
la banqueta irlandesa
la leñera
el foso, la zanja
el foso de agua, la ría
caer y partir

la caída
el obstáculo de fondo
el bull-finch (36.4)
el piano, el obstáculo en escalera (36.2)
el paso en alto (36.3)
las zanjas, los fosos (36.1)
el trakehnen, el vertical sobre zanja (36.5)
la mesa

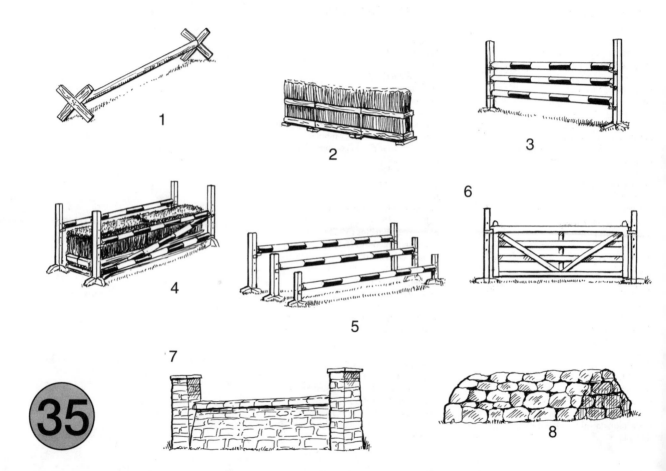

35

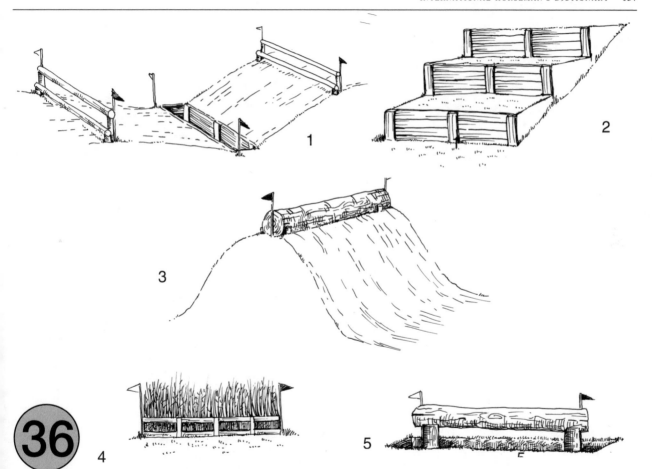

1

2

3

36

4

5

**Indexes**

**Index**

**Register**

**Indici**

**Indices**

# INDEX

above the contact 68
abscess 46
academic riding 78
to accept the bit 60
accident 94
action 8, 40, 58
action of one leg only 74
active 72
active leg 74
active rein 74
to adjust the reins 74
to adjust a saddle 136
admixture of new blood 6
advanced 92
advanced rider/trainer/
    instructor 90
affinity 4
African horse sickness 46
age specifications 108
aids 72
    diagonal 74
    lateral 74
    legs 72
    permeability to 64
    pushing 72
    rein 72
    seat 72
    on the 68
    weight 72
ailments 46
airs 42
airs above the ground 86
airs on the ground 86
alfalfa 12
allergic pruritic dermatitis 50
allergy, dust 48
amble 42
ambler 2
anaemia 46
anaesthetic 52
analgesic 52
ancestors 4

ancestry 4
angles 32
Anglo-Arab 2
to animate 2
anthelmintic 52
anti-inflammatory 52
antibiotics 52
antiseptic 52
anus 20
appeal 108
apprentice 108
apprentice's licence 110
to approach 94
apron 100
Arab, pure-bred 2
arched back 24
arched face 20
arched neck 22
arena 92
art of riding 78
arthritis 46
artificial airs 42
artificial insemination 8
ascarids 46
ascending parallel 154
to assess 94
assistant riding instructor 90
*Atropa belladonna* 10
attractive-looking fence 94
auction 110
auctioneer 108
automatic drinking bowl 126
automatic horse walker 130
automatic reverse 128
autumn crocus 10
azoturia 46

back 16, 24
    arched 24
    dipped 24
    hollow 24, 68
    long 24

muscles 72
protector 152
roach-backed 24
short 24
sores 46
stiff 68
straight 24, 112
strong 24
supple 68
sway 24
weak 24
well-coupled up 24
back at the knee 32
backward seat 72
bacteria 52
bad 92
badly set on head 22
badly muscled up neck 22
balance 8, 64
balanced 36
bald face 40
ballotade 86
balloting out 112
bandages 52, 126
    pressure 54
bank 154
bareback, to ride 80
barley 12
barrel 36, 58
barren mare 8
barrier draw 112
to bascule 94
base of support 60
bay 38
    blood 38
    bright 38
    bronze 38
    clear 38
    dark 38
    fawn 38
    golden 38
    light 38

tawny 38
at bay 102
beat 58
bed 126, 130
bedding 126
beget 8
beginner 90
behind the bit 68
behind the legs 68
belly 16, 24
    band 100
    cow-bellied 24
    greyhound-like 24
    herring-gutted 24
    normal 24
    pendulous 24
    pot-bellied 24
    tucked-up 24
belt 116, 118
bend 60
bent 60
    at the poll with head raised
    60
between legs and hands 68
bicorn 148
big head 20
bit 140-4
    to accept the 60
    behind the 68
    champ the 66
    contact with 60
    draw up behind the bit 68
    in front of 68
    on the 60
    take in the teeth 68
to bite 68
biting teeth 44
bitless bridle 140
bits 140
    bridoon 140
    curb 140
    eggbutt snaffle 140

gag 140
loose-ring snaffle 140
pelham 144
rubber snaffle 144
slide-mouth curb 144
snaffle 140
snaffle with cheeks 140
Weymouth curb 144
black 36, 116
    centre 44
    coal 36
    dull 36
    jet 36
    rusty 36
blacksmith 42
blanket clip 132
blaze 40
bleeding 52
blemishes 52
blindness 46
blinkers 100
blood bay 38
blood test 52
bloodline 4
blue 116
blue dun 38
blue roan 38
blue-grey 36
bodily defects/injuries 52
body 36, 58
body brush 126
body temperature 52
bog spavin 46
to bolt 68
bone 14
to bone 152
bone measurement 44
bone spavin 46
bonus points 94
bony withers 24
boot-hook 152
boot-jack 152

bootmaker 152
boots 126, 152
  to clean 152
  field 152
  hunting 152
  jockey 152
  jodphur 152
  polo 152
  to pull on 152
  racing 152
  riding 152
  to take off 152
  top 152
to bore 68
bots 46
bounce fence 154
bow-hocked 32
bow-legged 32
bowler 148
box (plant) 10
box spur 148
braces 116
bracken 10
brake 100
brake (transport) 128
brake (vehicle) 98
brake/stop light 128
bran 12
brand 10
to break in 64
breaking-in 120
breast bar 128
breast-plate 136
breastcollar harness 100
breeches 152
breeching 100
breeching strap 100
breed 2, 4
  create 6
  improve 6
breeder 4, 108
breeding 4-8
  line 6
  pure 6

selection 6
stock 2
brick wall 154
bridle 140
  bitless 140
  buckled 140
  double 140
  parts 140
  put on 140
  show 140
  snaffle 140
  stitched 140
  with studs 140
  take off 140
bridleway 80
bridoon 140
bright bay 38
broad croup 26
broken in 64
to be broken in 120
broken knees 46
broken wind 46
bronze bay 38
brood mare 8
brook 154
broom 126
brother 4
browband 140
brown 38, 116
bruise 52
brush 104, 152, 154
  to brush 130, 152
  to brush (a jump) 94
bucket 126
bucking 68
buckle 100, 148
buckskin dun 38
bull-necked 22
bullfinch 154
burns 52
buttercup 10
buttock 20
Buxus 10

cadence 42, 58
calf-kneed 32
calm 64
to calm 72
calves 72
cancer 46
cane 144
canine teeth 44
cannon 28
  bone 16
  circumference 44
  clearly defined 28
  free from gumminess 28
  long 28
  round 28
  short 28
  strong 28
  weak 28
  wide 28
canter 42, 84
  collected 84
  on the correct leg 84
  counter 76, 84
  disunited 68, 84
  extended 84
  left 76, 84
  medium 84
  near fore leading 84
  off fore leading 84
  on 76
  right 76, 84
  strike off at 76
  working 84
  on the wrong leg 84
to canter 76
cantle 136
capped elbow 46
capped hock 46
capriole 86
to be careless 94
caress 72
to caress 72
carriage 58, 98
carriage driving 78

carriage horse 2
carriage lamp 100
carrot 12
'carrousel' (French equestrian
  display) 80
to carry less 114
to carry over 114
cart horse 2
carty chested 22
to castrate 52
castration 52
category race 110
cavaletti 154
cavesson 144
central incisors 44
central nervous system 52
centre line 80
chaff 12
chain 126
chair seat 72
chambon 144
chamois leather 126, 128
champ the bit 66
change of direction 58
change of leg 76
  at every stride 76
change of rein
  in the circle 84
  through the circle 84
change of rider 112
to change 152
  in the air 76
  the diagonal 76
  direction 80
  gait 76
  the rein 76, 80
    down the centre line 80
    through the middle of
      the school 80
  speed 76
  tempo 76
changes (flying)
  every stride 76
  simple 76

changing the coat 130
changing the teeth 44
chaps 152
character 64-6
check squares 116
cheek snaffle 140
cheekpiece 140
cheeks 144
chest 16, 22
  carty chested 22
  chicken-breasted 22
  deep 22
  hollow 22
  narrow 22, 32
  pigeon-breasted 22
  thick in front 22
  well-proportioned 22
  wide 22, 32
chestnut 16, 36-8
  dark 36
  dark red 38
  golden 38
  light 36
  liver 36
  reddish liver 38
  roan 38
  washed-out 38
chicken-breasted 22
chin groove 16
chin strap 148
chrevrons 116
chronic obstructive pulmonary
  disease (COPD) 46
Cicuta virosa 10
circle 80
circuit of the track 114
circulatory system 52
circus rider 90
circus riding 78
class 120
classic race 110
classical equitation 76-8
to clean 130
to clean the boots 152

clean shoulder 26
cleaning kit 152
to clear 94
clear bay 38
clearly defined cannon 28
clench 42
clerk of the course 108
clerk of the scales 108
to clip 132
clipper blades 132
clippers 132
clipping 132
clips
   blanket 132
   full 132
   hunter 132
   trace 132
close breeding 6
close finish 122
close to the ground 32
close to the ground, hock 30
clover 12
club foot 42
coal black 36
coarse head 20
coarse mix 12
coarse shoulder 26
coat 14, 130
   changing 130
cob 2
coffin 154
*Colchicum autumnale* 10
cold 64
cold compress 52
cold hosing 52
cold-blooded 2
colic 46
collar 100
to collect the horse 60
collected canter 84
collected paces/gaits 42
collected trot 84
collected walk 84
collection 64

colour 14
colours 36-40
   racing 116, 148
colts 8, 108
comb 132
to comb 130
combination 154
combined driving 102
combined training 78
'coming through' 64
common head 20
compact 32
competition 78
competition riding 78
competitions 96
competitor's briefing 96
composite 36
compound feed 12
concave head 20
concave side 60
concussion 52
condition 64, 66
   out of 66
condition race 110
cones 102
confidence 64
confident contact 60
conformation 8, 14, 20
conformation of the legs 14,
   32
   defective 32
   normal 32
*Conium maculatum* 10
conjunctivitis 46
connections of the horse 108
consanguinity 4
constancy 6
constitution 8
contact
   above 68
   with bit 60
   confident 60
   soft 60
   unsteady 66

contagious 52
contagious equine metritis 46
contracted foot 42
convex profile 20
convex side 60
COPD *see* chronic obstructive
   pulmonary disease
corn 12
corner 80
corner incisors 44
corns 46
coronet 20
   white markings 40
cough 46
counter canter 76, 84
counter-change of hand 80
counter-rein 74
couple 102
courbette 86
'courbette' of the French
   School 86
course 80, 94, 154
   designer 94
   to walk 94, 96
covering 8, 10
cow-bellied 24
cow-hocked 32
cracked heels 46
cream 36, 116, 152
create a breed 6
cremello 36
crest 16
to be crooked 60
cross belts 116, 118
cross-country 78
   obstacles 96
   phase 96
crossing 6, 112
croup 16, 26
   broad 26
   flat 26
   goose-rumped 26
   long 26
   narrow 26

oval 26
overbuilt 26
   sharp 26
   short 26
   sloping 26
   strong 26
   too high 26
   weak 26
croup-high 36
croupade 86
crupper 100, 144
crushed 12
cryptorchid 8
cub-hunting 102
cubbing 102
cubes 12
curb
   bit 140
   chain 144
   on the curb only 74
   groove 16
   rein 140
   slide-mouth 144
   Weymouth 144
curb (ailment) 46
'curée' 102
curry comb 126
curved ribs 22
to cut 132

dagger 104
daily ration 14
dam 4
dandy brush 126
dappled grey 40
dark bay 38
dark blue 116
dark blue dun 38
dark chestnut 36
dark green 116
dark grey 38
dark head 40
dark red chestnut 38
dashboard 100

daughter 4
de Gogue 144
dead 116
dead mouth 66
dead-heat 114
deadly nightshade 10
declaration of riders 112
to declare forfeit 112
deep chest 22
deep litter 130
deep-set tail 26
defective conformation of the
   legs 32
degenerate 6
degree 4
degree of training 64-6
dehydration 52
delicate feeder 66
depth 32
derived 36
dermatophilosis 48
descendants 4
descent 112
to destroy a horse 52
diagonal
   aids 74
   change 76
   change of hand 80
   pairs 58
   trot on the left/right 76
diamonds 116, 118
diarrhoea 46
difficult temperament 64
digestive system 52
*Digitalis purpurea* 10
dimensions 36
dipped back 24
direct flexion 60
direct rein of opposition 74
direction
   to change 80
   change of 58
   indicator 128
   of movement 58

dirty white 36
to disappoint 120
disc 118
discharge 52
disease 46-50
dish-nosed head 20
to dismount 72
disobedience 66-71
disobedient 68
disqualification 98
to be disqualified 120
disqualified from final
    placings 110
distance 94, 112
distant 114
disunited canter 68, 84
dock 16, 132
to dock 132
docked tail 132
dog cart 98
donkey 2
dorsal band 40
double accumulator 96
double bridle 140
double obstacle 154
dovetail 44
down the centre line 80
drag-hunting 102
draught horse 2
draw up the tongue behind the
    bit 68
draw-reins 144
dress 148
to dress 152
dressage 58-64, 66
    driven 102
    horse 2
    to music 92
    phase 96
    saddle 132
    seat 72
    tail coat 152
    test 90, 92
    whip 148

dressings 52
to drive 98
driven dressage 102
driver 98
driving 98-102
    bridle 100
    trials 102
    whip 100
drop fence 154
drop noseband 140
dropped sole 42
drug (medicinal) 52
drug (prohibited substances)
    52
to dry 130
dry food 12
dry head 20
dual-purpose horse 2
dull black 36
dummy spur 148
dun 38
    blue 38
    buckskin 38
    dark blue 38
    grey 38
    light blue 38
    mouse 38
    yellow 38
dust allergy 48

ear 16
ease 60
eczema 52
eel stripe 40
eggbutt snaffle 140
elbow 16, 28
    capped 46
    inclined inwards 28
    inclined outwards 28
    loose 28
    tied-in 28
    weak 28
electrolytes 52
elementary 90

to eliminate 96
elimination 98, 112
empty weight 128
endurance ride 78
to engage the haunches/hind
    legs 60
engender 8
English measures 46
English Thoroughbred 2
to enter a horse 112
entire 8
entry 110
equerry 90
equestrian 90
equestrian centre 78
equestrian feel 76
equestrian games 78
equestrienne 90
equine influenza 48
equipment 125-54
    stable 126-8
Equisetum 10
equitation 76
ergot 20
error of course 92
error of test 92
evasions 66-71
event rider 96
eventer 2
eventer (horse) 96
eventing 78, 96
ewe-necked 22
excellent 92
execution of the test 92
to exercise 130
exercises to be carried out
    92
exhausted 66
expressive head 20
to extend 76
extended canter 84
extended paces/gaits 42
extended trot 84
extended walk 84

exterior of the horse 14-36
eye 16

to fail to respond 122
fairly bad 92
fairly good 92
fall 94
to fall 94, 98
false acacia 12
false curb 48
false start 112
family 4
faradism 52
farrier 42
farriery 42
fault and out 96
fawn bay 38
feather 20
to feed 130
feed stuffs 12-14, 126
feel 76
feet turned out 32
fences 92
    attractive-looking 94
    inviting 94
    solid 94
fencing 10
fetlock 16, 130
fever 48
field (hunting) 102
field (racing) 112, 122
field-boot 152
fiery 64
figure of eight 84
filly 8, 110
fine mouth 66
fine neck 22
finish 112
firm 114
first aid 54
first-aid kit 54
fistulous withers 48
fit 66
to be fit 120

to fit a saddle 136
fitness 66
flag start 112
flank 16
flap 136
flash noseband 140
flat croup 26
flat foot 42
flat forearm 28
flat knee 28
flat race 110
flat ribs 22
fleabitten grey 38
flexion
    direct 60
    lateral 60
    test 54
foal 10
    weaning 10
foaling 10
foaling mare 8
foam 66
follower of the hunt 102
foot 20, 42-4, 46
    club 42
    contracted 42
    flat 42
    to pick out 130
footboard 100
forage 126
to force the pace 120
forearm 16, 28
    flat 28
    large 28
    long 28
    narrow 28
    short 28
    wide 28
forehand 36, 58
forehead 16
forelegs 58
forelock 20, 130
forge 42
fork seat 72

form 64-6, 120
forward seat 72
forward thrust 64
forwards, not going 68
foundation 36
foundation sire 6
foundation stock 4
four-in-hand 98
fox-hunting 102
foxglove 10
fracture 54
frame 36
free generation 6
free paces/gaits 42
free walk 84
free-style 92
freedom 60
French hunting coat 148
fresh mouth 66
fresh (temperament) 64
frog 42
full brother 4
full clip 132
full collar harness 100
full sister 4
fungal infection 48
furlong 46

gag 140
gaits 40-2, 58
    to change 76
gallop 42
to gallop 76
gaskin 20, 30
    clearly defined 30
    full 30
    long 30
    strong 30
    well-muscled 30
gate 10, 154
to gather the horse 60
to geld 52
geldings 108
general equitation 78

general purpose saddle 132
general utility horse 2
gestation, period of 10
gig 98
girth 32, 136
    circumference 44
    to loosen 136
    strap 136
    to tighten 136
to give 74
to give up 120
giving away the rein 64
giving and retaking the rein 64
glanders 48
glove 148
going 114
golden bay 38
golden chestnut 38
'gone away' 102
good 92, 114
good bone 32
'good doer' 66
good feeder 66
goose-rumped 26
grakle noseband 140
Grand Prix 92
granddam 4
granddaughter 4
grandsire 4
grandson 4
grass 12
grass sickness 48
grass track 114
grassland 10
to graze 10, 94
green 64, 116
'green branch' 104
green fodder 12
green mouth 66
grey 38
    dappled 40
    dark 38
    dun 38
    fleabitten 38

iron 38
slaty blue 38
speckled 38
greyhound-like belly 24
grind the teeth 68
grinding surface 44
grinding teeth 44
groom 10, 102, 130
to groom 130
grooming
    quick 130
    thorough 130
groom's door 128
gross weight 128
ground jury 98
ground line 154
gullet 136
gymkhana 78

hack 2
hackamore 140
hacking 78
hacking jacket 148
hackney 102
hair 14
half brother 4
half a length 114
half pass 86
half sister 4
half-halt 74
half-moon mouthpiece 144
half-pirouette 86
half-turn on the haunches 86
half-volte 80
half-way mark 112
halt 58, 76, 84
to halt 76
halter 126
hame 100
hand (measurement) 44
hand-gallop 84
handicap 110
handicapper 108
hands 72

between legs and hands 68
simultaneous action of
    hand and leg 76
hang out the tongue 68
hard 114
hard mouth 66
harmonious 36
harmony 60
harness 98
harness horse 102
to harness up 100
harness-maker 136
hats
    bicorn 148
    bowler 148
    jockey skull 148
    polo 148
    riding 148
    silk 148
    top 148
    tricorn 148
haunches 58
    to engage 60
'haute école' 78
to have a narrow lead 120
to have racing ability 120
hay
    (first cut) 12
    (second cut) 12
hay-net 126
hay-rack 126
haylage 12
head 14, 20-2
    arched face 20
    badly set on 22
    big 20
    coarse 20
    common 20
    concave 20
    convex profile 20
    dish-nosed 20
    dry 20
    expressive 20
    heavy 20

lean 20
light 20
markings 40
noble 20
Roman-nosed 22
small 20
straight 20
to toss 68
to the wall 86
wedge-shaped 20
well set on 22
head collar 126
head groom 130
head lad 130
head (racing) 114
head (saddle) 136
head-rope 126
head-shaking 68
headpiece 140
health 8
heart disease 48
heavy 116
    head 20
    horse 2
    neck 22
heavyweight horse 2
hedge 154
heels 42
    hairy 20
heels (rider's) 72
height (at withers) 32, 44
hemlock 10
henbane 10
hepatitis 48
heredity 6
hernia 48
herring-gutted 24
heterogeneous 6
high at the withers 36
high croup 26
high school 78
high school airs 86
high school (circus) 78
high school horse 90

high school rider 90
high set-on neck 22
high withers 24
high-set tail 26
highly bred 36
highly strung 64
hind legs 58
　to engage 60
hindquarters 36, 58
hip 26
　normal 26
　point of 16
　pointed 26
　prominent 26
　ragged 26
hips (rider's) 72
to hit 72
hock 20, 30-2
　at an open angle 30
　capped 46
　close to the ground 30
　cow-hocked 32
　large 30
　lean 30
　long 30
　poorly defined 30
　sickle 32
　spongy 30
　straight 30
　strong 32
　weak 32
　well-defined 30
　wide 30
　woolly outline 30
to hog 132
hogged mane 132
holding 116
hollow back 24, 68
hollow chest 22
homogeneous 6
hood 126
hoof 20, 42-4
　grease 128
　oil 128

to pare 44
pick 126
hoof-bound 42
hooks 44, 144
hooped 116, 118
hormones 54
horny wall 42
horse ball 78
horse inspection 96
horse transport 128
horse trials 78, 96
horse walker 130
horsebox 128
horsetails 10
horsewoman 90
hot (temperament) 64
hound 102
hunt uniform 104
hunter 2, 102
hunter clip 132
hunter trials 78
hunting 78, 102
　boot 152
　dress 148
　horn 104
　saddle 132
　tie 148
　whip 104, 144
huntsman 102
hurdle race 110
hybrid 6
Hyoscyamus niger 10
Hypericum 12

identification document 10
immobility 58, 76
improve a breed 6
impulsion 58
in front of the bit 68
in front of the legs 68
in and out 154
in proportion 36
in the straight 112
in-foal mare 8

inactive leg 74
inactivity 60
inbreeding 6
incest breeding 6
inch 46
incisors 44
indicator 128
indirect rein of opposition
　behind the withers 74
indirect rein of opposition in
　front of the withers 74
individual 4
indoor school 80
infection, fungal 48
inflammation 54
influenza 48
infundibulum 44
inheritance 6
injury 50
innate defect 6
inner rein 74
insect bite 48
inseminate 8
insensitive to the legs 68
inside 58
inside leg (horse's) 86
insufficient 92
Intermediare 92
intermediary produce 6
interval training 98
inviting fence 94
Irish bank 154
Irish martingale 144
iron grey 38
irregular paces/gaits 42
itchiness 54

jab of the spurs 74
jag of reins 74
jaundice 48
jaw, lower 16
jerk the reins 74
jet black 36
jockey 90, 108

boot 152
seat 72
silk 148
skull cap 148
wheel 128
jockey's licence 110
jodphur boot 152
jodphurs 152
to jog 68
joint 14
joint disease 48
jointed mouthpiece 144
judge 108
to judge 94
judging, method of 94
jump 92
to jump 94
jump off 96
jumper 2, 92
jumping 92-6
　ability 92
　competition 78, 94
　faults 96
　lane 94
　loose 94
　race 110
　saddle 132
　seat 72
　style 92
jumps 154

keen 60
kennel 102
to kick 68
kill 102
to kill 102
knee 16, 28
　back at 32
　broken 46
　calf-kneed 32
　flat 28
　knotted 28
　large 28
　lean 28

long 28
over at 32
roll 136
rounded 28
tied-in below 28
well-defined 28
wide 28, 32
knee-caps 126
to knock down 94
to knock over 94
knock-kneed 32
knotted knee 28

laburnum 12
Laburnum 12
lad 108
lady jockey 108
lady owner 108
lady rider 90
lameness 48
laminitis 48
to land 94
large
　forearm 28
　hock 30
　knee 28
　stifle 30
laser therapy 54
lash 148
lash out 68 ·
last corner 112
lateral aids 74
lateral bend 60
lateral flexion 60
lateral incisors 44
lateral pairs 58
lateral work 86
lazy 64
lean
　head 20
　hock 30
　knee 28
　second thigh 30
　shoulder 26

stifle 30
withers 24
left canter 76, 84
left-handed track 114
leg-yielding 86
legs 58, 72
    action of one only 74
    active 74
    aids 72
    in the air 58
    behind the 68
    behind the girth 74
    between legs and hands 68
    conformation 14, 32
    in front of 68
    on the ground 58
    inactive 74
    insensitive to 68
    not going forward from 68
    passive 74
    sensitive to 68
    simultaneous action 74
    simultaneous action of hand
        and leg 76
leisure riding 78
length (racing) 114
to lengthen the reins 74
to let down 120
levade 86
level loins 24
levers 32
lice 48
ligament 14
light
    bay 38
    blue 116
    blue dun 38
    chestnut 36
    green 116
    head 20
    horse 66
    mouth 66
    neck 22
lightness 64

lightweight horse 2
Ligustrum 12
to like the going 120
limbs 14
    markings 40
to be of limited ability 120
line 4
line breeding 6
lineage 4
lines 32
linseed 12
lipstrap 144
list 40
list of runners 114
litter 130
liver chestnut 36
liver fluke 48
livery 130
load 128
loaded shoulder 26
to lodge an objection 110
loins 16, 24
    level 24
    long 24
    narrow 24
    short 24
    strong 24
    sunken 24
    weak 24
    wide 24
long
    back 24
    cannon 28
    croup 26
    forearm 28
    hock 30
    knee 28
    loins 24
    neck 22
    pastern 30
    reins 84, 144
        work in 90
    ribs 22
    shoulder 26

thigh 30
    upper arm 28
    withers 24
long-distance driving 102
long-distance ride 78
long-reining 66
longitudinal axis 60
loop 84
loose elbow 28
loose jumping 94
loose rein 74, 84
loose shoulder 26
loose-box 126
loose-ring snaffle 140
to loosen the girth 136
Lorraine cross 116, 118
lorry 128
loss of form 120
lotion 54
low school 78
low set neck 22
low set-on neck 22
low withers 24
low-set tail 26
to lower the head abruptly and
    with force 68
lower jaw 16
lower legs 72
lower part 36
lucerne 12
lungeing 66
    gear 144
    rein 144
    whip 144
lungworm infection 48
lupin 12
Lupinus 12
lymphangitis 48

made horse 66
maiden race 110
maintenance ration 14
maize 12
making up the bed 130

malnutrition 48
mane 20, 130
    hogged 132
    plaited 132
    pulled 132
mane comb 128
manège 80-90
mange 48
manger 126
marathon driving 100
mare 8
    barren 8
    brood 8
    with foal at foot 8
    foaling 8
    in-foal 8
    served 8
    tap-root 8
markers 92
markings 40
    without 40
maroon 116
martingales 144
    Irish 144
    running 144
    standing 144
mash 14
to massage 130
Master of the horse 90
master of hounds 102
match 110
mating 8
mauve 116
maximum weight 128
meadow 10
meadow saffron 10
measurement 44
    bone 44
    English 46
    metric 46
    taken with stick 44
    taken with tape 44
measures 44-6
measuring stick 44

measuring tape 44
measuring unit 44
medium 92
medium canter 84
medium trot 84
medium walk 84
meet 102
method of judging 94
metre 46
metric measures 46
mezair 86
microscopic examination 54
middle-distance horse 120
middleweight horse 2
mile 46
mile specialist 120
milk teeth 44
mites 48
mixed 6, 36
mixed breed 6
mobility 60
molars 44
molasses 12
moment of suspension 60
Monday morning disease 46
moulting 130
to mount 72
mounts 112
mouse dun 38
mouth 16, 66
    the bit 66
    dead 66
    fine 66
    fresh 66
    green 66
    hard 66
    light 66
    ruined 66
    sensitive 66
    spoiled 66
    wet 66
    yielding 60
mouthpiece 144
'mouthy' 66

move off at a trot 76
move off at a walk 76
movement 8, 40-2, 58
    direction of 58
to muck out the box 130
mud fever 48
mule 2
muscle-relaxant drug 54
muscles 14
musculoskeletal system 52

nail 42
    picked-up 42
nappy 68
narrow
    at the chest 32
    behind, at the hocks 32
    chest 22
    croup 26
    forearm 28
    loins 24
    neck 22
nationality plate 128
Nations Cup 96
native breed 2
natural paces/gaits 42
navel 16
navicular disease 48
near-side 58
neck 16, 22
    arched 22
    badly muscled up 22
    bull-necked 22
    ewe-necked 22
    fine 22
    heavy 22
    high set-on 22
    light 22
    long 22
    low set 22
    low set-on 22
    narrow 22
    oblique 22
    short 22

sloping 22
straight 22
stroking 64
strong 22
swan-necked 22
thick 22
well-muscled up 22
well-proportioned 22
neck (racing) 114
neck (spurs) 148
to neglect 94
nematodes 50
nerve 54
nerve-blocking 54
nerves 14
nervous 64
New Zealand rug 126
to nip 68
noble 36
noble head 20
normal
    belly 24
    conformation of the legs 32
    hip 26
    seat 72
nose 16
nose (racing) 114
nosebands 140
    drop 140
    flash 140
    grakle 140
nostrils 16
not eligible to race 110
not executed 92
not going forward from the leg
    68
not true to type 6
novice 120
    horse 66
    rider 90
    test 90
novices' race 110
number plate 128
numbness 54

numnah 136
to nurse 54
nutrition 54
nuts 12

oats 12
obedience 64
obesity 48
oblique neck 22
oblique shoulder 26
obstacle 92
obstacle driving 100
obstacles 154
off-side 58
offspring 4
oil 14
ointment 54
on the aids 68
on the bit 60
on the curb only 74
one beat 58
one step 58
one stride 58
one-day event 96
one-sided 60
open
    ditch 154
    jumping 96
    race 110
    stifle 30
    wound 54
opening rein 74
optimum time 98
orange 116
organs 14
Oriental horse 2
origin 4
out of condition 66
outbreeding 6
outcrossing 6
outdoor school 80
outer rein 74
outlines 32
outside 58

outside assistance 98
outsider 122
oval croup 26
over at the knee 32
over-reach boots 126
overbent 68
overbuilt croup 26
overreach injury 48
overridden 66
overshot fetlock 32
overrun brake 128
owner 108
owner-breeder 108
owner-trainer 108
oxer 154
oxyuris 50

pace 120
pacemaker 120
pacer 2
paces 40-2, 58, 84
pack 102
pack horse 2
pad 100
paddock 10
pain 54
pair (driving) 98
pairs of legs 58
palomino 38
panel 136
parade 112
parallels
    ascending 154
    square 154
paralysis 48
parasites 54
to pare the hoof 44
parting 40
partition 128
partnership 108
parturition 10
passage 86
passive 72
passive leg 74

passive rein 74
passport 110
pastern 20, 30
    long 30
    short 30
    sloping 30
    too long 30
    upright 30
    weak 30
pasture 10
to pat 72
pattern race 110
pedigree 6
pelham 144
pelvis 14
penalty points 96, 98
penalty zone 98
pendulous belly 24
penis 20
to perform surgery 54
performance 58
performance test 80
period of gestation 10
periods 44
peritonitis 48
permanent teeth 44
permeability to the aids 64
pesade 86
phaeton 98
phlegmatic 64
photo-finish 114
piaffe 86
to pick out the foot 130
picked-up nail 42
piebald 38
pigeon-breasted 22
pigeon-toed 32
pillars 144
pin firing 54
pink 116
pink coat 104
pirouettes 86
pitchfork 126
place bet 114

placing 96
plain 116, 118
plain mouthpiece 144
to plait 132
plaited mane 132
plaited tail 132
plaiting band 128
plaiting thread 128
plants, poisonous 10
to plunge 68
pneumonia 48
point of hip 16
point of shoulder 16
point to point 78
pointed hip 26
points of the horse 14, 20
poisoning 48
poisonous plants 10
pole 100, 154
polish 152
to polish 152
polishing bone 152
poll 16
    yielding 60
polo 78
    boot 152
    helmet 148
    saddle 136
pommel 136
pony 2
poorly defined hock 30
poorly defined withers 24
porcelain white 36
port 144
position (horse) 60
position (rider) 72
post 154
post and rails 154
pot-bellied 24
potency 6
poultice 54
powder 54
preliminary 90
preliminary canter to the

starting post 112
prepotency 6
presentation of stag's foot 104
pressure bandage 54
prick by farrier 42
principal paces/gaits 42
private sale 110
privet 12
Prix St Georges 92
prize 96
problem horse 64
procreate 8
produce 4
productive 8
prolific 8
prominent hip 26
pronounced shoulder 26
pronounced withers 24
prophet's thumb mark 40
prototype of the species 6
Pteridium aquilinum 10
public enclosure 114
'puissance' 96
to pull 68, 132
to pull on one's boots 152
to pull up 76, 120
pulled mane 132
pulled tail 132
puncture wound 48
to punish 72
punishment 72
punter 108
pupil 90
pure breeding 6
purple 116
purposeful 60
purses 108
pus 54
pushing aids 72
put on a bridle 140
to put to 100
put the tongue over the bit 68

quadrille 80

quality 8, 36, 120
quarry 102
quartered 118
quartering 130
quarters in 86
quarters out 86
quick grooming 130
to quicken 122
quiet 64

race 112
    card 114
    categories 110
    horse 2
    organisation 112-14
    riding 78
    whip 144
to race on the rails 122
racing 107-22
    administration 108
    boot 152
    colours 116, 148
    gallop 84
    performance 120-2
    personnel 108
    saddle 136
ragged hip 26
ragwort 10
rails 112
rain scald 48
raincoat 152
raiser 4
raising 4
ramp 128
randem 98
Ranunculus 10
to rap 94
rasp 42
rat tail 26
reactions of the ridden horse
    66-71
to rear 68
rearer (breeding) 4
rearing 4

to receive interference 120
rectangular 36
red roan 38
reddish liver chestnut 38
redworms 48
to refuse 94
registration certificate 110
regular paces/gaits 42
regularity 58
rein aids 72
rein back 76
reins 140
    active 74
    to adjust 74
    in both hands 74
    to change 76, 80
    change in the circle 84
    change through the circle 84
    completely loose 74
    counter-rein 74
    curb 140
    direct rein of opposition 74
    giving away 64
    giving and retaking 64
    indirect rein of opposition
        behind the withers 74
    indirect rein of opposition
        in front of the withers 74
    inner 74
    jerk/jag 74
    to lengthen 74
    long 84, 90, 144
    loose 74, 84
    lungeing 144
    manner of handling 74
    in one hand 74
    opening 74
    outer 74
    passive 74
    to separate 74
    to shorten 74
    snaffle 140
    taking down 64
relaxed 64

to remove the droppings 130
remove the shoe 44
renvers 86
to respect 94
respiratory system 52
to retire 98, 120
retrogressive 6
reversed pirouette 86
reward 72
to reward 72
rhythm 58
ribs 14, 16, 22
    curved 22
    flat 22
    long 22
    short 22
    well-sprung 22
ride 80
a ride 58
ride and drive horse 2
to ride against the clock 94
to ride astride 80
to ride bareback 80
to ride in 94
to ride side-saddle 80
riders 90, 92
    change of 112
    declaration 112
    weight 72
ridge of hair 40
riding
    boot 152
    dress 148
    fee 112
    hat 148
    horse 2
    to hounds 78
    instructor 90
    school 78
    for sport 78
    stables 78
    technique 72-6
    wear 148-52
    whip 144

rig 8
right canter 76, 84
right-handed track 114
ringbone 48
rings 144
ringworm 50
rise 112
rising trot 76
roach-backed 24
road crossing 154
roads and tracks 96
roan 38
   blue 38
   chestnut 38
   red 38
   strawberry 38
robinia 12
*Robinia pseudoacacia* 12
rolled 12
roller 126, 144
Roman-nosed 22
root of the tail 132
rose of Sharon 12
rosette 96
roughage 12
round cannon 28
rounded knee 28
roundworms 50
rowel 148
to rub 130
rubber riding boot 152
rubber snaffle 144
rug 126
ruined mouth 66
run 102
to run away 68
to run out 94
to run poorly 120
to run well 120
runners 114
running martingale 144
rusty black 36

saddle 132

to adjust 136
dressage 132
to fit 136
general purpose 132
horse 2
hunting 132
jumping 132
parts 136
polo 136
racing 136
side 136
soap 128
sores 50
synthetic 136
Western 136
to saddle a horse 136
saddle-room 136
saddler 136
saddler's shop 136
saddlery 132-44
St John's wort 12
sale
   with a reserve price 110
   without a reserve price 110
salt 14
   lick 14
salute 92
sand 80
sand track 114
sandcrack 42, 50
sarcoptic mange 50
satisfactory 92
scale of marks (dressage) 92
scarlet coat 104
scent 12
school 80, 92
   airs 42
   figures 80-90
   jumps 86
   rider 90
   riding 78
   trot 86
   walk 86
schooling 58-64, 66

to school a jumper 94
scissors 132
scratched 112
scrotum 20
scurry driving 100
scurry jumping 96
seams 116, 118
season 10
seat 72, 94
   aids 72
   backward 72
   bones 72
   chair 72
   dressage 72
   fork 72
   forward 72
   jockey 72
   jumping 72
   normal 72
   stiff 72
   supple 72
seat (driving) 100
seat (saddle) 136
second horse 102
second thigh 20, 30
   clearly defined 30
   full 30
   long 30
   strong 30
   well-muscled 30
seedy toe 50
selling race 110
*Senecio jacobea* 12
sensitive mouth 66
sensitive to the legs 68
to separate the reins 74
series race 110
serpentine 84
served mare 8
service 10
serving 8
set four-square 36
set of the legs 14
to set the pace 120

shaft 100
sharp 60
sharp croup 26
sharp spur 148
shavings 130
sheath 16
shelter 10
shoe 42
   removal 44
to shoe a horse 44
short
   back 24
   cannon 28
   croup 26
   forearm 28
   head (racing) 114
   loins 24
   neck 22
   neck (racing) 114
   pastern 30
   ribs 22
   shoulder 26
   tail 132
   upper arm 26
   withers 24
to be short of work 120
to shorten 76
to shorten the reins 74
shoulder 16, 26, 118
   clean 26
   coarse 26
   lean 26
   loaded 26
   long 26
   loose 26
   oblique 26
   point of 16
   pronounced 26
   short 26
   sloping 26
   straight 26
   upright 26
   weak 26
shoulder-in 86

show bridle 140
show class 80
show jumper 2
show jumping 78, 94
show jumping phase 96
shy 64
to shy 68
shy feeder 66
sickle hock 32
side saddle 136
side-reins 144
side-saddle
   habit 148
   to ride 80
sidebone 50
silk hat 148
silver eye 40
simple 36
simple change 76
simple obstacle 154
simultaneous action of the
   legs 74
single turnout 98
sire 8
sister 4
sitting
   on the fork 72
   square 72
   too far back 72
   trot 76
six bars 96
six-in-hand 98
to size up 94
skeleton 14
skewbald 38
ski jump 154
skilled rider 90
skin 14
to skip out 130
skirt 136
skull cap 148
slaty blue grey 38
slide-mouth curb 144
sloping

croup 26
  neck 22
  pastern 30
  shoulder 26
  thigh 30
  upper arm 28
to slow down 76
sluggish 64
small head 20
smithy 42
snaffle bit 140
  with cheeks 140
  eggbutt 140
  loose-ring 140
snaffle bridle 140
snaffle rein 140
to snap 68
snip 40
sock 40
soft 116
soft contact 60
sole 42
solid fence 94
'some white hairs' 40
son 4
soreness 54
sounding the bell 92
soundness 8, 52
spare wheel 128
species 4
  prototype 6
speckled grey 38
speed
  to change 76
  and endurance 96
spike 98
spine 14
splint 50
splinter bar 100
spoiled mouth 66
sponge 126
to sponge 130
spongy hock 30
spots 118

spotted 38
spread fence 154
springs 100
sprinter 118
spur-maker 148
spurs 144, 148
  box 148
  dummy 148
  jab of 74
  sharp 148
  strapped 148
square parallel 154
stability 6
stable 126-8
  companion 120
  lad 130
  management 130
  rubber 128
stag-hunting 102
staircase jump 154
stall 126
stallion 8
stallion man 10, 108
stamina 120
stand 154
standing
  martingale 144
  over a lot of ground 32
  stretched 32
  under 32
star 40
star-gaze 68
stars 118
start 112
  box 98
  false 112
  flag 112
  from the stalls 112
  tape 112
starter 108, 114
starting gate 112
starting signal 98
stayer 118
steeplechase 96, 110

steps 154
sterile 8
stewards 108
stick out the tongue 68
stiff 64
  back 68
  seat 72
stifle 20, 30
  large 30
  lean 30
  open 30
stirrup
  iron 136
  leather 136
stirrup-bar 136
stock 148
stock-pin 148
stocking 40
  rising above knee (hock) 40
stocky 32
stone 44
stone wall 154
to stop 76, 94
straight 58
  back 24
  course 114
  head 20
  hock 30
  horse 60
  line 80
  neck 22
  shoulder 26
  upper arm 28
straighten 58
straightness 58
strain 4
strained tendons 50
strangles 50
strapped spur 148
straps 148
straw 12
strawberry roan 38
stride 58
strike off at the canter 76

stringhalt 50
strip 116, 118
stripe 40
stripes 118
stroke of the whip 74
stroking the neck 64
strong
  back 24
  cannon 28
  croup 26
  hock 32
  loins 24
  neck 22
strongyles 48
stubborn 68
stud 8
  farm 4, 8
  groom 10, 130
  manager 10
stud (shoes) 44
stud-book 10
student 90
sturdy 32
style of jumping (of horse) 92
style of rider 94
submission 60
suck 10
sufficient 92
sugar 12
sugar-beet 12
summer coat 130
sunken loins 24
to supple 94
supple
  back 68
  seat 72
suppleness 58, 64
supplementary ration 14
suppleness 58, 64
surcingle 126, 136
surface 80
suspension, moment of 60
swab 54
swallow the tongue 68
swan-necked 22

sway back 24
sweat rug 126
sweat scraper 126
to sweep 130
sweet itch 50
swelling 54
swingle tree 100
swish the tail 68
syndication 108
synthetic saddle 136
syringe 54

table 94, 154
table (teeth) 44
tachograph 128
tack 132-44
tack room 126
tact 76
tail 16, 26, 130, 132
  carriage 26, 132
  deep-set 26
  docked 132
  going round 68
  high-set 26
  low-set 26
  plaited 132
  pulled 132
  rat 26
  root of 132
  swish 68
  to the wall 86
tail coat 152
tail line 4
tail/rear light 128
tailor 152
take the bit in the teeth 68
to take the lead 120
to take off 94
take off a bridle 140
to take off one's boots 152
to take to training 120
to take a wide turn 94
taking the rein down 64
tandem 98

tap-root mare 8
tap-root strain 6
tape start 112
tapeworms 50
tawny bay 38
*Taxus* 12
team 98
team jumping 96
teaser 8
technique, riding 72-6
teeth 44
  biting 44
  black centre 44
  canines 44
  changing 44
  dovetail 44
  grind 68
  grinding 44
  grinding surface 44
  hook 44
  incisors 44
  infundibulum 44
  milk 44
  molars 44
  periods 44
  permanent 44
  table 44
  take the bit 68
  tushes 44
temperament 8, 64-6
temperature, body 52
tempo 42, 58
  to change 76
ten-minute halt box 98
tendons 14
  strained 50
tense 64
terret 100
test 58, 78, 92
testicles 20
tetanus 50
tether 126
thick in front 22
thick neck 22

thick set 32
thick withers 24
thigh 20, 30
  long 30
  sloping 30
  well-muscled 30
thighs (rider's) 72
to thin 132
thin withers 24
thong 148
thorax 14
thorough grooming 130
thoroughbred, English 2
thoroughpin 50
threadworms 50
three-day event 96
throat 16
throatlash 140
to throw up the rider 68
throw-back 6
thrush 50
ticks 50
tied-in below the knee 28
tied-in elbow 28
to tighten the girth 136
time faults 96, 98
tired 64
titbit 14
toe 42
tongue
  clicking 72
  draw up behind the bit 68
  put over the bit 68
  stick/hang out 68
  swallow 68
top hat 148
top line 60
top score 96
top-boot 152
torsion 50
to toss the head 68
touch with the whip 72
touring on horseback 78
to tow 128

tow hitch 128
trace 100
trace clip 132
track 58, 80, 94, 114, 154
trailer 128
trainer 90, 108
trainer's licence 110
trainer's permit 110
training
  degree of 64
  terms 118-20
  track 114
trakehner 154
tranquilliser 54
transfer of entries 108
transition 60
transport 128
*travers* 86
treble obstacle 154
tree 136, 152
trekking 78
tricorn 148
to trim 132
trimming 130-2
triple bars 154
trophies 112
trophy 102
trot 42, 84
  collected 84
  extended 84
  medium 84
  move off at 76
  on 76
  rising 76
  school 86
  sitting 76
  working 84
to trot 76
  on the left diagonal 76
trotter 2
trough 126
true horseman 90
trunk 14
tucked-up belly 24

tuft 130
tug 100
tumour 50
turn 80, 112
turn on the forehand 86
turn on the haunches 86
to turn 94
to turn across the school 80
to turn sharply 94
to turn short 94
turning out to grass 10
turnout 98
turns 86
tushes 44
twisted gut 50
twitch 128
type, not true to 6
types 2, 4
typical 6

udder 20
ulcer 50
ultrasound scanning 54
unbroken 64
to be under pressure 120
to be under starter's orders 112
undershot fetlock 32
to undress 152
unfit 66
to be unfit 120
to unharness 100
unicorn 98
unload 128
unplaced 112
to unsaddle 136
to unseat the rider 68
unsteady contact 66
upholstery 100
upper arm 16, 26-8
  long 28
  short 26
  sloping 28
  straight 28
upper body 72

upper part 36
upright
  obstacle 154
  pastern 30
  shoulder 26
urinary system 52
urticaria 50
useful load 128
utility cross-breeding 6

vaccination 54
  certificate 110
variety 4
vaulting 78
vehicle 98
vehicle body 100
venereal disease 50
vertebra 14
very bad 92
very good 92
veterinary officer 108
veterinary surgeon 108
veterinary terms 50
vibration 74
vice 52
virus 54
voice 72
volte 80
voltige 78
vulva 20

waistcoat 148
walk 42, 84
  collected 84
  extended 84
  free 84
  long rein 84
  loose rein 84
  medium 84
  move off at 76
  on 76
  school 86
to walk 76
to walk the course 94, 96

wall eye 40
walls 80
  brick 154
  stone 154
warm-blooded 2
Warmblood 2
warts 50
to wash 130
washed-out chestnut 38
to water 130
water 14
  brush 126
  jump 154
water-bowl 126
waxed jacket 152
weak
  back 24
  cannon 28
  croup 26
  elbow 28
  hock 32
  loins 24
  pastern 30
  shoulder 26
to weaken 122
weakness 50
weaning a foal 10
wedge-shaped head 20
weigh-in 114
weigh-out 114
weighing room 114
weight
  for age event 110
  aids 72
  allowance 114
  cloth 136
  penalty 114
  racing 114
  rider's 72
to be well beaten 120
well set on head 22
well-coupled up back 24
well-defined hock 30
well-defined knee 28

well-muscled thigh 30
well-muscled up neck 22
well-proportioned chest 22
well-proportioned neck 22
well-schooled horse 66
well-sprung ribs 22
western riding 78
Western saddle 136
wet mouth 66
Weymouth curb 144
wheelbarrow 126
wheels 100
whip (driver) 98
whip (hunting) 102
whipper-in 102
whips 144
  dressage 148
  driving 100
  hunting 104, 144
  lungeing 144
  race 144
  riding 144
  stroke of 74
  touch with 72
whistling 50
white 36, 116
  cream 36
  dirty 36
  muzzle 40
  porcelain 36
white markings
  back of coronet 40
  front of coronet 40
  head 40
whole-coloured 40
whorl 40
wide
  at the chest 32
  at the knees 32
  behind, at the hocks 32
  cannon 28
  chest 22
  forearm 28
  hock 30

knee 28
  loins 24
win bet 114
win record 120
windgall 50
wing 154
winner 122
winning post 112
winnings 112
winter coat 130
withers 16, 24
  bony 24
  fistulous 48
  high 24
  lean 24
  long 24
  low 24
  poorly defined 24
  pronounced 24
  short 24
  thick 24
  thin 24
  too high 36
without markings 40
wolf-coloured 40
woodpile 154
woodshavings 130
woolly outline, hock 30
work
  in hand 90
  in long reins 90
  in the pillars 90
  on two tracks 86
working canter 84
working ration 14
working trot 84
'wormer' 52
worms 50

X-ray 54

yard 46
yard broom 126
yellow 116

yellow dun 38
yew 12
to yield 74
yielding 116
  the mouth 60
  at the poll 60
young stock 8
youngster 66

# INDEX

abandonnée, rêne 74
abandonner 98
abattre un cheval 52
abcès 46
aborder 94
abreuver 130
abreuvoir 126
automatique 126
abri 10
acariens 48
accepter l'action de la main 60
accessories 126-8
accident 94
accouplement 8
acculé 68
actif 72
action 8, 58
simultanée des jambes 74
d'une jambe isolée 74
administration des courses 108
agrafe 148
aides 72
de complaisance 98
diagonales 74
latérales 74
airs
d'école 86
de fantaisie 42
près de terre 86
relevés 86
aisance 60
ajuster
la selle 136
les rênes 74
alezan 36
brûlé 36, 38
clair 36
doré 38
foncé 36
lavé 38
pie 38
alimenter 130

allaitement 10
allée cavalière 80
allergie respiratoire 48
alliance 6
allocations 108
allongé
galop 84
pas 84
trot 84
allonger 76
les rênes 74
allure 58, 120
allures 40-2
d'école 42
artificielles 42
de l'école basse 84
étendues 42
irrégulières 42
libres 42
naturelles 42
principales 42
raccourcies 42
régulières 42
vives 42
amazone 90
selle de 136
amble 42
ambleur 2
améliorer une race 6
amputer 132
analgésiques 52
analyse de sang 52
âne 2
anémie 46
anesthésie diagnostique 54
anesthésiques 52
anglais 2
angles 32
anglo-arabe 2
animal 102
animer 72

anneaux 144
antérieurs 58
anti-inflammatoire 52
antibiotique 52
antiseptique 52
anus 20
aplomb 72
aplombs 14, 32
défecteux 32
normal 32
appareil
circulatoire 52
digestif 52
locomoteur 52
respiratoire 52
urinaire 52
appel 108
de langue 72
apprenti 108
appui 60
moelleux/franc 60
appuyer 86
aptitude au saut 92
arabe, pur sang 2
arçon de selle 136
ardoise, gris 38
arrivée 112
arqué 32
arracher 132
arrêt 58, 76, 84
arrêt de dix minutes 98
arrêter 76, 94, 120
l'entraînement 120
arrière des jambes 68
arrière-main 58
arrière-train 36
arrivée disputée 122
arrondies, côtes 22
arthrite 46
articulation 14
ascabiose 50
ascarides 46

ascendance 4
asseoir 60
assez bien 92
assez mal 92
assez souple 116
assiette 72
crispée 72
souple 72
association 108
assouplir 94
assurer
l'avantage 120
le train 120
astiquer 152
asymétrie 60
attache 132
attaque d'éperons 74
attaquer 94
atteinte 48
attelage 78, 98-102
à deux 98
en arbalète 98
en tandem 98
en tridem 98
à quatre 98
simple 98
à six 98
atteler 98, 100
attelle 100
attitude soutenue 58
au-dessus de la main 68
aubère 38
auteur 8
avalée, croupe 26
avaloire 100
avance 136
avant des jambes 68
avant de la main 68
avant-bras 16, 28
court 28
étroit 28
large 28

long 28
plat 28
avant-main 58
avoine 12
avoir l'aptitude
à la course 120
au terrain 120
axe longitudinal 60
azelan, brûlé 36

bactéries 52
bai 38
brun 38
cerise 38
clair 38
doré 38
fauve 38
pie 38
baisse de forme 120
balai 126
balayer 130
ballotade 86
balzane
grande 40
haut-chaussée 40
petite 40
trace de 40
principes de 40
bande 116, 118
bandes 52, 126
banquette 154
barbotage 14
barbour 152
barême 94
barrage 96
barre 154
d'appel 154
de poitrail 128
barres de spa 154
barrière 10, 154
bas d'état 66
bas, garrot 24

bas greffée/plantée, encolure 22
bas, jarret 30
bas jointé 32
bas jointé, paturon 30
bas plantée, queue 26
basculer 94
base de sustentation 60
    large 32
basse école 78
bassin 14
bat-flanc 128
bâti en descendant 36
    croupe 26
bâti en montant 36
battue 58
bave 66
béguin 126
beige 116
belladonne 10
belle face 40
betterave 12
bicorne 148
bien 92
bien dessinée, épaule 26
bien encadré 68
bien musclée
    cuisse 30
    encolure 22
    jambe 30
bien sculpté, genou 28
bien sculptée, jambe 30
bipèdes 58
    diagonaux 58
    latéraux 58
blanc 116
    isabelle aux crins blancs 36
    porcelaine 36
    rosé 36
    sale 36
blanc (de naissance) 36
bleimes 46
blessure 50
    de selle 46

bleu 116
    foncé 116
    gris 38
bleu-clair 116
bloc de sel 14
boit dans son blanc 40
boîte de départ 98
boiterie 48
bombe 148
bombé, genou 28
bon, terrain 114
bond 68
bonification 94
bonne attache de la tête 22
bonne ossature 32
boot 'jodphur' 152
bord supérieur de l'encolure 16
botte
    de campagne 152
    en caoutchouc 152
    d'équitation 152
    de polo 152
    à revers de jockey 152
    à revers de vénerie 152
botter 152
bottes 152
bottier 152
bouche 16, 66
    abimée 66
    aimable 66
    bavarde 66
    contractée 66
    dure 66
    fine 66
    fraîche 66
    légère 66
    moelleuse 66
    muette 66
    qui n'est pas faite 66
    souple 66
bouchon de chiendent 126
bouchonner 130
boucle 84, 100, 148

boule 128
boulet 16
bouleté 32
bourrelier 136
bourrer 68
bourses 20
bout de nez 40
boute-en-train 8
bouton
    noir 10
    d'or 10
box 126
bracelet de brancard 100
brancard 100
branche 4
branche-maîtresse 6
branches 144
bras 16, 26-8
    court 26
    long 28
    oblique 28
    vertical 28
brassage de sang 6
brassicourt 32
break 98
bretelles 116, 118
bricole 136
bride 100, 140
    à boucles 140
    cousue 140
    à crochets 140
    parties de la 140
    de présentation 140
brider 140
bridon 140
brochet, tête de 20
bronchiolite chronique obstructive 46
brosse douce 126
brosser 130, 152
brouette 126
brouter 10
brûlé, alezan 36, 38
brûlures 52

brun, bai 38
buis 10
bullfinch 154
busquée, tête 20
buste 72
butte 154

cabrer 68
cabriole 86
cadence 42, 58
cadre 36
café au lait 36
cagneux 32
caisse de la voiture 100
calme 64
calmer 72
camail 126
campé 32
camus, tête 20
cancer 46
canne 144
    à toise 44
canon 16, 28, 144
    brisé 144
    cintré 144
    court 28
    dégagé 28
    faible 28
    large 28
    long 28
    rond 28
    solide 28
    d'une pièce 144
canter 84, 112
cape de maure 40
capelet 46
capitonnage 100
caractère 64-6
cardiopathie 48
caresse 72
caresser 72
carotte 12
carpe, dos de 24
carrière 80

carrossier 102
carrousel 80, 130
casaque de jockey 148
casque 148
casque de polo 148
castration 52
castrer 52
cataplasme 54
catégories 110
causer des déceptions 120
cavaletti 154
cavalier
    de concours complet 96
    confirmé 90
    d'obstacle 92
cavalière 90
cavaliers 90
caveçon 144
cécité 46
céder 74, 120
    et reprendre le contact 64
ceinture 116, 118
centre équestre 78
cercle 80
cerclée 116, 118
cerf, encolure de 22
cerise, bai 38
certificat d'origine 6, 110
cession d'engagements 108
cession à la jambe 86
chaîne 126
châine métrique 44
chaleurs 4, 10
chambrière 144
chandelier 154
chanfrein 16
changement
    en diagonale 80
    de direction 58
    de ligne 112
    de monte 112
    de pied de ferme à ferme 76
changer 152
    d'allure 76

de diagonal au trot enlevé
76
de direction 76, 80
de main 76, 80
de main en prenant la
diagonale 80
de main sur le cercle 84
de pied 76
de pied au temps 76
de pied du tact au tact 76
de pied en l'air 76
de vitesse 76
chaps 152
charge utile 128
charnue
épaule 26
tête 20
chasse
à courre 78, 102-4
au renard 102
au renardeau 102
selle de 132
sur une piste odorante
artificielle 102
châtaigne 16
chaud 64
chausser 152
chef d'écurie 130
chef de piste 94
chenil 102
cheval
assoupli du dos 68
d'attelage 2, 102
de bât 2
de chasse 2, 102
de concours complet 2, 96
de concours d'obstacle 2
confirmé 66
de course 2
de course ayant du fond 118
croisé 6
débourré 64
de selle léger 2
à deux fins 2

difficile à nourrir 66
de distance moyenne 120
de dressage 2
dressé 66
droit 60
d'école 90
entier 8
facile à nourrir 66
de jeu 120
mis 66
d'obstacle 2
oriental 2
pif 8
pour cavalier de poids léger
2
pour cavalier de poids lourd
2
pour cavalier de poids
moyen 2
de rechange 102
de relais 102
de selle 2
sobre 66
de somme 2
à toute fin 2
de trait 2
cheval-père 6
chevillé, genou 28
chèvre
encolure de 22
poitrail de 22
chevron 116
chevrons 118
choc 52
chute 94, 98
des dents 44
ciguë 10
cirage 152
cirer 152
ciseaux 132
clair, alezan 36
classe 120
classement 96
clef de sellette 100

clignotant 128
cloches 126
clôture 10
clou
à cheval 42
de rue 42, 48
club hippique 78
coin 80
coins 44
coir 16, 132
colchique 10
colique 46
collant 116
collier 100
de chasse 136
colonne vertébrale 14
combinaison 154
combiné attelé 102
commissaire-priseur 108
commissaires 108
commune, tête 20
compagnon de box 120
compétition 78
composées 36
concassé 12
concave, tête 20
concours 78
complet 78, 96-8
complet d'attelage 102
complet de trois jours 96
complet d'une journée 96
de cross 78
de dressage 90-2
d'endurance attelé 102
hippique 78, 94
de modèles 80
de sauts d'obstacles 94
condition 66
conduire à deux mains 74
confiance 64
confirmé, cheval 66
conformation 8
du cheval 14
conique, tête 20

conjonctivite 46
consanguinité 4
constitution 8
contact 60
moelleux/franc 60
contagieux 52
contours 32
contre-bas 154
contre-changement de main 80
contre-galop 84
contre-sanglon 136
contrôlographe 128
contusion 52
convexes, côtes 22
copeaux 130
coquille 100
cor de chasse 104
corde 112
cornage 50
cornet dentaire externe 44
cornette à l'anglaise 104
corriger 72
costaud 32
costume de l'amazone 148
côté
concave 60
convexe 60
extérieur 58
hors-montoir 58
intérieur 58
montoir 58
côtes 14, 16, 22
arrondies 22
convexes 22
courtes 22
longues 22
plates 22
couchée, épaule 26
coude 16, 28
écarté 28
faible 28
plaqué 28
serré 28
coudé, jarret 32

couleurs d'écurie et les
dispositifs 116-18
coup
de cloche 92
de cravache 74
de lance 40
de sang 46
coupe
des Nations 96
couper 132
couple 102
courbette 86
classique 86
courir
bien 120
le cerf 102
mal 120
couronne 20
courroie de reculement
100
courroies 148
course 112
de catégorie 110
classique 110
à conditions 110
de haies 110
d'inédits 110
de maiden 110
à obstacles 110
en partie liée 110
plate 110
à poids pour âge 110
principale 110
publique 110
à réclamer 110
selle de 136
courses 78, 107-22
court
bras 26
canon 28
croupe 26
dos 24
encolure 22
garrot 24

lombes 24
paturon 30
rein 24
tête 114
courte
  encolure 114
  épaule 26
  queue 132
courtes, côtes 22
couteau de chaleur 126
coutelas 104
coutures 116, 118
couverture 126
  nid d'abeilles 126
  Nouvelle Zélande 126
cow-boy, selle 136
crampé 32
crampon 44
cravache 144
  de course 144
  de dressage 148
creux
  poitrail 22
  rein 24
crevasses 46, 48
crinière 20, 130
  raccourcie et désépaissie
    132
  rase 132
  tressée 132
crins 14, 130
crochet 152
crochets 44, 144
croisement 6
croisement irrégulier 6
croix de Lorraine 116, 118
croix de St André 116, 118
cross 78, 96
croupade 86
croupe 16, 26
  avalée 26
  bâti en descendant 26
  courte 26
  en dedans 86

en dehors 86
étroite 26
faible 26
horizontale 26
inclinée 26
large 26
longue 26
de mulet 26
ovale 26
puissante 26
tranchante 26
trop haute 26
croupière 100, 144
cryptorchide 8
cuisse 20, 30
  bien musclée 30
  inclinée 30
  longue 30
cuisses 72
culotte 152
culottée, jambe 30
cure-pied 126
curée 102
curer le pied 130
cygne, encolure de 22
cytise 12

dague 104
dame, selle de 136
damiers 116, 118
dans la ligne d'arrivée 112
dans les jambes 68
dead-heat 114
débotter 152
débourrage 120
débourrer 64
débrider 140
débutant 90
décharge 114
décharné, garrot 24
déchausser 152
déclaration
  de monte 112
  des partants 114

déclarer forfait pour un cheval
    112
décontraction de la mâchoire
    60
dedans de la main 68
défectueux, aplombs 32
défenses 66-71
déferrer le pied 44
défilé 112
dégagé, canon 28
dégarnir 100
dégénéré 6
degré 4
  de dressage 64-6
dégrossir 132
démangeaison 54
demi-arrêt 74
demi-frère 4
demi-longueur 114
demi-pirouette 86
demi-sang 2
demi-soeur 4
demi-train 84
demi-trait 2
demi-volte 80
dénominations 108
denrées 12-14
dents 44
  grincer des 68
  de lait 44
  de poulain 44
  de remplacement 44
dénutrition 48
départ 112
  à l'australienne 112
  au drapeau 112
  aux élastiques 112
  en stalles 112
déplacer 94
déposer une réclamation 110
dépôt d'étalons 8
dépourvu de type 6
dérivées, robes 36
dermite estivale récidivante 50

dernier tournant 112
dérober 94
derrière la main 68
désarçonner le cavalier 68
descendre 72
descendu
  rein 24
  ventre 24
descente 112, 154
  de l'encolure 64
  de jambes 74
  de main 64
désembarquer 128
désépaissir 132
déshabiller 152
déshydratation 52
désobéissances 66-71
desseller 136
dessous 36
dessus 36
désunir au galop 68
détendre 94
détendu 64
devant 36
diarrhée 46
difficile 64, 92
difficile à nourrir 66
difficulté moyenne 92
digitale pourprée 10
directeur de haras 10
direction du mouvement
    58
dispositifs de couleurs 118
disqualification 98
disque 118
distance 94, 112
distancé 110
dog-cart 98
donner
  à boire 130
  à manger 130
doppler 54
doré
  alezan 38

bai 38
clair 38
dos 16, 24
  de carpe 24
  court 24
  creux 68
  droit 24
  ensellé 24
  faible 24
  fort 24
  long 24
  de mulet 24
  solide 24
  vouté 24
dossard 96
doubler 80
  dans la longueur et changer
    de main 80
  et changer de main 80
douche 52
douleur 54
douve 48
drag 102
dressage 58-64, 66
  attelé 102
  selle de 132
dressé, cheval 66
droit 58, 154
  dos 24
  jarret 30
  jointé, paturon 30
droite
  encolure 22
  épaule 26
  tête 20

eau 14
ébranlement 52
écarté, coude 28
écartelée 118
échelle des notes 92
éclaircir 132
école d'équitation 78
écoulement 52

écourter 132
écurie 126-8
écuyer en chef 90
écuyer professeur 90
Écuyer-Cavalcadour 90
écuyers 90
eczéma 48, 52
effet d'ensemble 76
effleurer l'obstacle 94
égaliser 132
électrolytes 52
élémentaire 90
élevage 4-8
   dans la consanguinité 6
   dans la pureté de race 6
   en lignée 6
   en proche parenté 6
élève 4, 90
éleveur 4, 108
   propriétaire 108
élimination 98, 112
éliminer 96
emballer 68
embarquer 128
embauchoir 152
embouchures 140-4
empâté, jarret 30
emphysème pulmonaire 46
empoisonnement 48
empreinte 102
encadrement 152
encapuchonné 68
encastelé, pied 42
enceinte 10
encenser 68
enclos 10
   de départ 98
encolure 16, 22, 114
   bas greffée/plantée 22
   bien musclée 22
   de cerf 22
   de chèvre 22
   courte 22
   de cygne 22

droite 22
étroite 22
extension de 64
fine 22
grêle 22
grosse 22
haut greffée/plantée 22
horizontale 22
légère 22
longue 22
lourde 22
mal musclée 22
oblique 22
proportionée 22
renversée 22
rouée 22
endolorissement 54
enfoncée, queue 26
enfourcher le cheval 72
engagement 110
engager
   les postérieurs 60
   un cheval 112
engendrer 8
engorgement 54
engourdissement 54
enlever 94
   les crottins 130
enrênement
   Chambon 144
   Gogue 144
enrênements 144
ensellé, dos 24
entier 2
entourage du cheval 108
entraînement
   fractionné 98
   vocabulaire 118-20
entraîner 108
   à l'obstacle 94
entraîneur 90
entre main et jambes 68
épais, garrot 24
éparvin 46

éparvin sec 50
épaule 16, 26
   bien dessinée 26
   charnue 26
   couchée 26
   courte 26
   droite 26
   faible 26
   fine 26
   inclinée 26
   longue 26
   oblique 26
   prononcée 26
   relâchée 26
   sèche 26
   verticale 26
épaule en dedans 86
épaulettes 118
éperon
   à boîte 148
   à l'écuyère 148
   lisse 148
   pointu 148
éperonnier 148
éperons 148
épi 40
éponge 46, 126
éponger 130
épreuve 78
   à l'américaine 96
   avec barrage 96
   'choisissez vos points' 96
   au chronomètre 96
   des six barres 96
   de dressage 96
   de fond 96, 100
   nationale 96
   de performance pour jeunes
     chevaux 80
   de précision 96
   de puissance 96
   de saut d'obstacles 96
épreuves
   combinées 78

d'obstacles 78, 96
épuisé 66
équilibre 8, 64
équilibré 36
équitation
   académique 78
   artistique 78
   de cirque 78
   classique 76-8
   de fantaisie 78
   de loisir 78
   pratique 78
   de promenade 78
   savante 78
   sportive 78
   western 78
ergot 20
erreur
   de parcours 92
   de reprise 92
éruption des dents 44
espèce 4
   prototype de 6
estompé, jarret 30
étalon 8
   d'essai 8
étalonnier 108
état 66, 120
étendre 122
étirer 132
étoile 118
   en tête 40
étoiles 118
étonnement 52
être
   bien battu 120
   bousculé 120
   à court de travail 120
   débourré 120
   distancé 120
   en état 120
   froid 122
   hors de forme 120
   limité 120

à l'ouvrage 120
passé de forme 120
sous les ordres du juge du
   départ 112
étrier 136
étrille 126
étrivière 136
étroit
   avant-bras 28
   poitrail 22
   rein 24
étroite
   croupe 26
   encolure 22
euthanasier un cheval 52
examen
   microscopique 54
   radiographique 54
excellence héréditaire 6
excellent 92
exécution 92
exercice en liberté 94
   dans un couloir 94
expressive, tête 20
extension
   de l'encolure 64
   trot en 84
extérieur de cheval 14-32

faible
   canon 28
   coude 28
   croupe 26
   dos 24
   épaule 26
   jarret 32
faiblesse 50
faiblir 122
faire
   un écart 68
   une intervention
     chirurgicale 54
   souche 6
   le train 120

famille 4
fanon 20, 130
fatigué 64
fausse gourmette 144
fauve, bai 38
faux départ 112
faux ébénier 12
femme jockey 108
fer
  à cheval 42
  gris 38
ferme 114
  rein 24
ferrant, maréchal 42
ferrer
  clou à 42
  le pied 44
fesse 20
feu stop 128
feuillet de vaccination 110
feux en pointe 54
fièvre 48
figures de manège 80-90
filet 126, 140
  à aiguilles 140
  à anneaux 140
  chantilly 140
  en caoutchouc 144
  à olives 140
filet de mors de bride 140
filet releveur 140
fille 4
fine
  bouche 66
  encolure 22
  épaule 26
fistule du garrot 48
flanc 16
flèche 128
flegmatique 64
flexion
  directe 60
  de la nuque 60
fléxion, test de 54

floconné 12
flot 96
flyer 118
foin 12
  hâché 12
foncé
  alezan 36
  bai 38
  gris 38
  rouan et aubère 38
forcer
  l'allure 120
  l'animal 102
forge 42
forme 64, 66, 120
  catilagineuse 50
formes
  du paturon 48
  de la couronne 48
fort, dos 24
fossé 154
fossés 154
fouailler de la queue 68
fouet 100, 132
fouet de chasse 104, 144
fouets 144
fougère 10
foulée 58
fourburre 48
fourche 126
fourchette 42
fourmillière 50
fourrage 12-14, 126
fourrage 'sec' 12
fourrager 130
fourreau 16
fracture 54
franchir 94
franchise 60
frapper 72
frein 100, 128
frère 4
friandise 14
froid 64

froid aux jambes 68
front 16
frontal 140
frotter 130
frugal 66
furlong 46

gag 140
gagnant 122
gains 112
gale 48
gale sarcoptique 50
galop 42, 84
  allongé 84
  de course 84
  désuni 84
  à droit 76, 84
  à faux 76, 84
  à gauche 76, 84
  juste 84
  moyen 84
  rassemblé 84
  sur le mauvais pied 84
  sur le pied droit 84
  sur le pied gauche 84
  de travail 84
galope d'essai 112
galoper 76
galopeur 2
ganache 16
gant 148
garçon d'écurie 130
garde-crotte 100, 148
garnir 100
garrot 16, 24, 32
  bas 24
  court 24
  décharné 24
  épais 24
  maigre 24
  noyé 24
  prolongé 24
  prononcé 24
  saillant 24

taille au 32
tranchant 24
gastérophiles 46
gâteau 130
génération libre 6
genou 16, 28
  bien sculpté 28
  bombé 28
  chevillé 28
  grand 28
  large 28
  long 28
  net 28
  noué 28
  plat 28
genouillères 126
genoux
  couronnés 46
  creux 32
  déviés en dedans 32
genoux-clos 32
germe de fèves 44
gestation 10
geste à l'obstacle 92
gibier 102
gig 98
gilet 148
gilet de protection 152
glome 42
gorge 16
gourme 50
gourmette 144
graine de lin 12
grains 12
graisse à pied 128
grand
  genou 28
  grasset 30
  jarret 30
Grand Écuyer 90
Grand Prix 92
grand-mère 4
grand-père 4
grande

balzane 40
tête 20
granulés 12
grasset 20, 30
  grand 30
  net 30
  ouvert 30
grêle, encolure 22
grenat 116
grincer des dents 68
grippe equine 48
gris 38
  ardoise 38
  bleu 38
  fer 38
  foncé 38
  moucheté 38
  pommelé 40
  truité 38
groom 102
gros dos 68
gros mangeur 66
grosse
  encolure 22
  tête 20
guêtres 126
guides 66, 144
gymkana 78

habiller 152
habit 152
habit rouge 104
hack 2
hackamore 140
hackney 102
haie 154
haie vive 154
hallali 102
hanche 26
  normale 26
  pointue 26
  proéminante 26
  saillante 26
hanches 72

handicap 110
handicapeur 108
happer 68
haras 4, 8-10
harmonie 60
harmonieux 36
harnais 98
    avec une bricole 100
    avec un collier 100
haut de croupe 36
haut d'état 66
haut greffée/plantée, encolure
    22
haut plantée, queue 26
haut-de-forme 148
haute, croupe 26
haute école 78
hémoglobinurie 46
hémorrhagie 52
hépatite 48
herbages 10-12
herbe 12
herbe de Saint-Jean 12
hérédité 6
hernie 48
hétérogène 6
homme de cheval 90
homogène 6
hongres 108
honneurs du pied 104
horizontal, rein 24
horizontale
    croupe 26
    encolure 22
hormones 54
hors de forme 66
horse ball 78
huile 14
huit de chiffre 84
hunter 2
hybride 6

if 12
immobilité 58, 76

imperméable 152
impulsion 58
incesteuse, union 6
incisives 44
incliné, paturon 30
inclinée
    croupe 26
    cuisse 30
    épaule 26
incurvation 60
incurvé 60
individu 4
inédit 120
infection par strongles
    pulmonaires 48
inflammation 54
insémination artificielle 8
inséminer 8
inspection vétérinaire 96
instructeur d'équitation 90
insuffisant 92
irlandaise 154
isabelle aux crins blancs 36
isabelle (aux crins noirs) 38
    clair 38
    ordinaire 38
ischions 72

jacobée 12
jais, noir de 36
jambe 20, 30
    action 74
    active 74
    bien musclée 30
    bien sculptée 30
    cession à la 86
    culottée 30
    léger à 68
    longue 30
    passive 74
    solide 30
jambes 72
    action 74
    arrière des 68

avant des 68
dan les 68
descente de 74
entre main et jambes 68
froid aux 68
lourd aux 68
jarde 46
jarret 20, 30-2
    bas 30
    coudé 32
    droit 30
    empâté 30
    estompé 30
    faible 32
    large 30
    long 30
    net 30
    pauvre 32
    près de terre 30
    saillant 30
    sec 30
    solide 32
    tranchant 30
jarrets
    cambrés 32
jaune 116
jaunisse 48
jetage 52
jeux équestres 78
jockey 90, 108
jodhpur 152
juge 108
juge responsable de la pesée
    108
jument 2, 8
    pleine 8
    saillie 8
    suitée 8
    vide 8
jument-mère 8
jumenterie 8
jury de terrain 98
jusquiame 10

lâcher la sangle 136
lad 108
ladre 40
lancer 102
langue serpentine 68
lanterne 100
lanterne arrière 128
large
    avant-bas 28
    canon 28
    croupe 26
    genou 28
    jarret 30
    poitrail 22
    rein 24
lauréat 122
lavé, alezan 38
laver 130
léger à la jambe 68
légère
    encolure 22
    tête 20
légèreté 64
levade 86
leviers 32
levretté, ventre 24
l'habit 148
liberté
    de garrot 136
    de langue 144
libre, pas 84
licence
    d'apprenti 110
    d'entraîner 110
    de jockey 110
licol 126
ligament 14
ligne
    du dessus 60
    droite 80, 114
    d'en face 112
    du milieu 80
lignée 4
    élevage en 6

lion, poitrail de 22
liste
    étroite 40
    large 40
litière 126, 130
loin 114
lombes 24
long
    avant-bas 28
    bras 28
    canon 28
    dos 24
    genou 28
    jarret 30
    jointé, paturon 30
    paturon 30
    rein 24
long jointé 32
longe 144
    d'attache 126
longue
    croupe 26
    cuisse 30
    encolure 22
    épaule 26
    jambe 30
longues
    côtes 22
    rênes 144
longueur 114
losange 116, 118
losanges 118
lot 112, 122
lotion 54
lourd 64, 116
lourd aux jambes 68
lourde, encolure 22
louvet 40
lupin 12
luzerne 12
lymphangite 48

mâcher le mors 66
mâchoire inférieure 16

maigre, garrot 24
main 72
   accepter l'action de la 60
   au-dessus de la 68
   avant de la 68
   changer de 76, 80, 84
   contre-changement de 80
   dedans de la 68
   derrière la 68
   descente de 64
   entre main et jambes 68
   mise en 60
   rênes dans une seule 74
   sur la 60
   tirer à la 68
   travail à la main 90
mains, conduire à deux 74
maïs 12
maître 90
maître d'équipage 102
mal 92
mal musclée, encolure 22
mal teint, noir 36
maladie 50
   de l'herbe 48
   du lundi 46
   naviculaire 48
   vénérienne 50
maladies 46-50
mamelle 20
manège 80
manège couvert 80
mangeoire 126
maniabilité 100
maniement des rênes 74
manque d'activité 60
mantelet 100
marathon 100
marche arrière automatique
   128
marcher
   au galop 76
   au pas 76
   au trot 76

maréchal ferrant 42
marque (extérieure) de haras
   apposée au fer rouge 10
marron 116
martingale
   alliance 144
   à anneaux 144
   fixe 144
   irlandaise 144
mash 14
masser 130
match 110
matelassure 136
matériel 125-54
matériel de dressage 144
mauvaise attache de la tête
   22
mauve 116
maux 52
mèche 144
médicament 52
mélangées 36
mélasse 12
melon 148
membre
   à l'appui 58
   au lever 58
   au soutien 58
membres 14, 58
   particularitiés des robes 40
mener à grand allure 120
meneur 98
mensuration 44
mentonnière 148
mère 4
mesure
   à la chaine 44
   rigide 44
   souple 44
   sous potence 44
mesures 44
   anglaises 46
   métriques 46
métis 6

métisation 6
métissage 6
mètre 46
métrite equine contagieuse
   46
mettre
   en selle 72
   pied à terre 72
meurtrissure 52
meute 102
mezair 86
mi-parcours 112
microbes 52
mile 46
miler 120
milieu 36, 58
millepertuis 12
mis, cheval 66
mise
   à l'herbe 10
   en main 60
mise-bas 10
mitoyennes 44
mixte, selle 132
mobilité 60
modèle 8
moelleux 58
molette 50, 148
mollets 72
moniteur 90
montant 140
monte 8, 10, 112
montée 112
monter
   en amazone 80
   à califourchon 80
   au chronomètre 94
   à poil 80
   en selle 72
monture 148
mordre 68
mors 140
   de bride 144
   mâcher 66

à pompe 144
morve 48
moucheté, gris 38
mouton, tête de 22
mouvement 40-2, 58
moyen
   galop 84
   pas 84
   trot 84
mue 130
mulet 2
   croupe de 26
   dos de 24
mur 80
   de brique 154
   de pierre 154
muscles 14
muserolle 140
   allemande 140
   combinée 140
   à croisillon 140
mycose 48
myorelaxant 54

naissance de la queue 132
naisseur 4
naseaux 16
natter 132
négliger 94
nematodes 50
nerf 54
nerfs 14
net
   genou 28
   grasset 30
   jarret 30
nettoyer 130
   les bottes 152
   le box 132
nez 114
noble 36
noir 36, 116
   de jais 36
   mal teint 36

pie 38
nombril 16
non executé 92
non partant 112
non placé 112
normal
   aplombs 32
   ventre 24
normale, hanche 26
notions de base 14
noué, genou 28
nourriture composée 12
noyé, garrot 24
nuque 16
nutrition 54

obéissance 64
obésité 48
objets d'art 112
oblique
   bras 28
   encolure 22
   épaule 26
obstacle 92
   double 154
   fixe 94
   sautant 94
   selle de 132
   simple 154
   triple 154
   vertical 154
   de volée 154
obstacles 154
   de cross 96
oeil 16
oeil vairon 40
oeillières 100
onguent 54
orange 116
ordinaire, isabelle 38
oreille 16
organes 14
organisation des courses 112
orge 12

origine 4
    certificat 6, 110
os 14
os polissoir 152
ossature 14
outcrossing 6
outsider 122
ouvert, grasset 30
ovale, croupe 26
oxer
    au carré 154
    montant 154
oxyures 50

paddock 10
paille 12
paille hâchée 12
palefrenier 10, 130
palefrenier-chef 10
palmarès des victoires 120
palomino 38
palonnier 100
panard 32
panneau 136
pansage à fond 130
pansage sommaire 130
pansement 52
    compressif 54
    glacé 52
pansements 52
panser 130
papier 6
paralysie 48
parasites 54
parasitisme 54
parcours 94, 154
    de cross-country 96
    de maniabilité contre la
        montre 100
    de steeple-chase 96
    sur routes et sentiers 96
parenté 4
parer le pied 44
paresseux 64

pari simple gagnant 114
pari simple placé 114
paroi 42
partager les rênes 74
partants 114
particularités des robes 40
partir
    au galop 76
    aus pas 76
    au trot 76
pas 42, 58, 84
    allongé 84
    de coq 50
    de côté 86
    d'école 86
    libre 84
    moyen 84
    rassemblé 84
    les rênes abandonées 84
    les rênes longues 84
passage 86
    de gourmette 16
    de route 154
passeport 110
passer la langue au-dessus du
        mors 68
passif 72
pathologie articulaire 48
patte d'ours, paturon 30
pâturage 10
paturon 20, 30
    bas jointée 30
    court 30
    droit jointé 30
    inclinée 30
    long 30
    long jointé 30
    en patte d'ours 30
pauvre, jarret 32
peau 14
peau de chamois 126
pedigree 6
peigne 128, 132
peigner 130

pelham 144
pelote en tête 40
peloton 102
pelouse 114
pénalisation 96
pénalités
    pour fautes aux obstacles 96
    de temps 96, 98
pension 130
perçant 60
perche 154
père 8
performance 120-2
périodes 44
péritonite 48
permeabilité aux aides 64
permis d'entraîner 110
personnel de l'écurie de
        courses 108
pesade 86
pesée
    après la course 114
    avant la course 114
pesée de l'assiette 72
peste équine 46
petit mangeur 66
petit-fils 4
petite
    balzane 40
    fille 4
    porte 128
    tête 20
peureux 64
phaëton 98
photo-finish 114
phtiriase 48
piaffer 86
piano 154
pie 38
    alezan 38
    bai 38
    noir 38
pied 20, 42-4, 46, 154
    de dedans 86

encastelé 42
    plat 42
    de rampin 42
piliers 144
pince 42
pinces 44
piqueur 102
piqûre 48
piqûre d'insecte 48
pirouette
    ordinaire 86
    renversée 86
pirouettes 86
piste 58, 80, 92, 94, 114, 154
    d'entraînement 114
    de gazon 114
    à main droite 114
    à main gauche 114
    en sable 114
placer 60
plaie 54
    du garrot 46
    pénétrante 48
plaies dues au harnachement
        50
plantes vénéneuses 10-12
plaque
    de nationalité 128
    de police 128
plaqué, coude 28
plastron 148
plat
    avant-bras 28
    genou 28
    pied 42
plates, côtes 22
pli 60
ploiement 60
plonger 68
pneu de secours 128
pneumonie 48
poids 114
    du cavalier 72
    du corps 72

maximum 128
net 128
poil 14, 130
    d'été 130
    d'hiver 130
poils 14
point-to-point 78
pointe
    d'épaule 16
    de la hanche 16
pointer 68
points
    de pénalité 98
    de repère 92
pointue, hanche 26
pois 118
poitrail 16, 22
    de chèvre 22
    creux 22
    étroit 22
    large 22
    de lion 22
    profond 22
    proportionné 22
    saillant 22
    serré 22
polo 78
    selle de 136
pommade 54
pommeau 136
pommelé, gris 40
poney 2
poney-club 78
pont 128
porcelaine, blanc 36
port de queue 26, 130
porte-brancard 100
porte-étrivière 136
porter au vent 68
poser 58
position 60
    assis 72
    assis sur le trous,equin 72
    en avant 72

à cheval 72
en équilibre 72
du jockey 72
normale 72
sportive 72
sur l'enfourchure 72
postérieurs 58
poteau d'arrivée 112
pouce 46
poudre 54
poulain 8, 10, 66
poulains entiers 108
pouliche 8
pouliches 110
poulinage 10
poulinière 8
pourriture de fourchette 50
poursuite 102
pousse 46
poussée
    d'assiette 72
    des postérieurs 64
poux 48
prairie 10
pré 10
prèle des marais 10
premier garçon 130
premiers secours 54
prendre
    une légère avance 120
    le mors aux dents 68
près de terre 32
    jarret 30
pression, de selle 46
prestance 58
primitives, robes 36
principes de balzane 40
prix 96
Prix St Georges 92
procréer 8
producteur 8
produit 4
    dopant 52
    intermédiare 6

intermédiaire entre le foin et
    l'ensilage 12
produits 8
proéminante, hanche 26
profond, poitrail 22
profondeur 32
programme 114
prolifique 8
prolongé, garrot 24
promener 128
prononcé, garrot 24
prononcée, épaule 26
proportionné 36
    poitrail 22
proportionnée, encolure 22
propre frère 4
propre soeur 4
propriétaire 108
propriétaire-entraîneur 108
prototype de l'espèce 6
prurit 54
puissance, de génération 6
puissante, croupe 26
punir 72
punition 72
pur sang anglais 2
pur sang arabe 2
pus 54

quadrille 80
qualité 8
quartier 136
quelques poils en tête 40
queue 16, 26, 132
    d'aronde 44
    bas plantée 26
    désépaissie 132
    enfoncée 26
    haut plantée 26
    port de 26
    de rat 26
    de renard 104
    tressée 132
quilles 102

raccourcir 76
raccourcir les rênes 74
race 4
race indigène 2
races 2
rachis 14, 60
raid 78
raide 64
raie de mulet 40
ralentir 76
'rameau vert' 104
ramené 60
ramener 60
randonnée 78
râpe 42
rasoir 132
rassemblé
    galop 84
    pas 84
    trot 84
rassembler 60, 64
rat, queue de 26
râtelier 126
ration
    de croissance 14
    d'entretien 14
    journalière 14
    supplémentaire 14
    de travail 14
rayée 118
réactions du cheval monté
    66-71
recevoir 94
recevoir du poids 114
récompense 72
récompenser 72
reconnaître le parcours 94,
    96
rectangle 80
rectangulaire 36
rectitude 58
reculer 76
redingote de chasse à courre
    148

redresser 58
refaire la litière 130
refuser 94
regain 12
registre général 10
régression 6
régulariser 132
régularité 58
régulier 32
rein 16, 24
    court 24
    creux 24
    descendu 24
    étroit 24
    ferme 24
    horizontal 24
    large 24
    long 24
relâchée, épaule 26
remise de poids 114
remorque 128
rendez-vous 102
rendre 74
rendre du poids 114
rêne
    abandonnée sur l'encolure
        74
    active 74
    d'appui 74
    de bride 140
    contraire 74
    directe d'opposition 74
    en arrière du garrot 74
    en avant du garrot 74
    extérieure 74
    de filet 140
    intérieure 74
    d'ouverture 74
    passive 74
    résistante 74
    tendue 74
rênes 140
    abandonées 84
    ajuster 74

allemandes 144
allonger 74
coulissantes 144
dans une seule main 74
fixes 144
longues 74, 84
maniement 74
partager 74
raccourcir 74
tenue des 74
renouvellement du sang 6
renversée, encolure 22
renverser 94
reprise 58, 92
    Intermédiaire 92
    libre 92
    libre musicale 92
    Olympique 92
reproducteur 2, 8
reproductrice 8
résistance 120
résister au travail 120
respecter 94
ressorts 100
rétif 68
retour de race 6
retroussé, ventre 24
réunion des concurrents 96
réveiller 72
rivet 42
rivière 154
robe 14
robes 36-40
robinier faux acacia 12
rond
    canon 28
    ventre 24
rose 116
rosé, blanc 36
rouan 38
    foncé 38
roue jockey 128
rouée, encolure 22
roues 100

routier 96
ruban 44
ruer 68
rythme 58

sable 80
sabot 20, 42-4
saccade 74
safran des prés 10
saignement 52
saillant
   garrot 24
   jarret 30
   poitrail 22
saillante, hanche 26
saillie 8
sale, blanc 36
salle de balances 114
salut 92
sang
   analyse de 52
   brassage de 6
   renouvellement du 6
sangle 136
sangler 136
santé 8, 52
satisfaisant 92
saut
   en largeur 154
   de mouton 68
   de puce 154
sauter 94
   juste 94
   sans faute 94
sauteur 90, 92
sauts
   d'école 86
   d'obstacles 92
savon glycérine 128
seau 126
sec 114
   jarret 30
sèche
   épaule 26

tête 20
sécher 130
secousse 52
secrétaire de l'hippodrome
   108
sectionner 132
seime 42, 50
sel 14
   bloc de 14
selle 132-6
   ajuster 136
   arçon de 136
   blessure de 46
   cow-boy 136
   d'amazone 136
   de chasse 132
   de course 136
   de dame 136
   de dressage 132
   d'obstacle 132
   de polo 136
   mettre en 72
   mixte 132
   monter en 72
   parties de 136
   pression de 46
   synthétique 136
seller un cheval 136
sellerie 100, 126, 132-4, 136
sellette 100
sellier 136
séneçon 12
séparation 128
seringue 54
serpentine 84
serré
   coude 28
   poitrail 22
serrer la corde 122
servir l'animal 102
sevrage 10
siège 100, 136
signal de départ 98
signalement 10

simples, robes 36
sobre, cheval 66
soeur 4
soigner 54
soins à l'écurie 130
sol 80
sole 42
solide
   canon 28
   dos 24
   jambe 30
   jarret 32
son 12
sortir 130
   de l'entraînement 120
   la langue 68
souche 4
soumission 60, 64
souple 116
souplesse 58
souris 38
   clair 38
   foncé 38
sous lui 32
sous-écuyer 90
sous-gorge 140
sous-ventrière 100
sports
   équestres 78
   hippiques 78
sprinter 118
squelette 14
stabilité 6
stage 80
stalle 126
starter 108
station 58
stationata 154
stayer 118
steeple 96
steeple-chase 110
stère de bois 154
stérile 8
stimulation musculaire

électrique 52
strongles 48
stud-book 10
style du cavalier 94
sucre 12
suffisant 92
sur la bride seule 74
sur l'éperon 76
sur la main 60
surcharge 114
surface 80
surface de frottement 44
surfaix 126, 136, 144
surmené 66
suros 50
syndicat 108
synthétique, selle 136
système nerveux central 52

table 154
tablier 100
tact équestre 76
taille 32
taille au garrot 44
tailler 132
tailleur 152
talon 42
talons 72
talus 154
tampon 54
tapis
   de plomb 136
   de selle 136
tapoter 72
tare héréditaire 6
tares 46-50, 52
tarif de monte 112
taxer 94
technique de l'équitation 72-6
teigne 50
tempérament 8, 64-6
température corporelle 52
temps 58
   optimum 98

de suspension 60
tendinite 50
tendons 14
   chauffés 50
   claqués 50
tendu 64
ténias 50
tenue 148
   de cavalier 148-52
   de chasse à courre 148
   de l'équipage 104
   d'équitation 148
   des rênes 74
termes vétérinaires généraux
   50
terrain 114
test
   de dressage d'attelage 102
   de fléxion 54
testicules 20
tétanos 50
tête 14, 20-2, 114
   bonne attache de la 22
   de brochet 20
   busquée 20
   camuse 20
   charnue 20
   commune 20
   concave 20
   conique 20
   en dedans 86
   droite 20
   expressive 20
   grande 20
   grosse 20
   légère 208
   mauvaise attache de la 22
   de mouton 22
   au mur 86
   particularités des robes 40
   petite 20
   sèche 20
têtière 140
texte de la reprise 92

thorax 14
tige 148
tigré 38
timon 100
tiques 50
tirage des places à la corde
    112
tire-botte 152
tirer à la main 68
toilette 130-2
tomber 94, 98
tondeuse 132
tondre 132
tonte 132
    de chasse 132
    de couverture 132
    d'hiver 132
    totale 132
toque 148
torchon 128
tort-nez 128
toucher 94
    avec la cravache 72
toupet 20, 130
tour 114
    du canon 44
    de sangle 44
tournant 112
tourner 80, 94
    court 94
    large 94
toux 46
trace 102
trace de balzane 40
tracter 128
trait 100
traitement au laser 54
trakehnen 154
tranchant
    garrot 24
    jarret 30
tranchante, croupe 26
tranquille 64
tranquillisant 54

transition 60
transport de chevaux 128
trapu 32
travail
    aux longues rênes 66, 90
    aux piliers 90
    de deux pistes 86
    en guides 66
    à la longe 66
    à la main 90
traverser 60
trèfle 12
trempe 120
tresser 132
tricorne 148
troène 12
trompe 104
tronc 14
trop ouvert
    de derrière 32
    de devant 32
    de genoux 32
trop serré
    de derrière 32
    de derrière aplombs 32
    de devant 32
    de devant aplombs 32
trophée 102
trot 42, 84
    allongé 84
    assis 76
    d'école 86
    en extension 84
    enlevé 76
    moyen 84
    rassemblé 84
    de travail 84
trotter 76
    avec le diagonal gauche/
      droit 76
    à l'anglaise 76
    à la française 76
trotteur 2
trottiner 68

trousse
    de nettoyage 152
    de secours 54
troussequin 136
truité, gris 38
tube 148
tue-chien 10
tuméfaction 54
tumeur 50
turfiste 108
type 4
typé 6
types 2
typique 6

ulcère 50
uni 32
unie 116, 118
union incestueuse 6
unité de mesure 44
urticaire 50

vaccination 54
vainqueur 122
vairon, oeil 40
valet-de-chiens 102
van 128
variété 4
vénerie 78, 102-4
veneur 102
vente
    à l'amiable 110
    aux enchères 110
    avec réserve 110
    sans réserve 110
ventre 16, 24
    descendu 24
    levretté 24
    normal 24
    retroussé 24
    rond 24
verge 20
vermifuge 52
verrues 50

vers 50
vert 64, 116
    foncé 116
vert-clair 116
vertèbre 14
vertical, bras 28
verticale, épaule 26
vessignon
    articulaire 46
    tendineux 50
veste
    d'équitation 148
    huilée 152
vétérinaire 108
vétérinaires, termes généraux
    50
vibration 74
vice 52
violet 116
virus 54
vocabulaire d'entraînement
    118-20
voiture 98
voix 72
volée 100
volte 80
voltige équestre 78
volvulus 50
vouté, dos 24
voyages à cheval 78
vulve 20

yard 46

zain 40
zone de pénalité 98

# REGISTER

Aalstrich 40
Abarten 36-40
abfallende Kruppe 26
Abfangen des Wildes 102
abgedachte Kruppe 26
abgeleitete 36
abkauen (am Gebiss) 66
abklopfen 72
abkürzen 76
abladen 128
abreiben 130
abreiten 94
absatteln 136
Absätze 72
abschätzen 94
abschirren 100
abschneiden 132
abschüssige Kruppe 26
abschwammen 130
Abschwitzdecke 126
Absetzen 10
absitzen 72
abspringen 94
Absprung markierende Stange 154
Abstammung 4, 6
Abstammungsnachweis 6, 110
Abstand 94
abstehender Ellbogen 28
abstehendes Sprunggelenk 30
Abszess 46
abtrocknen 130
abwärts 112
abwerfen 94
abzäumen 140
Abzeichen 40, 118
Acht 84
Achtelmeile 46
achten 94
Adlerfarn 10
afrikanische Pferdepest 46
After 20

Afterklaue 20
Agraffe 148
Ahnen 4
akademische Reitkunst 78
Aktion 8, 40-2, 58
aktiv 72
aktiver
    Schenkel 74
    Zügel 74
Allergie der Atemwege 48
allgemeine tierärztliche
    Wörter 50
Altersgewichtsrennen 108, 110
Amazone 90
amerikanische Jagdspringen 96
an den Hilfen 68
Anbinderiemen 126
andersartig 6
Anfänger 90
angaloppieren 76
angeborene 36
angedrückter Ellbogen 28
angenehmes Maul 66
angerittenes Pferd 64
angewandte Reitkunst 78-80
Anglo-Araber 2
anhalten 76
An(In)-die-Hand-Stellen 60
ankleiden, sich 152
anlehnen 60
Anlehnung 60
Anreiten 64, 94, 120
anreiten im Schrift 76
anschlagen 94
Anschnallsporn 148
Anschwellen 54
anspannen 100
anspritzen 130
ansteckend 52
Antiobiotikum 52

antiseptisch 52
antraben 76
Anwelksilage 12
anziehen, sich 152
anziehendes Hindernis 94
Apfelschimmel 40
Arbeit
    mit der Doppellonge 66
    am langen Zügel 90
    an der Hand 90
    auf zwei Hufschlägen 86
    in den Pilaren 90
Arbeits-ration 14
Arbeitsgalopp 84
Arbeitstrab 84
Art 4
Art der Rennen 110
Aschfalb 38
Atemwege 52
Atmungssystem 52
auf die Hand stossen 68
Aufgalopp 112
aufgeben 98, 120
aufgeschürzter Bauch 24
aufgezogener Bauch 24
Auflauf-Bremse 128
aufmuntern 72
aufnehmen 74
aufnehmen, sich 94
aufpullen 120
aufschirren 100
aufsitzen 72
aufsteigendes Hindernis 154
aufwärts 112
aufzäumen 140
Aufzucht 4
Aufzüchter 4
Auge 16
Auktion 110
Auktionator 108
Ausbindezügel 144
ausbrechen 94

Ausdauer 120
ausdracksloses Sprunggelenk 30
ausdrucksvolle Schulter 26
ausdrucksvoller
    Kopf 20
    Unterschenkel 30
    Widerrist 24
Ausfluss 52
Ausführung 92
ausgeprägte Hüfte 26
ausgeprägtes
    Knie 30
    Vorderfusswurzelgelenk 28
ausgezeichnet 92
Ausgleicher 108
Ausgleichsrennen 110
auskratzen, Huf 130
Auslauf 10
Auslese 6
Auslosung 112
ausmisten 130
ausräumen 130
ausreichend 92
ausreissen 132
ausrichten 132
Ausschalten der Schenkel 74
ausscheiden 96
ausschlagen 68
Ausschluss 98
Aussengalopp 84
Aussenseiter 122
äussere
    Form 14
    Linien 32
    Seite 58
äusserer Zügel 74
aussitzen im Trabe 76
Austrocknung 52
Auswiegen 114
Auswieger 108
Auswiegeraum 114

Auswurf 52
Auszubilende-Lizenz 110
Azubi 108

Bach 154
Backenriemen 140
Backenzähne 44
Backsteinmauer 154
Bahnpeitsche 144
Bahnrunde 114
Bahntierarzt 108
Bakterien 52
Balance 58
Ballen 42
    weiss gesäumt 40
Ballentritt 48
Ballotade 86
Band 14
Bandagen 52, 126
Bande 112
Bänderstart 112
Bandmass 44
Bandwürmer 50
bärentatzige, Fessel 30
Barrierenspringen 96
Basis 60
Baskülе 94
Bauch 16, 24
    aufgeschürzter 24
    aufgezogener 24
    gesenkter 24
    hängender 24
    Heubauch 24
    normaler 24
Bauchfellentzündung 48
Bauchgert, kleine 100
Bäume 144
Becken 14
(Beeren-) Eibe 12
befriedigend 92
befruchten 8
begrentze Renneignschaft

120
Behaarung 14
behindert worden 120
behoster Unterschenkel 30
beidhändig führen 74
beidseitige 74
Beifahrer 102
beige 116
beigezäumt 60
Beine 58
    Abzeichen 40
Beinpaare 58
beissen 68
Beizäumung 60
belohnen 72
Belohnung 72
Bereiter 90
beruhigen 72
Beruhigungsmittel 54
berühren 72
besamen 8
Besamung, künstliche 8
Beschäler 8
beschlagen, Huf 44
Beschlagschmied 42
beschläunigen 122
Besen 126
besitzen, Renneigenschaft 120
Besitzer 108
    gleich Trainer 108
    gleich Züchter 108
Besitzerin 108
Beständigkeit 6
Bestandteile des Zaumzeugs
    140
Bestzeit 98
Beugeprobe 54
bewegen 130
Beweglichkeit 60
Bewegung 8, 40-2, 58
Biegsamkeit 58
Biegung 60
    in der Längsachse 60
    im Genick 60

Bitterlupine 12
blanke Kandare 74
Blassisabel 36
Blatt 136
blau 116
    Schimmel 38
Blendklappen 100
Blesse 40
Blindheit 46
Blinklicht 128
Blume 40
Blutarmut 46
Blutauffrischung 6
Bluten 52
Blutgemeinschaft 4
Blutlinie 4
Blutprobe 52
Blutstrom 4
Blutung 52
Blutwürmer 48
Bock 100
Bockbrett 100
Bockdecke 100
Bocken 68
Bockhuf 42
Bocksprünge 68
Boden 80
Boden deckend, viel 32
bodennahe 32
Bodenrick 154
bodenständig machen 6
bodenständige Rasse 2
Bogen 84
Box 126
Bracke 100
Brandwunden 52
Braun 38, 116
    Gold 38
    Hell 38
    Kirsch 38
    Reh 38
    Rot 38
    Schimmel (Stichelhaar) 38
    Schwarz 38

Break 98
Breeches 152
breite
    Brust 22
    Kruppe 26
    Niere 24
    Röhre 28
breiter Vorarm 28
breites
    Sprunggelenk 30
    Vorderfusswurzelgelenk 28
Breiumschlag 54
Bremse 100
Bremslicht 128
Bretthals 22
Bronchiolitis 46
Bruch 48, 54
Bruder 4
Brust 16, 22
    breite 22
    enge 22
    flache 22
    Habichtsbrust 22
    hohe 22
    Löwenbrust 22
    proportionierte 22
    schmale 22
    tiefe 22
    Ziegenbrust 22
Brustblattgeschirr 100
brusteng 32
Brustkorb 14
Brustriegel 128
Bruststütze 128
brustweit 32
brutaler Zügelanzug 74
Buchsbaum 10
Buggelenk 16
Bullfinch 154
'bunte' Mischung 6
Bürste 152
bürsten 130, 152

Cavaletti 154

Chambon 144
Chaps 152
Charakter 64-6
Chef-Bereiter 90
chirurgische Behandlung
    vornehmen 54
chronische
    Hufrollenentzündung 48
    obstruktive Bronchiolitis 46
Cob 2
Coffin 154
Cowboysattel 136

Damenreitkleid 148
Damensattel 136
Dampf 46
Darmverschlingung 50
'de Gogue' 144
Deckakt 8
Decke 126
Deckengurt 126
Deckvorgang 8, 10
Deichsel 100, 128
'deutsch' traben 76
diagonale
    Beinpaare 58
    Hilfen 74
    Diagonale wechseln 76
Diagonalwechsel 80
dicker
    Hals 22
    Widerrist 24
Disqualifikation 98
disqualifiziert
    für eine Placierung 110
    werden 120
Distanz 94
Distanzfahren 102
Distanzritt 78
Dogcart 98
Dopingmittel 52
Doppellonge 144
dreifaches Hindernis 154
dreijährige

Hengste 108
    Stuten 110
Dreimaster 148
Dreispitz 148
Dressur 58, 66
Dressurreiten 78
Dressuraufgabe 92
Dressurgerte 148
Dressurgrad 64-6
Dressurpferd 2
Dressurprüfung 90-2, 96
Dressurprüfung für
    Wagenpferde 102
Dressursattel 132
Dressursitz 72
Druck sein, unter 120
Druckverband 54
Druse 50
Dunkelfuchs 36
dunkelblau 116
dunkelgrün 116
durch
    den Zirkel wechseln 84
    die Länge wechseln 80
Durchfall 46
durchgehen 68
durchgehende Hornspalte 42,
    50
durchgetretene Fessel 30
durchlässiges Maul 66
Durchlässigkeit 58, 64
Dusche 52

Ecke 80
Eckzähne 44
edel 36
edler Kopf 20
egalisieren 132
Ehrenpreise 112
Eimer 126
Einbiss 44
Einbrechen 120, 122
einfache Körperfarben 36
einfacher Galoppwechsel 76

einfaches Hindernis 154
einflechten 132
Einfühlung 76
eingeflochtener Schweif 132
eingeklemmter Schweif 26
eingeritten sein 120
eingeschiente Röhre, gut 28
eingeschränktes Rennen 110
Einhorn 98
einseitige Hilfen 74
einseitiger Schenkeldruck 74
Einspänner 98
einspringen 94
Einstreu 130
einteiliges Mundstück 144
Einzelwesen 4
Eisenschimmel 38
Eisen abnehmen 44
Eiter 54
Ekzem 46, 48, 52
elastisch 116
elektrische
    Muskelstimulierung 52
Elektrolyte 52
Ellbogen 16, 28
    abstehender 28
    angedrückter 28
    gebundener 28
    loser 28
empfindliches Maul 66
Empfindlichkeit 54
Empfindungslosigkeit 54
Endkampf 112
enge
    Brust 22
    Verwandtschaftszucht 6
'englisch' traben 76
englische
    Masse 46
    Vollblut 2
Enkel 4
Enkelin 4
Eselskruppe 26
entartet 6

entfernt 114
Entfernung 112
entkleiden, sich 152
entladen 128
Entlastungssitz 72
entspannt 64
Entspannung 60
enttäuschen 120
Entzündung 54
entzündungshemmend 52
Erbanlage 6
Erbfehler 6
Erblichkeit 6
Erdwall 154
Erhaltungs-ration 14
erhöhen, Geschwindigkeit 120
Erkrankung der Gelenke 48
Erlaubnisgewicht 114
ernähren 130
Ernährung 54
Ersatzpferd 102
Ersatzzähne 44
erschöpft 66
erschrecken 68
Erschütterung 52
erste Hilfe 54
Esel 2
Euter 20
Exterieur 8, 14
Exterieur des Pferdes 14-36

Faden 128
Fahren 78, 98-102
Fahrer 98
Fahrgerte 100
Fahrpeitsche 100
Fahrpferd 102
Fahrt machen, die 120
Fahrtenschreiber 128
Fahrzaum 100
Falbe 38
fallen 94
falscher Galopp 84
Familie 4

Fang 154
Farbe 14
Farben 36-40
fassbeinig 32
faul 64
Federn 100
federnde Anlehnung 60
fegen 130
Fehler bei der Aufgabe 92
Fehler und Mängel 52
fehlerhafte Stellung der
    Gliedmassen 32
Fehlstart 112
Feiertagskrankheit 46
fein
    abgestimmte Zügel- und
        Schenkelhilfen 64
    gestimmt 68
    gestimmtes Maul 66
feiner Hals 22
Feld 102, 112
Feldstiefel 152
Fersen 72
Fessel 20, 30
    bärentatzige 30
    durchgetretene 30
    kurze 30
    lange 30
    schräge 30
    steile 30
    weiche 30
Fesselbehang 130
Fesselgelenk 16
Fesselhaare 130
Fesselkopf 16
fest 114
festes Hindernis 94
Fettleibigkeit 48
feurig 64
Fieber 48
Finish 112
fit sein 66, 120
flache
    Brust 22

Rippen 22
flacher Vorarm 28
flaches Vorderfusswurzelgelenk
    28
Flachhuf 42
Flachrennen 110
Flaggenstart 112
Flanke 16
flaues Maul 66
flechten 132
fleischiger Kopf 20
Fliegenschimmel 38
fliegend wechseln
    à tempo 76
    von Sprung zu Sprung 76
Flieger 118
Flocke 40
flüchtiges Überputzen 130
Fohlen 10
Fohlenzähne 44
Folge 102
Forellenschimmel 38
Form 64-6
Format 36
Fraktur 54
'französische' Kurbette 86
freie Jagd 102
freie Gangarten 42
freier Schritt 84
Freiheit 60
Freizeitreiten 78
fremdartig 6
fremde Hilfe 98
Fremdzucht 6
frisches Maul 66
Frisieren 130-2
fruchtbar 8
Fuchs 36-8
    Dunkel 36
    Gold 38
    Hell 36
    Kohl 38
    Lehm 38
Fuchsjagd 102

Fuchslunte 104
Fuchsschimmel 38
Führarbeit 120
Führung
    haben 120
    übernehmen 120
Fuss 20, 42-4, 46
    fliegend wechseln 76
    wechseln 76
fussen 94
Futter 12, 126
Fütter 130
Futter, pelletiertes 12
Futtermittel 12-14
füttern 130

Gabel 126
Gabelsitz 72
Gag 136, 140
Galle 50
Galopp 42, 84
    Arbeitsgalopp 84
    Aussengalopp 84
    falscher 84
    Handgalopp 84
    Innengalopp 84
    Konter 76, 84
    Kreuzgalopp 84
    links 76
    Linksgalopp 84
    Mittelgalopp 84
    rechts 76
    Rechtsgalopp 84
    reiten 76
    Renngalopp 84
    richtiger 84
    starker 84
    versammelter 84
galoppieren 76
Ganasche 16
Gang 58
Gangart 58
    wechseln 76
Gangarten 40-2

der Kampagneschule 84
künstliche 42
ganze Parade 58
Gatter 154
Gattung 4
Gebiss 60, 140
Gebisse 140-4
gebisslose Zäumung 140
gebogen (seitwärts) 60
gebogener Hals 22
Gebrauchskreuzung 6
Gebrauchspferd 2
gebrochenes Mundstück 144
gebundener Ellbogen 28
Geburt 10
gedeckte Stute 8
gedrosseltes Vorderfuss-
    wurzelgelenk 28
gedrungen 32
geflochtene Mähne 132
Gefühl des Reiters 76
gegen die Uhr reiten 94
gegenreiten 94
Gegenseite 112
Gehorsam 60, 64
Geländefahren 100
Geländehindernisse 96
Geländeprüfung 78, 96
Geländer 112
Geländestrecke 78, 96
Geländeritt 78
Geläuf 114-16
Geläuf mögen, das 120
gelb 116
    Schecke 38
    Schimmel 36
Gelbsucht 48
Gelenk 14
Gelenkentzündung 46
gemeiner Kopf 20
gemischt 6
gemischte Farben 36
Genick 16
gepflegte Mähne 132

gequetscht 12
gerade 58
    Linie 80
    Niere 24
    verlaufender Hals 22
Geradebahn 114
Geradewärter 10
Geradegerichtetsein 58
geradegerichtete Pferd 60
Geraden, in der 112
gerader
    Kopf 20
    Rücken 24
geraderichten 58
geringelt 116, 118
gerittenes Pferd 66
Gerste 12
Gesamtgewicht 128
Gesässknochen 72
Geschirr 98
Geschirrmacher 136
Geschlechtskrankheit 50
geschlossen 32
geschlossene Niere 24
geschnürtes Vorderfuss-
    wurzelgelenk 28
geschoren, komplett 132
geschorene Mähne 132
geschrotet 12
geschulter Reiter 90
'geschwätziges' Maul 66
Geschwindigkeit 120
    erhöhen 120
Geschwulst 50, 54
Geschwür 50
gesenkte Niere 24
gesenkter
    Bauch 24
    Rücken 24
Gespann 98
gespannt 64
gespannter Rücken 68
gespanntes Maul 66
gestreckt 32
gestreckte Gangarten 42

gestrichen 112
Gestüt 4, 8
Gestütsbrand 10
Gestütsbuch 10
Gestütsleiter 10
Gestütswärter 10
Gesundheit 8, 52
gevierteilt 118
Gewicht 114
Gewichtsdecke 136
Gewichtshilfen 72
Gewinne 112
Gewinnstatistik 120
gewölbte
    Rippen 22
    (steife) Seite 60
gewölbter, Rücken 24
gewölbtes
    Mundstück 144
    Vorderfusswurzelgelenk 28
Giftpflanzen 10
Gig 98
Glanzrappe 36
Glasauge 40
glatt geschlagen sein 120
gleichartig 6
Gleichgewicht 8, 36, 64
gleichzeitige Schenkelwirkung
    74
Gliedmassen 14
Glockenzeichen 92
Gold
    Braun 38
    Fuchs 38
Goldregen 12
Graben 154
Grad 4
Gras 12
Grasbahn 114
grasen 10
Graskrankheit des Pferdes 48
Grauschimmel 38
Grosse Vielseitigkeits-
    prüfungen 96

grosser Kopf 20
grosses
    Knie 30
    Sprunggelenk 30
    Vorderfusswurzelgelenk 28
Grossmutter 4
Grossvater 4
Grummet 12
grün 116
Grund-ration 14
Grundbegriffe 58-64
gründliches Putzen 130
grüne Bruch 104
Grünfutter 12
Gruppenrennen 110
Gruss 92
Gummiband 128
Gummigebiss 144
Gummiglocken 126
Gummistiefel 152
Gurte anziehen 136
Gurte lösen 136
Gürtel 116, 118
Gurtumfang 44
güsste Stute 8
gut 92, 114
gut aufgesetzter Kopf 22
gut bemuskelter
    Hals 22
    Oberschenkel 30
    Unterschenkel 30
gut eingeschiente Röhre 28
gut gelaufen 120
gut, ziemlich 92
guter
    Futterverwerter 66
    Zustand 66
Gutpunkte 94
Gymkhana 78
Gymnastikreihe 94

Haar 14
Haardecke 130
Haarkleid 14, 130

Haarlinge 48
haarlose Vorderfuss-
    wurzelgelenke 46
Haarwechsel 130
Haarwirbel 40
Habichtsbrust 22
Hackney 102
Häcksel 12
Hafer 12
Hahnenfuss 10
Hahnentritt 50
Hakenzähne 44
Halali 102
Halbbruder 4
halbe
    Länge 114
    Parade 74
    Reitschule 80
    Volte 80
halbem Wege, auf 112
Halbschwester 4
Halbtravers 86
Hals 16, 22, 114, 148
    Bretthals 22
    dicker 22
    feiner 22
    gebogener 22
    gerade verlaufender 22
    gut bemuskelter 22
    Hirschhals 22
    hochangesetzter 22
    kurzer 22
    langer 22
    leichter 22
    proportionierter 22
    schmaler 22
    schräggestellter 22
    schwach bemuskelter 22
    Schwanenhals 22
    schwerer 22
    steilgestellter 22
    tiefangesetzter 22
    waagerechter 22
Halten 58, 76, 84

Haltung 58, 60, 72
Hand
  hinter der 68
  schwer auf der Hand liegen
    68
  über der 68
  Verbindung zwischen Hand
    und Maul 60
  wechseln 76, 80
  Zügel in einer 74
  zwischen Hand und
    Schenkeln 68
Handgalopp 84
Handicap 110
Handicaprennen 110
Handschuh 148
hängender Bauch 24
Hanken 72
  setzen auf die 60
hannoverscher Reithalfter 140
Hardfutter 12
Harmonie 60
harmonisch 36
Harnorgane 52
harter Rücken 68
hartes Maul 66
Hasenhacke 46
(Haupt-) Gestüt 8
Hauptgangarten 42
Hauptgewicht 128
Hauptstamm 6
Haut 14
Hebel 32
Hechtskopf 20
heftig 64
hellblau 116
hellbraun 38
Hellfuchs 36
hellgrün 116
Hengst 8
Hengstdepot (Landgestüt) 8
Hengstwärter 10, 108
herausstrecken, Zunge 68
Herbstzeitlose 10

Herzerkrankung 48
heterogen 6
Hetzpeitsche 104, 144
Heu 12
Heubauch 24
Heuraufe 126
Hieb versetzen 72
Hilfen 72
Hilfs-Reitlehrer 90
Hilfszügel 144
Hindernis 92
  streifen 94
Hindernisfahren 100
Hindernisrennen nach Zeit 100
Hindernisse 154
  ohne Galoppzwischen-
    sprung 154
hingegebener Zügel 74
hinter
  den Schenkeln 68
  der Hand 68
Hinterbacke 20
Hinterbein weiss 40
Hinterbeine 58
Hinterfessel weiss 40
Hinterfuss hoch weiss 40
Hintergeschirr 100
Hinterhand 58
  heranstellen 60
Hinterhandwendung 86
Hinterknie 30
Hinterröhre 28
Hinterteil 36
Hinterzwiesel 136
Hirschfänger 104
Hirschhals 22
hochangesetzter
  Hals 22
  Schweif 26
Hochziehen der Zunge 68
Hofstallmeister 90
hohe
  Brust 22
  Kruppe 26

Schule 78
  Stiefel 152
hoher Widerrist 24
hohle
  Niere 24
  (schwierige) Seite 60
hohler Rücken 68
Holden 20
Holdensack 20
Holzscheit 154
Holzspäne 130
homogen 6
Hormone 54
Hornspalte 42, 50
Hornwand 42
Horse Ball 78
Huf 20, 42
  auskratzen 130
  beschlagen 44
  richten 44
Hufeisen 42
Huffett 128
Hufknorpelverknöcherung 50
Hufkratzer 126
Hufnagel 42
Hufraspel 42
Hufrehe 48
Hufrollenentzündung 48
Hufschlag 58, 80
Hufschlagfiguren 80-90
Hüfte 26
  ausgeprägte 26
  normale 26
  spitze 26
Hüfthocker 16
hüftige Kruppe 26
Hufverschlag 48
Hund 102
Hundsmann 102
Hürde 154
Hürdenrennen 110
Husten 46
hybrid 6
Impfpass 110

Impfung 54
Influenza 48
Innengalopp 84
innere Seite 58
innerer Fuss 86
innerer Zügel 74
Insektenstich 48
Interessenten 108
Intermédiaire 92
Intervalltraining 98
Inzestzucht 6
Inzucht 6
inzuchtfreien Ahnenreihen 6
irische Bank 154
irische Martingal 144

jagdbares Tier 102
Jagddress 104
Jagdfrack 148
Jagdherr 102
Jagdhorn 104
Jagdkrawatte 148
Jagdmartingal 144
Jagdpferd 2, 102
Jagdreiten 78
Jagdreiter 102
Jagdrennen 110
Jagdrock 148
Jagdsattel 132
Jagdstiefel 152
Jagduniform 104
Jagdzeug 136
Jockey 90, 108
Jockey-Lizenz 110
Jockeystiefel 152
Jodhpurstiefel 152
Johanniskraut 12
Jucken 54
Juckreiz 54
junge
  Remonte 64
  Stute 8
Jungfuchsjad 102
Junghengst 8

Jungpferd 66
Jungpferde-Ration 14

Kadenz 58
Kakerlakenauge 40
kaltblütige Schlag 2
Kaltblutpferd 2
Kamm 132
Kamm-Messer 132
Kammdeckel 100
kämmen 130
Kammer 136
Kampagne-Reiterei 78
Kandare 140, 144
Kandarenzaum 140
Kanonenspringen 96
Kanter 84
kantiges Sprunggelenk 30
Kappzaum 144
Kapriole 86
Kardätsche 126
kariert 116, 118
Karpfenrücken 24
Karren 126
Kastanie 16
Kastensporn 148
Kastration 52
Kastrieren 52
Kegel 102
Kehlkopf 16
Kehlkopfpfeifen 50
Kehlriemen 140
keilförmiger Kopf 20
Kette 126
Kinnbacke 16
Kinnkette 144
Kinnkettengrube 16
Kinnkettenhaken 144
Kinnriemen 148
Kirsch, Braun 38
Kissen 136
Klasse 8, 90, 120
klassische
  Reitkunst 76-8

Rennen 110
klebend 68
Klee 12
Kleie 12
kleine Bauchgurt 100
kleiner Kopf 20
Kleinpferd 2
Klopphengst 8
knappe Führung haben 120
Knie 20, 30
    ausgeprägtes 30
    grosses 30
    offenwinkeliges 30
knieeng 32
Kniekappen 126
knieweit 32
Kniewulst 136
knirschen 68
Knochen 14
    viel 32
Knochengerüst 14
Kohl, Fuchs 38
Kolik 46
Kombination 154
kombinierte Prüfung 78, 102
kombinierte Reithalfter 140
komplett geschoren 132
Kondition 66
konkaver Kopf 20
Konstanz 6
Konstitution 8
kontagiöse equine Metritis 46
Kontakt 60
Konter-Wechsel 80
Kontergalopp 76, 84
Kopf 14, 20-2, 68, 114
    Abzeichen 40
    ausdrucksvoller 20
    edler 20
    fleischiger 20
    gemeiner 20
    gerader 20
    grosser 20
    gut aufgesetzter 22

Hechtskopf 20
keilförmiger 20
kleiner 20
konkaver 20
leichter 20
Ramskopf 20
Schafskopf 22
schlecht aufgesetzter 22
schwerer 20
trockener 20
Kopfgestell 140
Kopfräude 50
Kopfstück 100, 126
Koppel 10, 102
Kornfutter 12
Körperbau 8
    des Pferdes 14
Körperfarben 36-40
Körperinnentemperatur 52
korrigieren 72
Kötenbehang 20
Kötenhaare 130
kräftiger Unterschenkel 30
kräftiges Sprunggelenk 32
Krankheit 50
Krankheiten 46-50
Krebs 46
Kreislaufsystem 52
Kreuz 72
Kreuzen 112
kreuzen (im Galopp) 68
Kreuzgalle 46
Kreuzgalopp 84
Kreuzkraut 12
Kreuzung 6
Kreuzverschlag 46
Kreuzzucht 6
Krippe 126
Krone weiss gesaumt 40
Kronengelenk 20
Kruppade 86
Kruppe 16, 26
    abfallende 26
    abgedachte 26

abschüssige 26
breite 26
Eselskruppe 26
hohe 26
hüftige 26
kurze 26
lange 26
ovale 26
schmale 26
schwache 26
starke 26
überbaute 26
waagerechte 26
Kruppeherein 86
Kuh-Heubauch 24
kuhhessig 32
Kühlverband 52
Kumt 100
Kumtbügel 100
Kumtgeschirr 100
Kunde 44
künstliche Besamung 8
künstliche Gangarten 42
Kunst-Reiterei 78
Kunststoffsattel 136
kupieren 132
Kupplung 128
Kür 92
    mit Musik 92
Kurbette 86
Küree 102
Kurve 112
kurz wenden 94
kurzbeinig 32
kurze
    Fessel 30
    Jagdhorn am Sattel
        geschnallt 104
    Kruppe 26
    Niere 24
    Rippen 22
    Röhre 28
    Schulter 26
kurzegefesselt 32

kurzer
    Hals 22, 114
    Kopf 114
    Oberarm 26
    Rücken 24
    Vorarm 28
    Widerrist 24
kurzes Ende 122
Kurzkehrtwendung 86
kurzscheren 132
Kutsche 98
Kutschpferd 102

Lahmheit 48
Lähmung 48
landen 94
Landeskennzeichen 128
lang bemuskelter Unter-
    schenkel 30
lange
    Fessel 30
    Kruppe 26
    Niere 24
    Reithose 152
    Rippen 22
    Röhre 28
    Schulter 26
    Zügel 144
langer
    Hals 22
    Oberarm 28
    Oberschenkel 30
    Rücken 24
    Schritt 84
    Unterschenkel 30
    Vorarm 28
    Widerrist 24
langes
    Sprunggelenk 30
    Vorderfusswurzelgelenk 28
Längsachse (Wirbelsäule) 60
Lanzenstich 40
Lappen 128
Lasertherapie 54

Laterne 40
Leberegelbefall 48
Leberentzündung 48
Leckerbissen 14
Leckstein 14
Leergewicht 128
Lehm, Fuchs 38
Lehrgang 80
Lehrling 108
Lehrlings-Lizenz 110
Leibstallmeister 90
leichtfütterig 66
leicht 90
leicht an dem Schenkel stehen
    68
leichten Trab übergehen 76
leichter
    Hals 22
    Kopf 20
    Schlag 2
    Sitz 72
Leichtigkeit 64
leichttraben 76
Leinenklebeband 128
Leinenschlüssel 100
Leinsamen 12
Leistungsprüfung 80
Lende 16, 24
letzte Ecke 112
Levade 86
lichten 132
Lidbindehautentzündung 46
Liguster 12
Linienzucht 6
linke Seite 58
linken Diagonale traben, auf
    der 76
Linksbahn 114
Linksgalopp 84
loben 72
lockern 136
Longe 144
Longier-und Dressurzeug 144
Longiergurt 144

Longierien 66
lose
 Schulter 26
 Wand 50
lösen 94
loser Ellbogen 28
Losgelassenheit 58, 60
Lothringer Kreuz 116, 118
Lotion 54
Löwenbrust 22
Lungenentzündung 48
Lungenwurm-Infektion 48
Luzerne 12
Lymphangitis 48

Mächtigkeitsspringen 96
Madenwürmer 50
Magenbremsen 46
magerer Widerrist 24
Mähne 20, 130
Mähnenbürste 126
Mähnenflechtringe 128
Mähnenhaare 130
Mähnenkamm 16, 128
Mais 12
malvenfarbig 116
Manager der Rennbahn 108
Mängel 46-50
mangelhaft 92
Mannschaftsspringen 96
Markiertafeln 92
Mash 14
Masse 44
massieren 130
Master 102
Material 125-54
Materialprüfung 80
Matratze 130
Matratzenlager 130
Mauer 80, 154
Mauke 46
Maul 16, 66
 empfindliches 66
 rohes 66

Maulesel 2
Mausfalb 38
Mausgrau 38
Medikament 52
mehr tragen 114
mehrere 'V' 116, 118
Mehrgewicht 114
Mehrzwecksattel 132
Meile 46
Meiler 120
Meister 90
Melasse 12
Melone 148
Messband 44
Messeinheit 44
Messtock 44
Messung 44
Meter 46
metrische Masse 46
Meute 102
mexikanische Reithalfter 140
Mezair 86
mikroskopische Untersuchung
 54
Milben 48
Milchmaul 40
Milchschimmel 36
Milchzähne 44
Military 78
Militarypferd 96
Mischblut 6
Mischfutter 12
Mischling 6
mittel 92
Mitteldistanzpferd 120
Mittelgalopp 84
Mittelhand 58
Mittellinie 80
Mittelschritt 84
Mittelstück 36
Mitteltrab 84
Mittelzähne 44
Mixtur 54
Mohrenkopf 40

Mohrrübe 12
Moment der frien Schwebe 60
müde 64
Mundstück 144
munter 64
Muskeln 14
muskelrelaxierende
 Medikament 54
Mutter 4
Mutterstute 8

Nabel 16
nachgeben 74
Nachgeben des Unterkiefers
 60
Nachkommenschaft 4
nachlässig springen 94
Nachwuchspferd 66
Nachzucht 4, 8
Nageltritt 42, 48
Nähte 116, 118
Nase 114
Nasenbremse 128
Nasenriemen 140
Nasenrücken 16
natürliche Gangarten 42
Nennung 110
Nerv 54
Nerven 14
Nervenblockade 54
Nesselausschlag 50
Netz 126
Neuseeland-Decke 126
nicht ausgeführt 92
niedere Schule 78
niedriger Widerrist 24
Niere 16, 24
 breite 24
 gerade 24
 geschlossene 24
 gesenkte 24
 hohle 24
 kurze 24
 lange 24

schmale 24
Niete 42
normal, Stellung der
 Gliedmassen 32
normale Hüfte 26
normaler Bauch 24
Notenschlüssel 92
Notfallapotheke 54
Nummerschild 128
Nüstern 16
Nutzlast 128

'o'-beinig 32
Oberarm 16, 26-8
 kurzer 26
 langer 28
 schräger 28
 steiler 28
Oberbau 36
Oberbereiter 90
Obergurt 136
Oberkörper 72
Oberlinie 60
Oberschenkel 20, 30, 72
 gut bemuskelter 30
 langer 30
 schräger 30
offene Verletzung 54
Öffenerennen 110
offenes Sprunggelenk 30
Öffentliche-Rennen 110
Öffentlichkeitsring 114
offenwinkeliges Knie 30
ohne Abzeichen 116, 118
ohne Galoppzwischensprung
 154
ohne jegliche Abzeichen 40
Ohr 16
Öl 14
Olivenkopftrense 140
Olympia-Dressurprüfung 92
orange 116
Organe 14
orientalisches/morgenländisches

Pferd 2
Ortscheit 100
ovale Kruppe 26
Oxer 154

Packpferd 2
Paddock 10
Palomino 38
Parade 76, 84, 112
Parasiten 54
Parasitenbefall 54
Parcours besichtigen 96
Parcoursbesichtigung 94
Parcourschef 94
parieren 72
Passage 86
Passgang 42
Passgänger 2
passiv 72
passiver
 Schenkel 74
 Zügel 74
Paste 152
Peitschen 144-8
Peitschenschmitz 148
Peitschenschnur 148
Pelham 144
pelletiertes Futter 12
'Pellets' 12
Pension 130
pensionieren 120
Perioden 44
Peritonitis 48
Personentür 128
Pesade 86
Pferd
 angerittenes 64
 in die Ecke stellen 120
 euthanasieren 52
 mit schwingendem Rücken
 68
 nennen 112
 schlachten 52
 töten 52

Pferdefreund 90
Pferdeführanlage 130
Pferdekenner 90
Pferdelänge 114
Pferdemann 90
Pferdepass 110
Pferdetransport 128
Pferdetransport-Anhänger 128
Pferdetransporter 128
Pferdetransportwagen 128
Pferdewärter 130
pflegen 54
Pfleger 108
Pfriemenschwänze 50
Phaeton 98
phlegmatisch 64
Piaffe 86
Piephacke 46
Pikör 102
Pilaren 144
Pilzerkrankung 48
Pirouette 86
Pirouetten 86
Placierung 96
Plastron 148
Platzewette 114
'Point-to-Point' 78
polieren 152
Polierknochen 152
Polo 78
Polohelm 148
Polokandare 144
Polosattel 136
Polostiefel 152
Polsterung 100, 136
Pony 2
Ponyhof 78
Porzellanschimmel 36
Potenz 6
Preis 96
Prellung 52
Presi der Nationen 96
Privatverkauf 110
Probierhengst 8

Produkt 4
Promenadenreiten 78
proportionierte 36
    Brust 22
proportionierter Hals 22
Protest einlegen 110
Prototyp der Gattung 6
Prüfung 78, 92
    'Jagd um Punkte' 96
Puissance 96
pullen 68
Pulver 54
Pumpgebiss 144
Punkt 118
Punktbrennen 54
Punkte 118
putzen 130
Putzzeug 152

Quaddelausschlag 50
quadratisch 36
Qualität 8
Querfeldeinstrecke 96

Räder 100
Rahmen 36
Rails laufen, an den 122
Ramskopf 20
Random 98
Rappschimmel (Stichelhaar)
    38
Rappe 36
    Glanz 36
    Sommer 36
Rasse 4
    verbessern 6
Rassen 4
Rattenschweif 26
Räude 48
Rauhfutter 12
Raute 116, 118
rautiert 118
Reaktion des Reitpferdes
    66-71

Rechtsbahn 114
rechte Seite 58
rechteckig 36
Rechtsgalopp 84
regelmässige Gangarten 42
Regelmässigkeit 58
Regenmantel 152
Rehbraun 38
Rehe 48
Reibfläche 44
reinigen 130
Reinzucht 6
Reisen im Sattel 78
Reit- und Wagenpferd 2
Reitbahn 80-90
reiten 76
    im Damensattel 80
    im Gelände 78
    im Herrensitz 80
    ohne Sattel 80
    zu Hirschhunden 102
    zu Hunden 78
Reiter 90
Reiter abwerfen 68
Reiter-Karussell 80
Reiter-Quadrille 80
Reiterei 76
Reitererklärung 112
Reiterin 90
Reiterpfad 80
Reiterspiele 78
Reitertakt 76
Reiterwechsel 112
Reitfrack 148, 152
Reitgeld 112
Reitgerte 144
Reithalle 80
Reithose 152
Reithut 148
Reitjackett 148
Reitjagd 102-4
Reitkappe 148
Reitkleidung 148-52
Reitkunst 76

Reitkünstler 90
Reitlehrer 90
Reitmeister 90
Reitpferd 2
Reitplatz 80, 92
Reitschule 78, 80
Reitschüler 90
Reitsport 78
Reitsport-Fachgeschäft 136
Reitstall 78
Reitstiefel 152
Reitstock 144
Reittechnik 72
Reitverein 78
Reitwart 90
Reitweg 80
Remonte 66
Rendez-vous 102
Rennsteifel 152
Rennbahn 96, 114
Rennbehörde 108-10
Renndress und Abzeichen
    116-18
Renneigenschaft
    begrenzte 120
    besitzen 120
Rennen 107-22
Rennen machen 120
Rennfarben 118
Rennform 120
Renngalopp 84
Rennjacke 148
Rennleistung 120
Rennleitung 108
Rennorganisation 112-14
Rennpeitsche 144
Rennpferd 2
Rennpreise 108
Rennprogramm 114
Rennreiten 78
Rennsattel 136
Rennsitz 72
Rennstall 120
Rennverein 108

Renvers 86
Reprise 58
Reservereifen 128
respektieren 94
Rhythmus 58
richten, den Huf 44
Richter 108
Richtergruppe 98
richtiger Galopp 84
Richtung
    der Bewegung 58
    wechseln 76, 80
Richtungswechsel 58
Richtverfahren 94
Rick 154
Riemer 136
Ringbein 48
Ringe 144
Ringelflechte 50
Ringtrense 140
Rippen 14, 16
    flache 22
    gewölbte 22
    kurze 22
    lange 22
Ritte 112
Robustpferd 2
roh 64
rohes Maul 66
Rohrbein 16
Röhrbeinumfang 44
Röhre 16, 28
    breite 28
    gut eingeschiente 28
    kurze 28
    lange 28
    runde 28
    schwache 28
    starke 28
Rohren 50
Röntgenuntersuchung 54
rosè 116
Rosette 96
Rosse 10

Rot
  Braun 38
  Schecke 38
rotbraun 116
rote Rock 104
roter Fingerhut 10
Rotz 48
rückbiegig 32
Rücken 16, 24
  gerader 24
  gesenkter 24
  gespannter 68
  gewölbter 24
  harter 68
  hohler 68
  Karpfenrücken 24
  kurzer 24
  langer 24
  schwingende 68
  schwacher 24
  Senkrücken 24
  starker 24
  weicher 24
Rückfahrautomatik 128
Rücklicht 128
Rückschlag 6
rückschlägig 6
Rückwärtsrichten 76
ruhig 64
Rumpf 14
runde Röhre 28
Rundwürmer 50
Rute 20

säbelbeinig 32
St Georg Preis 92
Sakkade 74
Salbe 54
Salz 14
Sand 80
Sandbahn 114
Sattel 132-6
  Bestandteile 136
  Reisen im 78

verpassen 136
Sattelbaum 136
Satteldecke 136
Satteldruck 46, 50
Sattelkammer 126, 136
Sattelkranz 136
satteln 136
Sattelseife 128
Sattelzeug 132, 136
Sattler 136
Sattlerei 136
sauber springen 94
säubern 130
Säugen 10
Schafskopf 22
Schale 48
Schanze 154
scharf 94
scharfe Sporn 148
scharfer, Widerrist 24
Schärpen Überkreuz 116,
  118
Schaum 66
Schecke 38
  Gelb 38
  Rot 38
  Schwarz 38
Scheide 20
Schenkel
  aktiver 74
  passiver 74
schenkelfaul 68
schenkelgehorsam 68
Schenkelhilfen 72
Schenkeltrense 140
Schenkelweichen 86
Schere 100, 132
Scheren 132
Scherenriemen 100
Scherenträger 100
Schermaschine 132
Scherriemen 144
scheu 64
scheuen 68

schief sein 60
Schiefe der Achse 60
Schierling 10
Schimmel (Stichelhaar) 38
  Braun 38
  Rapp 38
Schimmel (veränderlich)
  38-40
  Apfel 40
  Blau 38
  Eisen 38
  Fliegen 38
  Forellen 38
  Grau 38
  Schwarz 38
Schimmel (weissgeboren) 36
  Blassisabel 36
  Gelb 36
  Milch 36
  Porzellan 36
schläfrig 64
Schlag 4
Schlangenlinie 84
Schlauch 16
Schlaufzügel 144
schlecht 92
  aufgesetzter Kopf 22
  gelaufen 120
  ziemlich 92
schlechter
  Fresser 66
  Futterverwerter 66
  Zustand 66
Schleimbeutelentzündung des
  Sprunggelenks 50
Schleppjagd 102
schmale
  Brust 22
  Kruppe 26
  Niere 24
schmaler
  Hals 22
  Vorarm 28
Schmerz 54

Schmerzausschaltung am Nerv
  54
schmerzstillendes Mittel 52
Schmiede 42
schmieren 152
Schnalle 100, 148
Schnallen, Zaummit 140
schnappen 68
schneiden 132
Schneider 152
Schneidezähne 44
schnelle Gangarten 42
Schnippe 40
Schopf 20, 130
schräge
  abfallende Schulter 26
  Fessel 30
  Schulter 26
schräger
  Oberarm 28
  Oberschenkel 30
schräggestellter Hals 22
Schritt 42, 84
  am hingegebenen Zügel 84
  am langen Zügel 84
  freier 84
  langer 84
  reiten 76
  versammelter 84
Schrulreiter 90
Schub 64
Schubrine 20
Schulen
  auf der Erde 86
  über der Erde 86
Schulgangarten 42
Schulgänge 86
Schulpferd 90
Schulreiter 90
Schulreiterei 78
Schulreiterin 90
Schulschritt 86
Schulsprünge 86
Schulter 16, 26

ausdrucksvolle 26
kurze 26
lange 26
lose 26
schräge 26
schräge abfallende 26
steile 26
trockene 26
überladene 26
Schulterherein 86
Schultern 118
Schultrab 86
Schur 132
Schutzhütte 10
Schutzweste 152
Schwäche 50
schwache
  Kruppe 26
  Röhre 28
schwacher
  Hals 22
  Rücken 24
schwaches Sprunggelenk 32
schwammiges Sprunggelenk
  30
Schwanenhals 22
Schwann 126
schwarz 116
  Braun 38
  Schecke 38
  Schimmel 38
schwarze
  Harnwinde 46
  Tollkirsche 10
schwarzes Bilsenkraut 10
Schwebephase 60
Schweif 16, 26, 68, 130, 132
  eingeklemmter 26
  hoch angesetzter 26
  Rattenschweif 78
  tief angesetzter 26
Schweifansatz 132
Schweifes, Tragen des 26
Schweifriemen 100, 144

Schweifrübe 16, 132
Schweissmesser 126
schwer 92, 116
schwer auf der Hand liegen 68
schwerer
   Hals 22
   Kopf 20
   Schlag 2
Schwester 4
schwierig 64
Schwung 58
schwungvoll 60
Sechserzug 98
Sechsspänner 98
Sehnen 14
Sehnenentzündung 50
Sehnenklapp 50
sehr gut 92
sehr schlecht 92
sehr weich 116
Seitengänge 86
seitliche Beinpaare 58
Selbsttränke 126
Sellett 100
Senkrücken 24
Serie in Rennen 110
Servicetür 128
seuchenhafte Husten 48
Sheuklappen 100
Sieger 122
siegloses Hindernispferd 120
Sieglosenrennen
   in Flachrennen 110
   in Hürdenrennen 110
Siegwette 114
Sielengeschirr 100
Signalement 10
Sitz 72, 100, 136
Skelett 14
Skelett und die Muskeln 52
Sohle 42
Sohn 4
Sommerrappe 36
Sommerekzem 50

Sommerhaar 130
spanische Tritt 86
Spat 46
Spielbein 58
spitze Hüfte 26
Sporen 144-8
Sporer 148
Sporn 20
Spornrädchen 148
Spornriemen 148
Spornstich 74
sportliches Reiten 78
Springbahn 94, 154
Springen 92-6
Springfehler 96
Springkonkurrenzen 96
Springpferd 2, 92
Springprüfung 96
   Klasse 'S' 96
   ohne Teilnahmebeschrän-
     kungen 96
Springreiten 78
Springreiter 92
Springsattel 132
Springsitz 72
Springstil 94
Springtechnik des Pferdes 92
Springturnier 78, 94
Springübung im Couloir 94
Springvermögen 92
Sprinter 118
Spritzbrett 100
Spritze 54
Sprung 58, 88
Sprungfolge 94, 154
Sprunggelenk 20, 30-2
   abstehendes 30
   ausdrucksloses 30
   breites 30
   grosses 30
   kantiges 30
   kräftiges 32
   langes 30
   offenes 30

säbelbeinig 32
   schwaches 32
   schwammiges 30
   steiles 30
   tief am Boden 30
   trockenes 30
   verschwommenes 30
   zu stark gewinkeltes 32
Sprunggelenke
   zu eng 32
   zu weit 32
Spulwürmer 46
Spur 102
Staccionata 154
Stall 126-8
Stallbursche 130
Stalldienst 120, 130
Stallgefährte 120
Stallgerät 126-8
Stallhalfter 126
Stallmeister 130
Stamm 4
Stamm gründen 6
Stammbaum 6
Stammgrunder 6
Stammstute 8
Stammutter 8
Stammvater 6
Stand 126
Stand ausräumen 130
Standbein 58
Ständer 118
Stange 140, 144, 154
   greifen 68
Stangenzaum 140
Stangenzügel 140
stark 32
stark gewinkelte Sprunggelenk
   32
starke
   Kruppe 26
   Röhre 28
starker
   Galopp 84

Rücken 24
   Schritt 84
   Trab 84
starre Martingal 144
starres Hindernis 94
Start 112
   von der Startmaschine 112
Startbox 98
Startboxe 112
Starter 108, 114
Starterauslosung 112
Starterfeld 122
Starterliste 114
Starterskommando, unter 112
Startliste 114
Startzeichen 98
stätisch 68
Stechen 96
stehen-bleiben 94
Steher 118
steif 64
steifer Sitz 72
Steigbügel 136
steigen 68
Steigebiss 140
Steigriemen 136
steile
   Fessel 30
   Schulter 26
steiler Oberarm 28
steiles
   Hindernis 154
   Sprunggelenk 30
steilgefesselt 30
steilgestellter Hals 22
Steingallen 46
Steinmauer 154
Stelldichein 102
Stellen 102
Stellung 60
Stellung der Gliedmassen 14,
   32
   fehlerhaft 32
   normal 32

steril 8
Stern 40, 118
Sterne 118
Stichwunde 48
Stiefel 152
   anziehen 152
   ausziehen 152
   putzen 152
   reinigen 152
Stiefelblock 152
Stiefelette 152
Stiefelhaken 152
Stiefelknecht 152
Stiefelleiste 152
Stiefelmacher 152
Stillstehen 58, 76, 84
Stimme 72
Stirn 16
Stirnriemen 140
Stockhieb 74
Stockmass 44
Stollbeule 46
Stolle 44
störrisch 68
Strafe 72
   anzeigen 112
strafen 72
Strafpunkte 96, 98
Strafzone 98
Strahl 42
Strahlfäule 50
Streckenfahren 100
streicheln 72
streichen 68
Streichkappen 126
Streifen 116, 118
Streu 126
   erneuern 130
   richten 130
Strich 40
Striegel 126
Strippe 136
Stroh 12
Strohbett 130

Stufen 154
Stuhlsitz 72
Stulpenstiefel 152
Stummelschweif 132
'stummes' Maul 66
stumpfer Sporn 148
Sturz 94, 98
stürzen 94, 98
Sturzfeder 136
Sturzkappe 148
Stutbuch 10
Stute 8
   gedeckte 8
   güsste 8
   junge 8
   mit Fohlen bei Fuss 8
   Mutterstute 8
   tragende 8
Stuterei 8
Stutmeister 10
Stützrad 128
Sumpf-Schachtelhalm 10
symmetrisch 72
Syndicat 108

Tagesnorm 14
Tagesration 14
Takt 58
Tandem 98
tätiger 74
Tätigkeit 60
taxieren 94
Teilhaberschaft 108
Teilnehmer-Besprechung 96
Temperament 8, 64-6
Tempo 42, 58
Tempo wechseln 76
tief 116
   am Boden, Sprunggelenk 30
   angesetzter Schweif 26
Tiefe 32
tiefe Brust 22
tiefer Hals 22
Tiefsprung 154

tierärztliche, allgemeine
   Wörter 50
Tiger 38
Tisch 154
Tochter 4
Tod 102
Tor 10, 154
totes Rennen 114
Tour 58
Trab 42, 84
   Arbeitstrab 84
   Mitteltrab 84
   reiten 76
   starker 84
   versammelter 84
traben 76
Traber 2
Trabpferd 2
Trächtigkeit 10
Tragen des Schweifes 26
tragende Stute 8
Trageöse 100
Tragferd 2
Tragweite des Schweifes 132
Trainer 90, 108
Trainer-Lizenz 110
Trainerausweis 110
Trainierbahn 114
Training nehmen, in 120
Trainingsvokabeln 118-20
Trakehner 154
Tränke 126
tränken 130
Travers 86
Traversale 86
Traversalverschiebung 86
traversieren 86
treibender Schenkel 74
Trekking 78
Trennwand 128
Trense 140
Trensenzaum 140
Trensenzügel 140
Trippelbarre 154

Tritt 58
trocken 114
trockene Schulter 26
trockener
   Kopf 20
   Widerrist 24
trockenes
   Sprunggelenk 30
   Vorderfusswurzelgelenk 28
Trockenschnitzel 12
Trophäe 102
Tupfer 54
Turnier 78
Turnierreiten 78
Turniersport 78
Turniertrense 140
'tuschieren' 72
Typ 4
Typen 2
typisch 6
typlos 6

über der Hand 68
überbaut 36
überbaute, Kruppe 26
Überbein 50
Übergang 60
überladene Schulter 26
überständig 32
Überstreichen 64
überwinden 94
überzäumt 68
Überzug über der Sturzkappe
   148
Ultraschalluntersuchung 54
umankleiden, sich 152
umanziehen, sich 152
umwerfen 94
Umzäunung 10
unachtsam springen 94
Unarten 66-71
unempfindlich machendes
   Mittel 52
Unfall 94

unfruchtbar 8
Ungehorsham 66-71
ungeritten 64
Ungezwungenheit 60
unplaziert 112
unqualifiziert für Rennen 110
unregelmässige Gangarten 42
unruhiges Maul 66
unstetes Maul 66
Untätigkeit 60
unter Druck sein 120
unter Starterskommando 112
Unterbau 36
Unterernährung 48
Untergesicht 16
Unterkiefers, Nachgeben des
   60
Unterlegtrense 140
Unterschenkel 30, 72
   ausdrucksvoller 30
   behoster 30
   gut bemuskelter 30
   kräftiger 30
   lang bemuskelter 30
   langer 30
Untugend 52
Ursprung 4

'V' 116, 118
Vater 8
Vatertier 8
Verband 52
Verbände 52
Verbandmaterial 52
Verbindung zwischen Hand
   und Maul 60
Verdauungssystem 52
verdorbenes Maul 66
veredeln 6
Vererbungsfähigkeit 6
Verfassungsprüfung 96
Vergiftung 48
Vergleichsrennen 110
verhalten 68

Verkauf
   mit Mindestpreis 110
   ohne Mindestpreis 110
   mit Reservepreis 110
   ohne Reservepreis 110
Verkaufsrennen 110
verkürzte Ganagarten 42
Verladeklappe 128
verladen 128
Verladerampe 128
verlängern 76
verlesen 132
verletzte Linie 46
Verletzung 50
Verlieren von Rennform 120
Vernageln 42
Veröffentlichung der
   Nennungen 108
Verreiten 92
versammeln 60
versammelte Gangarten 42
versammelter
   Galopp 84
   Schritt 84
Versammlung 64
verschwommenes
   Sprunggelenk 30
vershwommener Widerrist 24
verstärken 76
Versteigerer 108
Vertrauen 64
vertrauende Anlehnung 60
Verwaltung 108-10
Verwandtschaft 4
Verwandtschaftszucht 6
verweigern 94
verziehen 132
verzogene Mähne 132
verzogene Schweif 132
viel Boden deckend 32
viel Knochen 32
Vielseitigkeitspferd 2, 96
Vielseitigkeitsprüfung 78,
   96-8, 102

Vielseitigkeitsreiter 96
Viererzug 98
Vierspänner 98
violett 116
Virus 54
Vollblut 2
Vollblut-Araber 2
Vollbruder 4
Vollschwester 4
Volte 80
Voltigieren 78
vor dem Zügel 68
Vorarm 16, 28
  breiter 28
  flacher 28
  kurzer 28
  langer 28
  schmaler 28
vorbiegig 32
Vorderbein weiss 40
Vorderbeine 58
Vorderfessel weiss 40
Vorderfuss hoch weiss 40
Vorderfusswurzelgelenk 16, 28
  ausgeprägtes 28
  breites 28
  flaches 28
  gedrosseltes 28
  geschnürtes 28
  gewölbtes 28
  grosses 28
  langes 28
  trockenes 28
Vorderknie 16
Vorderröhre 28
Vorderteil 36
Vorderzeug 136
Vorderzwiesel 136
Vorfahren 4
Vorhand 58
vorn zu hoch 36
Vorwärtssitz 72

waagerechte Kruppe 26
waagerechter Hals 22
Wachsmantel 152
Wagen 98
Wagenkasten 100
Wagenlampe 100
Wagenpferd 2
Wagenpferde 102
Waidmesser 104
Wall 154
Wallache 108
Wand 80
Wanderritt 78
warmblütiger Schlag 2
Warmblutpferd 2
Warzen 50
Waschbürste 126
waschen 130
Waschleder 126
Wasser 14
Wassergraben 154
wecken 72
Wegstrecke 96
Wegübergang 154
weich 116
weiche Fessel 30
weicher
  Rücken 24
  Sitz 72
weiches Maul 66
weichgefessel 32
Weide 10
Weidegang 10
Weideland 10-12
weiss 116
weisse Robinie 12
Weitsprung 154
wenden 80, 94
Wendung 112
  auf der Hinterhand 86
  um die Hinterhand 86
  auf der Vorhand 86
Wendungen 86
weniger tragen 114

werfenlassen 76
Weste 148
Western-Reiten 78
Wettbewerb 78
Wetter 108
Wichse 152
Widerrist 16, 24
  ausdrucksvoller 24
  dicker 24
  hoher 24
  kurzer 24
  langer 24
  magerer 24
  niedriger 24
  scharfer 24
  trockener 24
  vershwommener 24
Widerristfistel 48
Widerristhöhe 32, 44
Widersetzlichkeit 66-71
Widerspruch 108
Widerstand 122
wienern 152
Wiese 10
Wild 102
Winkelung 32
Winterhaar 130
Wirbel 32
Wirbelsäule 14
Wischtuch 128
Witterung 102
wohlgeformt 36
Wolfsfarbe 40
Wundstarrkrampf 50
Würmer 50
Wurmkur 52
Wurmmittel 52
Wurzelbürste 126

Yard 46

zackeln (in Schritt) 68
Zähne 44
Zahnwechsel 44

Zangen 44
Zaum
  Knöpfen 140
  mit eingenähtem Gebiss 140
  Schnallen 140
Zaumzeug 140
Zaumzeugs, bestandteile des 140
Zaun 10
Zecken 50
Zehe 42
zeheneng 32
zehenweit 32
Zeitfehler 96, 98
Zeitspringen 96
Zeitspringen mit Stechen 96
Zelter 2
Zentralnervensystem 52
zeremonielle Überreichung eines Hirschlaufs 104
zeugen 8
zeugungsfähig 8
Zeugungsfähigkeit 6
Ziegenbrust 22
ziehen 128
Ziel 112
Zielfoto 114
ziemlich
  gut 92
  schlecht 92
Zirkel 80
Zirkusreiter 90
Zirkusreiterei 78
Zirkusreiterin 90
Zoll 46
zu stark gewinkeltes Sprunggelenk 30
Zubehör 136
Zucht 4-8
Züchter 4, 108
Zuchtpferd 2
Zuchtstute 8
Zuchtwahl 6
Zucker 12

Zügel 60, 68, 140
  aktiver 74
  in einer Hand 74
  lange 144
  passiver 74
  teilen 74
  verkürzern 74
  verlängern 74
  verpassen 74
Zügelführung 74
Zügel-aus-der-Hand-kauen-lassen 64
Zügelhaltung 74
Zügelhilfen 72
Zugstrang 100
Zugtrense 140
zulegen 76
Zunge herausstrecken 68
Zunge über das Mundstück legen 68
Zungenfreiheit 144
Zungenschlag 72
zurücktreten 76
Zurückwiegen 114
zusammengesetzte 36
zusätzliche Ration 14
Zusätzlichegewicht 114
Zustand 66
Zwanghuf 42
Zwanglosigkeit 60
Zwangspause 98
zwei Streifen 116, 118
zweifaches Hindernis 154
Zweig 4
  zweijährige Hengste 108
  zweijährige Stuten 110
Zweimaster 148
Zweispänner 98
Zweispitz 148
Zwinger 102
zwischen Hand und Schenkeln 68
Zwischenprodukt 6
Zylinderhut 148

# INDICE

abattuta di tronchi 155
abbaiare (della muta) 103
abbassatesta 145
abbastanza
  bene 93
  male 93
abbattere un cavallo 53
abbeverare 131
abbeveratoio 127
  automatico 127
acari 49
accarezzare 73
accettare l'azione della mano
  61
accorciare 133
  le redini 75
acqua 15
addestramento 59-65, 67
  all'ostacolo 95
adenite equina 51
affaticato 65
affinità 5
affrontare 95
affumicato, morello 37
affunato, ginocchio 29
aggancio 129
aggiustare
  le redini 75
  la sella 137
agitare la coda 69
agostano 13
aiuti 73
  du compiacenza 99
  diagonali 75
  laterali 75
aiuto-istruttore 91
albero genealogico 7
alcuni peli bianchi 41
alimentare 67, 131
allattamento 11
allattare 11
alleggerire (la coda o la

criniera) 133
allenamento
  intervallato 99
  vocobolario di 119
allenatore 91, 109
allentare le cinghie 137
allergia alla polvere 49
allevamento 5-11
  secondo la famiglia 7
  in stretta parantela 7
allevare 5
allevatore 5, 109
  proprietario 109
allievo 91
allievo fantino 109
allungare 77
  le redini 75
allungato
  galoppo 85
  passo 85
  trotto 85
alt 77, 85
alta scuola 79
altezza al garrese 33, 45
alzarsi 95
ambiatore 3
ambio 43
ammazone 91
ammazzone (amateur) 109
amministrazione 109
ammorbidire 95
analgesici 53
anca 27
  cornuta 27
  normale 27
  sporgente 27
anche 73
andare
  in partenza 113
  in testa 121
andatura 59, 121
  forzare 121

andature 41-3
  allungate 43
  artificiali 43
  della bassa scuola 85
  corte 43
  irregolari 43
  libere 43
  naturali 43
  principali 43
  regolari 43
  riunite 43
  di scuola 43
anelli 145
anello 'reggiguide' 101
anemia 47
anestesia 53
  diagnostica 55
anglo-arabo 3
angoli 33
angolo 81
animare 73
ano 21
antenati 5
anteriore 37, 59
anteriori 59
antibiotici 53
antielmintico 53
antinfiammatorio 53
antisettico 53
aperta, grassella 31
aperto
  davanti 33
  garretto 31
  di gomiti 29
apparato
  circulatorio 53
  digerente 53
  locomotore 53
  muscolo-scheletrico 53
  respiratorio 53
  urinario 53
appiombi 15, 33

appoggiare 113
appoggiare (sulla diagonale)
  87
appoggio 61
  fiducioso 61
  franco 61
  morbido 61
  per il ginocchio 137
appuntamento 103
arabo, purosangue 3
arcata, testa 21
arcione 137
arco anteriore 137
arcuata, incollatura 23
ardesia, grigio 39
arie
  alte 87
  basse 87
  di scuola 43, 87
  vincino a terra 87
armonia 61
armonioso 37
arpeggio 51
arrancione 117
arrivo 113
  combattuto 123
arrotondato, ginocchio 29
arti 15, 59
articolazione 15
arto in appoggio 59
arto in sostegno 59
artrite 47
ascaridi 47
ascendenza 5
ascesso 47
asciugare 131
asciutta
  grassella 31
  spalla 27
  testa 21
asciutto
  garrese 25

garretto 31
ginocchio 29
asino 3
asse longitudinale 61
assetto
  del cavaliere 73, 95
  contratto 73
  flessible 73
  morbido 73
  rigido 73
assimetria 61
asta 149
aste 145
atipico 7
attaccare 99, 101
attaccaticcio 117
attaccato al torace 29
attacchi 79, 99-103
attacco 99, 103
  della coda 133
  del singolo 99
  con lo sperone 75
  in pariglia 99
attitudine 93
attivo 73
attrezzi 125-55
avambraccio 17, 29
  corto 29
  largo 29
  lungo 29
  piatto 29
  sottile 29
avena 13
avere attitudine
  alla corsa 121
  al terreno 121
avere un piccolo vantaggio
  121
avvallata, groppa 27
avvallato, ventre 25
avvelenamento 49
avvicinare 95

azione 9, 41-3, 59
    simultanea delle gambe 75
    di una gamba isolata 75
azoturia 47
azzurro 117

bacchetta 145
bacino 15
baio 39
    ciliegia 39
    dorato 39
    fulvo 39
    lavato 39
    oscuro 39
    pezzato 39
    scuro 39
ballottata 87
ballottaggio 113
balzana 41
    alto calzata 41
    calzata 41
banchina 155
banditore 109
barbabietola 13
barbetta 131
barbozza 17
barbozzale 145
bardatura della testa 141
barra 129
barriera 155
    di richiamo 155
basculare 95
base
    d'appoggio 61
    di appoggio larga 33
    della coda 17
bassa
    groppa 27
    scuola 79
basso
    garrese 25
    garretto 31
basso-giuntato, pastorale 31
batteri 53

battistrada 121
battuta 59
battuto da lontano 121
beige 117
bella faccia 41
belladonna 11
ben bilanciato 37
ben disegnata, spalla 27
ben inquadrato 69
ben scolpito, ginocchio 29
bendaggio compressivo 55
bende 53
bene 93
bevente in bianco 41
beverone 15
bianco 37, 117
    porcellana 37
    sauro isabella 37
    sporco 37
bicorno 149
bilanciato, ben 37
bilancino 101
bipedi 59
    diagonali 59
    laterali 59
birilli 103
blu 117
blu scurro 117
bocca 17, 67
    amabile 67
    chiacchierona 67
    contratta 67
    dura 67
    fine 67
    fresca 67
    leggera 67
    morbida 67
    muta 67
    non fatta 67
    rovinata 67
    sempre in movimento 67
    sensibile 67
bolsaggine 47
bombetta 149

bordo superiore
    dell'incollatura 17
bosso 11
box 127
braca 101
bracciale portastanga 101
braccio 17, 27-9
    corto 27
    dritto 29
    lungo 29
    obliquo 29
braga 101
break 99
bretelle 117, 119
breve, groppa 27
brevi, reni 25
briglia 101
    completa 141
    cucita 141
    con la fibbia 141
    con i ganci 141
    mettere la 141
    parti della 141
    da presentazione 141
    togliere la 141
bronchite ostruttiva cronica
    47
brucare l'erba 11
bruciato, sauro 37, 39
brusca (di setola) 127
bruscone di saggina 127
bull-fence 155
buona attaccatura 23
buona condizione 67
buona ossatura 33
buono 115
buono-morbido 117
busto 73

caccia
    con i cani 79
    a cavallo 103
    al cervo 103

ai piccoli della volpe 103
    alla strusa 103
    alla volpe 103
cacciatore 103
cadenza 43, 59
cadere 95, 99
caduta 45, 99
caffelatte, sauro 37
cagnolo 33
calare 123
caldo 65
calmare 73
calori 11
calzare gli stivali 153
cambiamento
    diagonale 81
    di direzione 59
    longitudinale 81
    di monta 113
    di piede passando al passo
      75
    di piede passando al trotto
      75
    traversale 81
cambiare
    andatura 77
    diagonale di trotto 77
    direzione 77, 81, 113
    di mano 77, 81
    di mano all'interno del
      circolo 85
    di piede 77
    di piede in aria 77
    di piede a tempo 77
    velocità 77
cambiarsi 153
camminare
    galoppo 77
    al passo 77
    trotto 77
campo 95
    dei partenti 113, 123
camusa, testa 21
cancello 11

sbarrato 155
cancro 47
cane da seguito 103
canile 103
cannone 145
    circonferenza del 45
    curvo 145
    rigido 145
    snodato 145
canter 113
cantoni 45
cap 149
capezza 127
capezza di moro 41
capezzina 141
    con chiudibocca 141
    incrociata 141
    sotto-filetto 141
capezzone 145
    a leva 141
capo palafreniere 11
caporazza 11
caposcuderia 131
cappelletto 47
capriola 87
capuccio 127
carattere 65-7
caratteristiche 15, 21
cardiopatia 49
carenato, petto 23
carezza 73
carica di carne, spalla 29
carico utile 129
carnosa, testa 21
carosello 81
carota 13
carriola 127
carrozza 99
carrozziere 3, 103
casco 149
cassa 101
cassetta 101
    del pronto intervento 55
castagna 17

castrare 53
castrazione 53
castroni 109
cataplasma 55
categoria di salto
   all'americana 97
   delle sei barriere 97
   al cronometro 97
   nazionale 97
   coppa delle nazioni 97
   di potenza 97
   di precisione 97
   a punti 97
   con spareggio 97
categorie
   di corse 111
   di salto 97
catena 127
cattiva attaccatura 23
cattiva condizione 67
cava-stivali 153
cavaliere 91
   di circo 91
   da concorso completo 97
   esperto 91
   da ostacoli 93
   professore 91
   seduto sulla paletta 73
   sfilato indietro 73
cavallerizza 81
cavallerizzo 91
cavalletto 155
cavalli 109
cavallino 3
cavallo
   addestrato 67
   all'inizio dell'-
      addestramento 65
   d'attacco 103
   di bassa taglia e robusto 3
   da caccia 103
   da carrozza 103
   da concorso completo 3, 97
   da concorsi di

addestramento 3
che fa la distanza 119
che monta con il dorso 69
con il dorso morbido 69
confirmato 67
da corsa 3
debuttante 67
difficile da alimentare 67
diritto 59, 61
domato 65
   a doppio uso 3
   da dressage 3
   facile da nutrire 67
   intero 9
   leggero 3
   messo 67
   da milleotto a due mila 121
   orientale 3
   da passeggio 3
   piccino 3
   di ricambio 103
   di riserva 103
   da salto ostacoli 3
   di scuola 91
   da sella 3
   da sella e da carrozza 3
   sobrio da nutrire 67
   da soma 3
   da tiro 3
   da tiro pesante 3
cecità 47
cedere 75, 121
   e riprendere 65
centro
   equestre 79
   ippico 79
cerata 153
cerchiata 117
certificato
   d'origine 111
   di vaccinazione 111
cervato 41
cervo, incollatura di 23
cessione

alla gamba 87
   delle iscrizioni 109
charrette inglese 99
chiaro
   sauro 37
   sorcino 39
chiave passaredini 101
chiodo 43
   da strada 43, 49
ciambella 87
cicuta 11
ciliegia
   baio 39
   sauro 39
cilindro 149
cinghia 137
   della braga 101
cinghie
   allentare 137
   passaggio delle 45
   stringere 137
cinghietti 149
circhiata 119
circolo 81
circonferenza
   del canone 45
   dello stinco 45
   al torace 45
circulatorio, apparato 53
ciuffo 21, 131
classe 121
classifica 97
claudicazione 49
club ippico 79
coccarda 97
coda 17, 27, 133
   aggitare la 69
   attaccata alta 27
   attaccata bassa 27
   attacco della 133
   base della 17
   corta 133
   intrecciata 133
   portamento della 27

di rondine 45
serrata 27
sfoltita 133
di sorcio 27
torso della 17
della volpe 105
coffin 155
colchico 11
coliche 47
collana 101
collo 17
   di cigno 23
colonna vertebrale 15
colore 15, 37
colori 37-41
   delle giubbe 117
   di scuderia 117
colpire 73
colpo
   di frusta 75
   di lancia 41
coltello da sudare 127
combinazione 155
commissari 109
commissario al peso 109
commozione cerebrale 53
compagno di scuderia 121
compatto 33
composti 37
comproprietà 109
concava, testa 21
concavo, dorso 25, 69
concorso 79
   di addestramento 91-3
   al campanile 79
   per cavalli debuttanti 91
   completo 79, 97-9
   completo di attacchi 103
   completo di una giornata 97
   con la solaprova di
      campagna 79
   di fondo attaccato 103
   ippico 95
   da punto a punto 79

di salto ostacoli 79, 95
concussione (del piede) 53
condizionata 111
condizione 67, 121
   buona 67
   cattiva 67
   patologica 51
condurre con due mani 75
conduttore 99
conformazione 9, 37
congiuntivite 47
conica, testa 21
consanguineità 5
consistente 115
contagioso 53
contatto 61, 65
contorni 33
contorno confuso 31
contratto, ventre 25
contro-cambiamento di mano
   81
contusione 53
convesse, costole 23
convesso, dorso 25
coperta 127
   per asciugare 127
   da paddock 127
copertina 101
   imbottita 137
   per i piombi 137
coppa delle nazioni 97
coppia 103
copricasco 149
copripantaloni in pelle 153
corba 47
corda 113, 127, 145
cordone 149
corneggio laringeo 51
corno da caccia (Inghilterra)
   103
cornuta, anca 27
corona 21
coronature 47
corpo del cavallo 15-37

correggere 73
correre bene 121
correre male 121
corsa 107-23
    al campanile 79
    di categoria 111
    classica 111
    di gruppo 111
    ostacoli 111
    a peso per età 111
    in piano 111
    pubblica 111
    da punto a punto 79
    di serie 111
    di siepi 111
    a vendere 111
corse 79
    organizzazzione delle 113
corso 81
corta 79
    groppa 27
    incollatura 23, 115
    spalla 27
    testa 115
corte
    andature 43
    costole 23
corto
    avambraccio 29
    braccio 27
    dorso 25
    garrese 25
    di lavora 121
    pastorale 31
    stinco 29
corvetta 87
    classica 87
corvino, morello 37
cosce 73
coscia 21, 31
    inclinata 31
    lunga 31
    muscolosa 31
cosciali 15

costanza 7
costituzione 9
costole 15, 17, 23
    convesse 23
    corte 23
    lunghe 23
    piatte 23
cravatta a plastron 149
creare una razza 7
crini 15, 131
crini, fare i 133
criniera 21, 131
    accorciata e sfoltita 133
    rasata 133
    con le treccine 133
criptorchide 9
croce
    di Lorena 117, 119
    di St Andrea 117, 119
cross 79
cross country 97
crusca 13
cuciture 117, 119
curare 55
    il piede 131
curasnetta 127
cure in scuderia 131
curva 113
    della serpentina 85
cuscinetto 137

daga 105
danneggiato 121
dare il foraggio 131
dare leggeri colpi a mo' di
    carezza 73
davanti alla mano 69
davanti alle gambe 69
debole
    dorso 25
    garretto 33
    gomito 29
    groppa 27
    spalla 29

stinco 29
debolezza 51
debuttante 121
debuttanti 111
decontrazione della mascella
    61
degenerato 7
deludente 121
denti 45
    decidui 45
    digrignare i 69
    incisivi 45
    da latte 45
    permanenti 45
    prendere il morso fra i 69
denutrizione 49
deposito stalloni 9
depresse, reni 25
derivati, mantelli 37
dermatite estiva 51
diarrea 47
discesa delle gambe 75
dichiarare forfeit 113
dichiarazione
    della monta 113
    dei partenti 115
dietro
    le gambe 69
    la mano 69
difese 67-9
difetto ereditario 7
difettoso (appiombi) 33
difficile 65, 93
digerente, apparato 53
digitale 11
digrignare i denti 69
dimensioni 37
direttore di campo 95
direttore dell'allevamento 11
direzione del movimento 59
dirittura 115
    di fronte 113
diritto 59, 61
disarcionare il cavaliere 69

discarico 115
discendenti 5
discesa 113, 155
    delle gambe 75
    dell'incollatura 65
    della mano 65
disegni dei colori 119
disellare 137
disidratazione 53
disinvoltura 61
distanza 95, 113
distanziato 111
distendere 95
distendersi 123
disteso 65
    anteriormente e
        posteriormente 33
distomatosi 49
distribuzione della carne ai
    cani 103
disubbidiente 69
disubbidienze 67-9
disunirsi al galoppo 69
doccia fredda 53
dog-cart 99
dolore 55
dolori 47
domare 65, 121
domatura 121
dominio 7
doping 53
doppia gabbia 155
dorato
    baio 39
    sauro 39
dorso 17, 25
    concavo 25, 69
    convesso 25
    corto 25
    debole 25
    dritto 25
    insellato 25
    lungo 25
    di mulo 25

orizzontale 25
robusto 25
dorso del naso 17
dritta
    incollatura 23
    spalla 27
    testa 21
dritto 155
    braccio 29
    dorso 25
    garretto 31
    giuntato 33
    giuntato, pastorale 31
droghe 53
duro 115

eccelente 93
ecografia 55
eczema 53
    del dorso 49
effetto
    del peso del corpo 73
    d'insieme sullo sperone 77
elementare 91
elenco delle vittorie 121
elettroliti 53
elevato, garrese 25
eliminare 97
eliminazione 99, 113
elmetto da polo 149
emorragia 53
epatite 49
equilibrio 9, 65
equiseto 11
equitazione 77
    accademica 79
    artistica 79
    di circo 79
    classica 77-9
    di fantasia 79
    di passeggio 79
    pratica 79
    sapiente 79
    sportiva 79

di svago 79
erba 13
erba medica 13
ereditarietà 7
ernia 49
erpete tonsurante 51
errore
  di percorso 93
  di ripresa 93
eruzione 45
esame
  ematologico 53
  microscopico 55
  radiografico 55
  del sangue 53
escursione equestre 79
esecuzione 93
esercizi 81-7
esploratore 9
espressiva, testa 21
essi e l'uncino 145
estastici per le treccine 129
estensione dell'incollatura 65
esteriore 15
estrazione del numero di
    partenza 113
estro 11
età 109
eterogeneo 7

fabbricante di speroni 149
faccia, bella 41
facilità 61
falbo 41
falcata 59
falce, garretto a 33
falsa
  acacia 13
  corva 49
  martingala 145
  partenza 113
falso barbozzale 145
famiglia 5
fanale

di arresto 129
di direzione 129
illuminazione targa 129
posteriore 129
fantina 109
fantino 91, 109
farmaco 53
fasce 127
fascia 117, 119
fascie 53
fascione 145
fattrice 9
  coperta 9
  piena 9
  con puledro 9
  vuota 9
fava porcina 11
febbre 49
felce aquilina 11
femmine 111
ferita 51
  aperta 55
fermare 77, 121
fermarsi 95
fermata 59, 77, 85
ferrare 45
ferro 43
  grigio 39
fiaccatura 47, 51
fianco 17
fibbia 101, 149
fiducia 65
fiducioso, appoggio 61
field 103
fieno 13
fieno tritato 13
figlia 5
figlio 5
figure 81-7
filetto 141
  ad anelli 141
  della briglia 141
  da corsa 141
  elevatore 141

di gomma 145
  a olive 141
  da presentazione 141
  con le stanghette 141
filo per le treccine 129
finimenti 99
finimento
  a collana 101
  a petto 101
finish 113
finito 67
fiocco 131
fiocco 21
fiore 41
flemmatico 65
flessibilità 59
flessione della nuca 61
flogosi 55
focatura 55
foraggio 13, 127, 131
  verde 13
forbici 133
forca 127
forchetta 43
forgia 43
forma 65-7, 121
  fuori 67, 121
  passato di 67, 121
  perdita di 121
  poca 121
formelle 49
forte
  gamba 31
  groppa 27
forti, reni 25
forzare
  l'andatura 121
  l'animale 103
fosso 155
  tra ostacoli 155
foto-finish 115
franchezza 61
franco, appoggio 61
fratello pieno 5

frattura 55
freddo 65
  alle gambe 69
freno 101
  inerziale 129
frontale 141
fronte 17
frugale 67
frusta 101, 145
  da addestramento 149
  da caccia 105, 145
  da corsa 145
fruste 145
frustone 145
fulvo, baio 39
fuori forma 67, 121
fusto 17, 133

gabbia 155
gabbie di partenza 113
galoppare 77
galoppo 43, 85
  allungato 85
  camminare al 77
  da corsa 85
  a destra 85
  destro 77
  disunirsi al 69
  disunito 85
  falso 85
  giusto 85
  di lavoro 85
  lento 85
  medio 85
  partire al 77
  riunito 85
  rovescio 77, 85
  a sinistra 85
  sinistro 77
  sul piede destro 85
  sul piede sinistro 85
  a una velocità media 85
gamba 21, 31
  attiva 75

azione di una 75
ben definita 31
forte 31
lunga 31
muscolosa 31
passiva 75
piena 31
gambale 153
gambe 73
  azione simultanea delle 75
  davanti alle 69
  dietro le 69
  discesa delle 75
  freddo alle 69
  particolarità delle 41
  pesante alle 69
  tra mani e gambe 69
ganascia 17
gancio 153
gara 79
  combinata 79
  combinata di attacchi 103
garrese 17, 25
  asciutto 25
  basso 25
  corto 25
  elevato 25
  grasso 25
  lungo 25
  mal del 49
  piatto 25
  pronunciato 25
  tagliente 25
garretti
  larghi 33
  stretti 33
  valghi 33
  vari 33
garretto 21, 31
  aperto 31
  asciutto 31
  basso 31
  ben definito 31
  contorno confuso 31

debole 33
dritto 31
a falce 33
grande 31
largo 31
lungo 31
mal definito 31
netto 31
solido 33
spugnoso 31
vicino a terra 31
gastrofili 47
gemizio 53
generazione libera 7
germe di fava 45
gesto di mordere, fare 69
giacca
  da cavallo 149
  rossa 105
giallo 117
gig 99
gincana 79
ginocchia
  arcate 33
  chiuse 33
  da montone 33
  valghe 33
ginocchiere 127
ginocchio 17, 29
  affunato 29
  arrotondato 29
  asciutto 29
  ben scolpito 29
  grande 29
  largo 29
  lungo 29
  netto 29
  piatto 29
  strozzato 29
giocatore 109
giochi a cavallo 79
gioco di palla a cavallo 79
giostra sgambatura 131
girare 81, 95

intorno alle anche 87
stretto 95
giubba del fantino 149
giubbotto protettivo 153
giudice all'arrivo 109
giuntato
  dritto 33
  obliquo 33
giuria 99
gola 17
gomito 17, 29
  aperto di 29
  attaccato al torace 29
  debole 29
  serrato ai 29
governare 131
governo a fondo (dopo il
    lavoro) 131
gradazioni 37
grado 5
gran mangiatore 67
Gran Premio 93
granata 117
grande
  garretto 31
  ginocchio 29
  grassella 31
  testa 21
grani 13
granoturco 13
grassella 21, 31
  aperta 31
  asciutta 31
  grande 31
  netta 31
grasso
  garrese 25
  per i piedi 129
grigio 39
  ardesia 39
  ferro 39
  moscato 39
  pomellato 41
  scuro 39

trotinato 39
grigionato 39
groom 103
groppa 17, 27
  avvallata 27
  bassa 27
  breve 27
  corta 27
  debole 27
  in dentro 87
  forte 27
  in fuori 87
  larga 27
  lunga 27
  a mandorla 27
  di mulo 27
  obliqua 27
  orizzontale 27
  scesa tagliente 27
  stretta 27
  troppo alta 27
groppiera 145
  e la sottocoda 101
grossa, incollatura 23
grosso 33
  davanti 23
guanto 149
guida 99-103
guidare 99
guidatore 99
guide 145

hack 3
hackamore 141
hackney 103
handicap 111
handicapper 109

iardo 47
ibrido 7
ignipuntura 55
imboccatura 141-5
imboccature 141
imbottitura 101, 137

immettere nuovo sangue 7
immobilità 59, 77
impacco 55
  raffreddante 53
impegnare le anche 61
impermeabile 153
impulso 59
imputridimento del fettone 51
inattività 61
incalzato 121
incappucciato 69
incastellato, piede 43
incavato, petto 23
incensare 69
inchiodatura 43
incidente 95
inclinata
  coscia 31
  spalla 27
inclinato, pastorale 31
incollatura 17, 23, 115
  alta attaccata 23
  arcuata 23
  attaccata bassa 23
  bene muscolata 23
  di cervo 23
  corta 23, 115
  dritta 23
  grossa 23
  leggera 23
  lunga 23
  male muscolata 23
  obliqua 23
  orizzontale 23
  pesante 23
  proporzionata 23
  rovesciata 23
  stretta 23
incrociamento 7
incrocio
  incestuoso 7
  puro 7
  tra non parenti 7
incurvamento 61

incurvato 61
indietreggiare 77
individuo 5
indolenzimento 55
infestazione da strongili
    polmonari 49
infiammazione 55
influenza equina 49
iniziare l'addestramento 65
inizio dell'inseguimento 103
inquadramento 155
insegnante di equitazione 91
inseguimento 103
insellato, dorso 25
inseminare 9
inseminazione artificiale 9
insensibilità 55
insufficiente 93
intelaiatura 37
interrompere l'allenamento
    121
intervallo di dieci minuti 99
intervenire chirurgicamente 55
intorpidimento 55
iperico 13
ippometro 45
isabella (con crini neri) 39
ischi 73
iscrivere un cavallo 113
iscrizione 111
istruttore 91
itterizia 49

laburno 13
lami 133
laminite 49
lanterna 101
larga, groppa 27
larghe, reni 25
largo 155
  avambraccio 29
  garretto 31
  ginocchio 29
  petto 23

stinco 29
laserterapia 55
lato
  concavo 61
  convesso 61
  destro 59
  esterno 59
  interno 59
  sinistro 59
lavare 131
lavato
  baio 39
  sauro 39
lavoro
  alla corda 67
  galoppo di 85
  alla mano 91
  ai pilieri 91
  alle redini lunghe 67, 91
  su due piste 87
  trotto di 85
leccornia 15
legamento 15
leggera
  incollatura 23
  testa 21
leggerezza 65
leggermente pesante 117
leggero alla gamba 69
lettiera 127, 131
lettiera permanente 131
levata 87
leve 33
levriero, ventre di 25
libere, andature 43
libero, passo 85
libertà di lingua 145
libro genealogico 11
ligustro 13
limfangite 49
limitato 121
linea 5
  di centro 81
  d'origine 7

retta 81
lingua
  far uscire la 69
  serpentina 69
  sopra il morso 69
liscio fra le nari 41
lista (larga) 41
lista (stretta) 41
livre 105
locomotore, apparato 53
lombi 17, 25
losanga 117, 119
losanghe 119
lozione 55
lucidare 153
lucido 153
lugliatico 13
lunga
  coscia 31
  gamba 31
  groppa 27
  incollatura 23
  spalla 27
lunghe
  costole 23
  reni 25
lunghezza 33, 115
  mezza 115
lunghezze, molte 115
lungo
  avambraccio 29
  e basso, pastorale 31
  braccio 29
  dorso 25
  garrese 25
  garretto 31
  ginocchio 31
  pastorale 31
  stinco 29
lungo-giuntato, pastorale 31
lupia 47
lupino 13

macchinetta tosatrice 133

maceria 155
madre 5
maggengo 13
maggiociondolo 13
maglia dei ferri 101
maiden 111
mal del garrese 49
malattia 51
  da erba 49
  venerea 51
male 93
mallattie 47-51
maltinto
  morello 37
  sorcino 39
mammella 21
mancino 33
mandorla, groppa a 27
maneggio 79, 81-91
  all'aperto/scoperto 81
  coperto 81
maneggevolezza 101
mangiatoia 127
mangimi 13-15
  composti 13
mani 73
  tra mani e gambe 69
maniscalco 43
mano
  cambiare di 77, 81, 85
  contro-cambiamento di 81
  davanti alla 69
  dietro la 69
  discesa della 65
  lavoro alla 91
  messa in 61
  redini in una 75
  sopra la 69
  sulla 61
  tirare la 69
  tuffarsi sulla 69
mantelli 37-41
mantello 15, 131
  estivo 131

invernale 131
maratona 101
marchio 11
marcia 97
marrone 117
marsina 153
martingala
  falsa 145
  fissa 145
  con forchetta ad anelli 145
martingale 145
mascella inferiore 17
maschi 109
masseggiare 131
massiccia, spalla 29
masticare il morso 67
mastro 103
match 111
materiale 133-45
media difficoltà 93
mediani 45
medicazioni 53
medicina 53
medio
  galoppo 85
  passo 85
  trotto 85
melassa 13
mentoniera 149
mescolanza 13
mescolati 37
messa in mano 61
metà corsa 113
meticcio 7
metrite contagiosa equina 47
metro 47
  di stoffa 45
mettere
  la briglia 141
  dritto 59
  al prato 11
  a riposo 121
mettersi gli stivali 153

mezza
  fermata 75
  lunghezza 115
  piroetta 87
  sorella 5
  volta 81
mezzani 45
mezzaria 87
mezzo
  fratello 5
  sorella 5
mezzosangue 3
  per lavoro 7
micosi 49
miglia 47
migliorare una razza 7
miler 121
miorilassante 55
misto 7
misurazione 45
  con metro rigido 45
  con metro di stoffa 45
misure 45, 47
  inglesi 47
  metriche 47
mobilità 61
modo di usare le redini 75
molari 45
molletta 51
molte lunghezze 115
molto
  bene 93
  male 93
mondo del cavallo 109
monta 9, 11
  americana 79
  Western 79
montante 141
montare
  da amazzone 81
  a calvalcioni 81
  a cavallo 73
  in concorsi 79
  a pelo 81

in sella 73
monte 113
montonina, testa 23
morbida 67
morbidezza 59
morbido 117
    appoggio 61
mordere 69
morello 37
    affumicato 37
    corvino 37
    maltinto 37
morso 141
    della briglia 145
    a pompa 145
morte 103
    delle galline 11
morva 49
moscato, grigio 39
movimento 41-3, 59
    direzione del 59
mozzare 133
mozzone 149
mula 3
mulo 3
    groppa di 27
    ventre di 25
muraglia 43
muro 155
muscoli 15
muscolo-scheletrico, apparato 53
muscolosa
    coscia 31
    gamba 31
muta 103, 131

nari 17
narice 115
narici 17
natica 21
nematodi 51
nero 117
    pezzato 39

nervi 15
nervo 55
nervoso centrale, sistema 53
netta, grassella 31
netto
    garretto 31
    ginocchio 29
    sorcino 39
    stinco 29
nipote 5
nobile 37
    testa 21
nodello 17
nomenclatura 15
non eseguito 93
non partente 113
non piazzato 113
non qualificato 111
nonna 5
nonno 5
normale
    anca 27
    gli appiombi 33
    ventre 25
novizio 91
nuca 17
nutrizione 55

obesità 49
obliqua
    groppa 27
    incollatura 23
    spalla 27
obliquo
    braccio 29
    giuntato 33
occhio 17
    gazzuolo 41
olio 15
ombelico 17
omogeneo 7
onori del piede 105
orecchio 17
organi 15

organizzazione delle corse 113
originari 37
origine 5
orizzontale
    dorso 25
    groppa 27
    incollatura 23
orizzontali, reni 25
ormoni 55
orzo 13
oscuro, baio 39
ossificazione della cartilagine alare 51
ossiuri 51
osso 15
    per pulire e lisciare gli stivali 153
ostacoli 155
    salto 93-7
ostacolo 93
    fisso 95
    invitante 95
    semplice 155
    di volata 155
ostacoli di cross country 97
otto 85
outcross 7
outsider 123
oxer
    pari 155
    in salita 155

paddock 11
padre 9
paglia 13
    tritata 13
palafreniere 131
paletta 137
palla 119
palle 119
palomino 39
panciotto 149
pantaloni da cavallo 153

pantaloni da cavallo lunghi 153
parafango anteriore 101
paraglomi 127
paralisi 49
paraocchi 101
parassiti 55
pareggiare il piede 45
parete 43, 81
parete divisoria 129
pariglia 99
    di cavalli con cavallo davanti 99
parità 115
parte
    inferiore 37
    superiore 37
partenti 115
partenza 113
    con la bandiera 113
    dalle gabbie 113
    con i nastri 113
particolarità 41
partire
    al galoppo 77
    al passo 77
    al trotto 77
parto 11
pascolare 11
pascolo 11-13
paseggio 87
passaggio
    delle cinghie 45
    di strada 155
passaporto 111
passar la brusca 131
passare 95
    la brusca 131
    la lingua sopra il morso 69
    l'osso 153
passato di forma 67, 121
passeggiare 131
passeggio 87
passi

indietro 77
laterali 87
passivo 73
passo 43, 59, 85
    allungato 85
    camminare 77
    libero 85
    medio 85
    partire al 77
    con le redini abbandonate 85
    con le redini lunghe 85
    riunito 85
    di scuola 87
pastoia 31
pastone 15
pastorale 21, 31
    basso-giuntato 31
    corto 31
    dritto-giuntato 31
    inclinato 31
    lungo 31
    lungo e basso 31
    lungo-giuntato 31
patente
    da allenatore 111
    da allievo fantino 111
    da fantino 111
patologia articolare 49
patrimonio ereditario 7
pauroso 65
pedana 101
pedigree 7
pelham 145
peli 15
pelle 15
    di camoscio 129
pellettati 13
penalità 99
    agli ostacoli 97
    per il tempo 97, 99
penalizzazione 97
pendente, ventre 25
pendenza, reni in 25

pene 21
pensione 131
percorso 95, 155
    su strade e sentieri 97
    a tempo 95
    di velocità 101
perdita di forma 121
perimetro toracico 33
periodi 45
periodo di gestazione 11
peritonite 49
permeabilità agli aiuti 65
permesso di allenare 111
personale della scuderia da
        corsa 109
perspicacia (l'azione)
        penetrante 61
pesante 65, 117
    alle gambe 69
    incollatura 23
    testa 21
pesata 87
peso 115
    del cavaliere 73
    dopo la corsa 115
    (omologato) massimo 129
    prima della corsa 115
    a vuoto 129
pesta equina 47
pettinare 131
pettine 129, 133
petto 17, 23
    carenato 23
    incavato 23
    largo 23
    di pollo 23
    profondo 23
    proporzionato 23
    stretto 23
pettorale 137
    da caccia 137
pezzato 39
    baio 39
    nero 39

sauro 39
phaeton 99
piaffo 87
pianoforte 155
piantarsi 95
piante velenose 11
piatte, costole 23
piatto
    avambraccio 29
    garrese 25
    ginocchio 29
    piede 43
piazzato 115
piccola, testa 21
picozzi 43
pidocchi 49
piede 21, 43, 47, 155
    concussione 53
    incastellato 43
    interno 87
    pareggiare il 45
    piatto 43
    rampino 43
    a terra 73
piego
    diretto 61
    laterale 61
    verticale 61
piena, gamba 31
pigro 65
piliere 155
pilieri 145
piroetta rovesciata 87
piroette 87
pista 59, 81, 93, 115, 155
    d'allenamento 115
    d'erba 115
    a mano destra 115
    a mano sinistra 115
    riservata ai cavalieri 81
    di sabbia 115
più V 117, 119
plastron 149
poca forma 121

podoflemmatite 49
pollice 47
pollo, petto di 23
polminite 49
polo 79
polpacci 73
polvere 55
pomata 55
pomellato, grigio 41
pomo 137
ponte 129
pony 3
pony club 79
porpora 117
porta laterale 129
porta di servizio 129
portamento 59
    della coda 27, 133
portare
    meno peso 115
    più peso 115
portastaffile 137
portata 129
posata 59
posizione 61
    accademica 73
    a cavallo 73
    da fantino 73
    sportiva 73
    sull'inforcatura 73
posta 127
posteriore 37, 59
posteriori 59
potente 33
potenza 7
prato 11
    mettere al 11
premi 109, 113
premio 97
Premio San Giorgio 91
premiture 47
prendere
    bene il lavoro 121
    il morso fra i denti 69

prepuzio 17
presentare un reclamo 111
prestazione 121
prezzo della monta 113
procreare 9
prodotti giovani 9
prodotto 5
    intermedio 7
profilo convesso 21
profondità del torace 33
profondo, petto 23
progenie 5
programma 115
prolifico 9
pronto soccorso 55
pronunciata, spalla 27
pronunciato, garrese 25
proporzionata, incollatura 23
proporzionato 37
    petto 23
proprietaria 109
proprietario 109
prototipo della specie 7
prova
    di addestramento 97
    di addestramento degli
        attacchi 103
    di attitudine 81
    di flessione 55
    di fondo 97, 101
    di modello 81
    di salto ostacoli 97
prurito 55
puledra 9
puledro 9, 11, 67
pulire 131
    il box 131
    gli stivali 153
punire 73
punizione 73
punta 43, 149
    dell'anca 17
    della spalla 17
punti

di bonifico 95
di riferimento 93
puntura 49
    d'insetti 49
purosangue arabo 3
purosangue inglese 3
pus 55

quadrato 37
quadriglia 81
qualificato 111
qualità 9, 121
quarti 119
quartiere 137

rabattitura 43
raccorciare 75
rachide 15, 61
ragadi 47, 49
ragazzo di scuderia 11, 131
raggiungersi 49
raid 79
rallentare 77
ramazza 127
ramazzare (la scuderia) 131
rampa (di salita) 129
rampino, piede 43
rampone 45
randem 99
ranuncolo 11
raschiatoio 127
raspa 43
rastrelliera 127
razione
    giornaliera 15
    di lavoro 15
    di mantenimento 15
    supplementare 15
razza 5
    creare una 7
    indigena 3
    migliorare una 7
razze 3
reagire 123

reazioni del cavallo montato
   67-9
recinto 11
   di partenza 99
   del pubblico 115
recinzione 11
reclamo 109
redine
   abbandonata 75
   d'apertura 75
   d'appoggio 75
   attiva 75
   contraria 75
   contraria d'opposizione
     davanti al garrese 75
   contraria d'opposizione
     davanti alle spalle 75
   contraria d'opposizione
     dietro al garrese 75
   contraria d'opposizione
     dietro le spalle 75
   diretta d'opposizione 75
   esterna 75
   del filetto 141
   gogue 145
   interna 75
   del morso 141
   passiva 75
   che resiste 75
   di ritorno 145
redini 141
   abbandonate 85
   accorciare le 75
   aggiustrare le 75
   allungare 75
   fisse 145
   lunghe 85, 145
   in una mano 75
   modo di usare le 75
   separare 75
   speciali 145
   tenuta delle 75
regolarità 59
regolarizzare 133

regressivo 7
remolino 41
reni 17, 25
   brevi 25
   depresse 25
   forti 25
   larghe 25
   lunghe 25
   orizzontali 25
   in pendenza 25
   strette 25
respiratorio, apparato 53
restio 69
rete 127
retratto, ventre 25
retromarcia automatica 129
retta d'arrivo 113
rettangolare 37
rettangolo 81
ribattitura 43
riceversi 95
ricognizione del percorso 95
   fare la 97
ricompensa 73
ricompensare 73
ricovero 11
rifare la lettiera 131
rifiutare 95
riga mulina 41
rigido 65
rimorchio 129
ripassare il cavallo (prima di
   uscire) 131
ripresa 59, 93
   intermedia 93
   libera 93
   libera con musica 93
   Olimpica 93
riproduttore 3
riproduttrice 3
riproduzione
   per consanguinità 7
   per selezione 7
riscontro della sella 137

rispettare 95
risvegliare 73
ritirare dall'allenamento 121
ritirarsi 99
ritmo 59
ritorno indietro 7
riunione 65
   dei concorrenti 97
riunire 61
riunito
   galoppo 85
   passo 85
   trotto 85
riviera 155
roano 39
robinia 13
robusto, dorso 25
rogna 49
   sarcoptica 51
rosa 117
rotella 149
rovesciare 95
rovesciata, incollatura 23
rullo di sale minerale 15
ruota di scorta 129
ruote 101
ruotino anteriore 129

sabbia 81
sala bilance 115
sale 15
salire 129
salita 113
saltare 95
   nel corridoio 95
   giusto 95
   in libertà 95
   netto 95
saltatore 93
salti di scuola 87
salto 79
   ostacoli 93-7
   da pulce 155
salute 9, 53

saluto 93
sapone di glicerina 129
sarto 153
sauro
   bruciato 37-9
   caffelatte 37
   chiaro 37
   ciliegia 39
   dorato 39
   isabella 37
   lavato 39
   pezzato 39
   scuro 37, 39
scacchi 117, 119
scaglioni 45
scala dei voti 93
scalciare 69
scanalatura tra i due cuscinetti
   137
scappare 69
scarpa alta per i pantaloni
   lunghi 153
scartare 95
scarto, fare uno 69
scendere 129
scesa tagliente, groppa 27
scheletro 15
schiacciato 13
schinella 51
schiocco della lingua 73
schiume 67
scolo nasale 53
scroto 21
scuderia 127-9
scuola di equitazione 79
scuro
   baio 39
   grigio 39
   sauro 37, 39
   sorcino 39
secchio 127
sedile 101
seduto 69
   in appiombo 73

seggio 137
segnale di partenza 99
segretario della società di
   corse 109
seguito 103
sella 133
   di addestramento 133
   aggiustare 137
   d'amazzone 137
   da caccia 133
   da corsa 137
   cowboy 137
   generica 133
   parti della 137
   da polo 137
   da salto ostacoli 133
   sintetica 137
sellaio 137
sellare un cavallo 137
selleria 127, 133-45
selleria (il materiale) 137
selleria (il negozio) 137
selleria (la stanza) 137
sellino 101
selvatico 103
seme di lino 13
semplici, mantelli 37
senecio 13
senecione 13
sensibilità 77
separare le redini 75
serpentina 85
serrata, coda 27
serrato
   davanti 33
   ai gomiti 29
servizio per la pulizia degli
   stivali 153
setola 43, 51
sezionare 133
sferrare 45
sfilata 113
sfiorare l'ostacolo 95
sfoltire 133

sgroppata 87
siepe 155
sindacato 109
sindrome navicolare 49
siringa 55
sistema nervoso centrale 53
slattare 11
smontare 73
smontonata 69
soddisfacente 93
solano insano 11
solido
  garretto 33
  stinco 29
solo colore 117
sopra la mano 69
sopraffascia 127, 137
soraccapo 141
sorcino 39
  chiaro 39
  maltinto 39
  nero 39
  scuro 39
sorcio, coda di 27
sorella 5
  piena 5
sospensione, tempo di 61
sottile, avambraccio 29
sotto di sé dietro e davanti 33
sottocoda 101
sottogola 141, 149
sottomissione 61, 65
sottopancia della dorsiera 101
sovraccarico 115
sovrallenato 67
spalla 17, 27
  asciutta 27
  ben disegnata 27
  carica di carne 27
  corta 27
  debole 27
  in dentro 87
  dritta 27
  inclinata 27

lunga 27
massiccia 27
obliqua 27
pronunciata 27
punta della 17
spalline 119
spareggio 97
spavenio 47
spazzola 153
spazzolare 131, 153
specie 5
sperone 21
  con la punta 149
  alla scuderia 149
  senza cinghietti 149
  senza rotelle 149
speroni 145, 149
spettatori 103
spilla da plastron 149
spinta
  dell'assetto 73
  dei posteriori 65
spogliarsi 153
sporco, bianco 37
sporgente, anca 27
sport
  equestri 79
  ippici 79
spostare 95
spugna 127
spugnare 131
spugnoso, garretto 31
squalifica 99
squalificato 121
staccionata 155
  sul fosso 155
stadio 47
staffa 137
staffile 137
stallone 9
  di origine 7
stamina 121
stanga 101
stare allo steccato 123

start 113
starter 109, 113
stato 67
  segnaletico 11
stazione 59
steccato 113
steeplechase 97, 111
stella 41, 119
stelle 119
sterile 9
stile all'ostocolo 93
stimare l'ostacolo 95
stimolazione elettrica della
muscolatura 53
stinchiere 127
stinco 17, 29
  circonferenza dello 45
  corto 29
  debole 29
  largo 29
  lungo 29
  netto 29
  solido 29
  tondo 29
stivalaio 153
stivali 153
  da caccia 153
  da campagna 153
  da cavallo 153
  di gomma 153
  mettere gli 153
  osso per pulire e lisciare
    153
  da polo 153
  pulire 153
  con risvolto 153
  con risvolto da fantino 153
  servizio per la pulizia degli
    153
  togliersi 153
stock 149
strattone 75
stretta
  groppa 27

incollatura 23
strette, reni 25
stretto, petto 23
striglia 127
stringere le cinghie 137
striscia 117, 119
striscie 119
strofinaccio 129
strofinare 131
strongili 49
strozzato, ginocchio 29
sudore 127
sufficiente 93
sulla
  mano 61
  sola redine del morso 75
suola 43
suolo 81
suono della campana 93
superare 95
superficie masticatoria 45
sverzino 149
svestire 101

tabella 95
tachigrafo 129
tagliare 81, 133
tagliente, garrese 25
tallone 43
talloni 73
talus 155
tampone 55
tandem 99
tare e difetti 53
targa 129
targhetta di nazionalità 129
tarlo dello zoccolo 51
tasso 13
tatto equestre 77
tavolo 155
tecnica equestre 73
temperamento 9, 65-7
temperatura corporea 53
tempo 43, 59

di sospensione 61
tempo ottimo 99
tendini 15
tendinite 51
tenie 51
tenuta
  da amazzone 149
  da caccia 149
  da caccia francese 149
  del cavaliere 149
  da equitazione 149
  (inglese) 149
  delle redini 75
termini veterinari generali
  51-5
terreno 115-17
teso 65
testa 15, 21, 115
  arcata 21
  asciutta 21
  camusa 21
  carnosa 21
  concava 21
  conica 21
  corta 115
  in dentro 87
  dritta 21
  espressiva 21
  grande 21
  leggera 21
  montonina 23
  al muro 87
  nobile 21
  particolarità 41
  pesante 21
  piccola 21
  al vento 69
  volgare 21
testicoli 21
testiera 141
testo della ripresa 93
tetano 51
tettoia 11
tigna 51

tigrato 39
timone 101, 129
tipico 7
tipo 5
tirante 101
tirare la mano 69
tiro
    a quattre 99
    a sei 99
toccare 95
    con la frusta 73
tocco 149
toeletta 131-3
togliere
    la briglia 141
    le fiande 131
togliersi gli stivali 153
tondo, stinco 29
torace 15
    circonferenza al 45
torcinaso 129
torso 133
    della coda 17
tosare 133
tosatura 133
    da caccia 133
    completa 133
    a coperta (completa) 133
    da corsa 133
    a mezza coperta 133
tosse 47
tra le gambe 69
tra mani e gambe 69
traccia 103
    di balzana al tallone 41
    di balzana davanti 41
tracciato della pista 115
traguardo 113
trailer 129
trainare 129
trainer 109
tranquillante 55
tranquillo 65
transizione 61

trasporto dei cavalli 129
traversarsi 61
travone sul fosso 155
tre cavalli in fila 99
treccine, fare le 133
trekking 79
tricorno 149
trifoglio 13
triplice 155
trofei 113
trofeo 103
tromba da caccia (Francia) 105
tronchi 155
tronco 15, 37, 59
troppo alta, groppa 27
troppo alto
    davanti 37
    dietro 37
trotinato, grigio 39
trottare 77
    con il diagonale destro 77
    con il diagonale sinistro 77
trottatore 3
trottignare 69
trotto 43, 85
    allungato 85
    camminare 77
    all'inglese 77
    di lavoro 85
    medio 85
    partire al 77
    riunito 85
    di scuola 87
    seduto 77
    sollevato 77
trucioli (di legno) 131
tuba 149
tuffarsi sulla mano 69
tumefazione 55
tumore 51
turismo equestre 79

ubbidienza 65
ubero 39

uccidere l'animale 103
uguagliare 133
ulcera 51
ultima curva 113
ultimo boccone 105
uncino 145
unguento 55
unicorn 99
unità di misura 45
uomo
    di cavalli 91
    di scuderia 109
    dello stallone 109
urinario, apparato 53
urticaria 51
uscire 131
    la lingua 69
usta 103
ustioni 53
utensili 127-9

V 117, 119
vaccinazione 55
van trailer 129
van (trasporto) 129
varietà 5
velenose, piante 11
velocista 119
vendita
    all'asta 111
    con riserva sui premi 111
    senza riserva sui premi 111
ventre 17, 25
    avvallato 25
    contratto 25
    di levriero 25
    di mulo 25
    normale 25
    pendente 25
    retratto 25
verde 65, 117
    chiaro 117
    scuro 117
vermi 51

vermifugo 53
verruche 51
vertebra 15
verticale 155
vescicone
    del garretto 45, 51
    trafitto 51
vestire 101
vestirsi 153
veterinari, termini generali
    51-5
veterinario di servizio 109
viaggio a cavallo 79
vibrazione 75
vicino a terra 33
    garretto 31
vincente 115
vincitore 123
viola 117
virus 55
visita veterinaria 97
vizio 53
voce 73
vocabolario di allenamento
    119
volata 101
volgare, testa 21
volta 81
volteggio 79
volvolo 51
vulva 21

whipper-in 103

zaino 41
zecche 51
zoccolo 21, 43
zona di penalità 99
zoppia 49
zucchero 13

# INDICE

abatir 103
abierta, babilla 31
abierto
    de codos 29
    corvejón 31
abrevadero 127
abrevadero automático 127
abrevar 131
abrigo impermeable 153
abrir las riendas 75
abrochar la cincha 137
absceso 47
abuela 5
abuelo 5
abúlico 65
acacia falsa 13
acariciar 73
acarnedada, cabeza 23
ácaros 49
accelerar 123
accidente 95
acción 9, 41-3, 59
    de la espalda 73
    de las manos 73
    del peso 73
    de las piernas 73
    simultánea de las piernas 75
    de una sola pierna 75
aceite 15
aceptar le embocadura 61
acercar 95
ación 137
acodada, rodilla 29
acoplamiento 129
acortar 77
acortar las riendas 75
activo 73
adaptar la montura 137
adiestrador 91
adiestramiento 67
administración 109
afinidad 5

agotado 67
agrión 47
agua 15
aguantar el trabajo 121
ahogadero 141
aire 59
aires 41-3
    de alta escuela 87
    básicos de escuela 85
    cortos 43
    de escuela 43
    de fantasía 43
    fundamentales de alta
        escuela 87
    irregulares 43
    largos 43
    libres 43
    naturales 43
    principales 43
    regulares 43
    reunidos 43
ajustar las riendas 75
alacranes 145
alargar 77
    las riendas 75
alazán 37
    cereza 39
    claro 37, 39
    encendido 39
    guinda 39
    lavado 39
    oscuro 37, 39
    pío 39
    tostado 37
albino 37
alcance 49
alergia respiratoria 49
alfalfa 13
alfiler (de adorno y sujeción)
    149
algodón 55
algunos pelos blancos 41

alheña 13
alimentar 131
alimento verde 13
almohaza 127
alrededor del caballo 109
alta
    cruz 25
    escuela 79
    grupa 27
alumno 91
alzada 33, 45
amarillo 117
amazona 91, 109
aminorar 123
amplio de pecho 33
analgésicos 53
análisis sanguíneo 53
ancha
    caña 29
    grupa 27
    rodilla 29
ancho
    antebrazo 29
    corvejón 31
    pecho 23
anchos, riñones 25
anemia 47
anestésicos 53
anglo-árabe 3
ángulos 33
anilla 101
anillas 145
animar 73
ano 21
antebrazo 17, 29
    ancho 29
    corto 29
    estrecho 29
    largo 29
    plano 29
anteojeras 101
antibiótico 53

antiinflamatorio 53
antiparasitario 53
antiséptico 53
aparato
    digestivo 53
    respiratorio 53
    urinario 53
aparejar 101
aplastado 13
aplomado 73
aplomos 15, 33
apósito 55
apósitos 53
apostador 109
apoyarse en las riendas 69
apoyo 87
apoyo de la boca 61
apoyo-rodillas 137
aprendíz 109
aproximar 95
aptitud 93
árabe, pura sangre 3
arena 81
arestín 49
armonía 61
armoniosa 37
arpeo 51
arqueado, cuello 23
articulación 15
artritis 47
áscaris 47
ascendientes 5
asegurarse la plaza 121
asiento 73, 101, 137
    adelantado 73
    atrasado 73
    de Caprilli 73
    de carreras 73
    de doma 73
    flexible 73
    rígido 73
    de salto 73

asimétrico 61
atalajar 101
atípico 7
atreos 133-45
atruchado, tordo 39
avena 13
ayudas 73
    diagonales 75
    exteriores 99
    laterales 75
azabache, negro 37
azúcar 13
azul 117
    claro 117
    marino 117
    oscuro 117

babilla 21, 31
    abierta 31
    grande 31
    nítida 31
bacteria 53
baja, cruz 25
bajo, corvejón 31
ballestras 101
balotada 87
banda 117, 119
banqueta 155
    irlandesa 155
bara 101
barbour 153
baremo 95
barra 155
    delantera 129
    de llamada 155
barras 119
barrer 131
barrera 11, 155
bascular 95
base de sustentación 61
bastante bien 93
bastante mal 93

larga 29
redonda 29
canal 137
canal de babilla 17
cáncer 47
cansado 65, 67
canter preliminar 113
capa 15
capas 37-41
carácter 65-7
características fijadas 7
cardiopatía 49
careta 127
careto 41
carga útil 129
carnaza 103
carrera 79, 107-23
 abierta 111
 de debutantes 111
 lisa 111
 de obstáculos 111
 primera 111
 principal 111
 pública 111
 en serie 111
 de vallas 111
 de venta 111
carrera con condiciones 111
carrera 'point to point' 79
carreras
 con handicaps 111
 en serie 111
carretilla del estiércol 127
carruaje 99
carrusel 81
carta genealógica 7
carta de orígen 111
casco 21, 43-5
 amulado 43
 de cross 149
 encastillado 43
 equitación 149
 de polo 149
 protector 149

castaña 17
castaño 39
 cereza 39
 claro 39
 encendido 39
 giunda 39
 normal 39
 oscuro 39
 pío 39
castigar 73
castigo 73
castracíon 53
castrados 109
castrar 53
categorías 111
causar decepción 121
caza 79
cazador 103
cebada 13
ceder 75, 121
ceguedad 47
celos 11
cepillado
 completo 131
 rápido 131
cepillar 131, 153
cepillo 153
 de raíces 127
 suave 127
cerca de tierra 33
cercado 11
ceremonia de presentación
 francesa 105
cereza
 alazán 39
 castaño 39
cerneja 21
cerrado
 de codos 29
 de corvejones 33
 de rodillas 33
certificado de origen 7
certificado de vacunación 111
cerviz 17

cesar la acción de las piernas
 75
cesión 65
 de entradas 109
 a la pierna 87
chaleco 149
chaps 153
chaqueta
 de caza 149
 roja 105
 de sport 149
charnela 137
chasquido de la lengua 73
chevrons 117, 119
cicuta 11
ciervo, cuello de 23
cincha 101, 137
 abrochar la 137
 desabrochar la 137
cinchuelo 127, 145
cinta métrica 45
circuito 81
círculo 81
círculos 117, 119
cisne, cuello de 23
claro
 alazán 37, 39
 castaño 39
clase 121
clasificación 97
clavadura 43
clavo 43
club hípico 79
cobertizo 11
cobro de la pieza 103
cocear 69
cochero 99
codeso 13
codillo 17
codo 29
 débil 29
codos
 abierto de 29
 cerrado de 29

coger
 los palos 123
 sólo las riendas del bocado
  75
cojera 49
cola 17, 27, 133
 de caballo 11
 corta 133
 entresacada 133
 entresacar 133
 hundida 27
 de inserción alta 27
 de inserción baja 27
 nacimiento de la 133
 porte de la 27, 133
 protestar con la 69
 de rata 27
 trenzada 133
 del zorro 105
cólico 47
collerón 101
colmillos 45
colocación 61
colocados 115
colores de cuadra 117-19, 149
colores de cuadra (de carrera)
 149
cólquico 11
columna vertebral 15
combinación 155
comisarios 109
comitiva 103
compacto 33
compañero de cuadra 121
compresa fría 53
compuestas 37
común, cabeza 21
con buenos huesos 33
cóncava, cabeza 21
concha 101
concurso 79
concurso combinado de
 enganches 103
concurso completo 79, 97

caballo de 97
 de enganches 103
 jinete de 97
 de tres días 97
 de un día 97
concurso morfológico 81
concursos de categoría A, B 93
confianza 65
conformación 9, 15
cónica, cabeza 21
conjunctivitis 47
conjunto 81
conmoción 53
'conos' 103
consanguinedad 5
constitución 9
contacto 61
contacto con la mano 61
contacto franco 61
contacto muelle 61
contagioso 53
contornos 33
contracambio de mano 81
contraído, vientre 25
contusión 53
convexa, cabeza 21
convexo, lomo 25
copete 21, 133
copropietarios 109
cordón corrido 41
corona 21
corona blanca 41
correa
 de la barbilla 149
 del reculante 101
correíllas 149
correr
 bien 121
 mal 121
corta
 cabeza 115
 caña 29
 cruz 25
 cuartilla 31

espalda 27
grupa 27
cortar 133
la cola 133
cortas, costillas 23
corto
  antebrazo 29
  brazo 27
  cuello 23
  lomo 25
cortos
  aires 43
  riñones 25
corvaza 47
corvejón 21, 31-3
  abierto 31
  ancho 31
  bajo 31
  bien definido 31
  débil 33
  derecho 31
  empastado 31
  fuerte 33
  grande 31
  largo 31
  mal definido 31
  nítido 31
  recto 31
  remetido de atrás 33
corvejones
  cerrado de 33
  hueco de 33
corveta
  clásica 87
  a la francesa 87
corvo 33
costilla del collar 101
costillas 15, 17, 23
  cortas 23
  curvadas 23
  largas 23
  planas 23
costuras 117, 119
crear una raza 7

cremello 37
cría 5-9
  de pura raza 7
criador 5, 109
criador-proprietario 109
crin 15, 21, 131
  entresacar 133
  esquilada 133
crines
  entresacadas 133
  rapadas 133
  trenzadas 133
criptórquido 9
cross 79
cruce 7
  de consanguinidad 7
  con línea distinta 7
  con raza distinta 7
  mestizo 7
  siguiendo una línea 7
cruz 17, 25
  alta 25
  baja 25
  corta 25
  delgada 25
  destacada 25
  empastada 25
  fina 25
  larga 25
  de Lorena 117, 119
  plana 25
  de S. Andrés 117, 119
cruzado 7
cuadra 109
cuadrado 37
cuadro 37
cuadros 117, 119
cuartilla 21, 31
  corta 31
  débil 31
  inclinada 31
  larga 31
  recto de 33
  vertical 31

cuartillón 31
cuarto 51
cubo 127
cuchillas 133
cuchillo de sudor 127
cuello 17, 23, 115
  arqueado 23
  bien musculado 23
  de cabra 23
  de ciervo 23
  de cisne 23
  corto 23
  estrecho 23
  grueso 23
  horizontal 23
  inserción alta 23
  inserción baja 23
  largo 23
  ligero 23
  medio 115
  oblicuo 23
  pesado 23
  poco musculado 23
  proporcionado 23
  recto 23
cuerda 113, 127
  para dar cuerda 145
cuerno de caza 105
cuerpo 115
  medio 115
cuidado 131
cuidar 55
curas 53
cursillo 81
curva 113
curvadas, costillas 23

dar brillo 153
dar kilos 115
dar más peso 115
dar peso 115
dar una palmada 73
débil
  caña 29

codo 29
corvejón 33
cuartilla 31
espalda 27
grupa 27
lomo 25
debilidad 51
debut 111
debutante 121
decidido 61
declaración
  de forfait 113
  de monta 113
  de partants 115
dedalera 11
defectos y taras 53
defectuoso (aplomos) 33
defensas 67-9
degeneración 7
dejar el caballo en un prado 11
delante
  de la mano 69
  de la pierna 69
delgada, cruz 25
delicado 67
demasiado
  alto de la cruz 37
  alto de la grupa 37
dentadura 45
deportes hípicos 79
depósito 9-11
depósito, de sementales 9
derecha 77, 115
  espalda 27
derecho 59
  corvejón 31
derechos de monta 113
derivadas 37
dermatitis estival 51
derribar 95
desabrochar la cincha 137
desatalajar 101
desbocarse 69
descalificación 99

descendientes 5
descenso 113
  del cuello 65
  de mano 65
descargo de peso 115
descolar 133
descontracción de la boca 61
desembarcar 129
desempate 97
desfile 113
desherrar 45
deshidratación 53
desmontar 73
desnudarse 153
desnutrición 49
desobediencias 67
desobediente 67-9
despapado 69
destacada, cruz 25
destete 11
desveno 145
detrás
  de la mano 69
  de la pierna 69
diarrea 47
dibujos 117-19
dibujos de los colores 119
dientes 45
  cambio de 45
  definitivos 45
  de leche 45
  temporales 45
difícil 65
digital 11
dimensiones 37
director
  de cacería 103
  de la yegua 11
dirección del movimiento 59
disco de nacionalidad 129
distancia 95, 113
  clásica 111
distanciado 111, 115
distensión de tendones 51

doblar 81
doblar y cambiar de mano 81
doble tronco 99
dócil 65
dog-cart 99
dolencia 51
dolor 55
doma 59-65, 67, 121
    clásica 79, 93
dorso 17
    cóncavo 69
droga 53
ducha de agua fría 53
duro 115

echar la cama 131
ecografía 55
eczema 53
eczema del dorso 49
eje longitudinal 61
ejecución 93
ejercicios
    en el callejón 95
    en libertad 95
elasticidad 59
electrolitos 53
elevada 87
eliminación 99, 113
eliminar 97
embarcar 129
embocadura 145
    acceptar le 61
    articulada 145
    curva 145
    'en media luna' 145
    rígida 145
embocaduras 141-5
embridar 141
empastada, cruz 25
empastado, corvejón 31
empate 115
emplasto 55
empujar con los posteriores 65
en forma 67

en la mano 61
encabritarse 69
encendido, castaño 39
enderezar 59
enfermedad 51
    articular 49
    de la hierba 49
    del navicular 49
    venérea 51
enfermedades 47-51
enganchar 101
enganche 99, 129
    de cuatro caballos 99
    de seis caballos 99
engancher 101
enganches 79, 99
ensillado, lomo 25
ensillar 137
entrenador 109
entrenadores, terminología de
    119-21
entrenamiento
    del caballo de salto 95
    por fases 99
entresacar 133
entumecimiento 55
envenenamiento 49
equilibrado 37
equilibrio 9, 65
equipo 125-55
    caballeriza 127-9
equiseto 11
equitación 77
    académica 79
    de adorno 43
    de alta escuela 79
    clásica 77-9
    de fantasía 79
    práctica 79
    de recreo 79
    'Western' 79
error
    de recorrido 93
    de reprise 93

escala de notas 93
escaparse 95, 121
escarapela 97
escoba 127
escofina 43
escroto 21
escuela
    básica 79
    de equitación 79
    de iniciación 79
espalda 17, 27
    acción de la 73
    adentro 87
    corta 27
    débil 27
    derecha 27
    inclinada 27
    larga 27
    oblicua 27
    pastosa 27
    pronunciada 27
    seca 27
esparaván 47
especialista del terreno 121
especie 5
especificaciones de la edad
    109
espejuelo 17
espiga 149
espolín 149
esponja 127
espuela
    ciega 149
    de coreíllas 149
    con gallo 149
espuelas 149
espuma 67
esqueleto 15
esquilado
    de caza de zorro 133
    de enganches 133
    de manta 133
    total 133
esquilador 133

esquilar 133
    la crin 133
esquina 81
estadio 47
estar
    bajo presión 121
    cerrado 121
    distanciado 121
    domado 121
    en forma 121
    frío 123
    a las ordenes del juez de
        salida 113
    puesto 121
estéril 9
estevado 33
estilo del jinete 95
estimulación elétrica de los
    músculos 53
estrecha, grupa 27
estrechamiento debajo de la
    rodilla 29
estrecho
    antebrazo 29
    cuello 23
    de pecho 33
    pecho 23
estrechos, riñones 25
estrella 119, 149
estribera 137
estribo 137
estróngilos 49
eutanasiar un caballo 53
examen miscroscópico 55
excelente 93
expresiva, cabeza 21
exterior 15-37
extremidades, particularidades
    41
extremos 45

fabricante de espuelas 149
fácil para la comida 67
faeton 99
faldón 137

falsa barbada 145
'falsa corvaza' 49
falta de actividad 61
falto de preparación 121
familia 5
farol 101
fasciola hepática 49
fibrocartilago lateral 51
fiebre 49
figuras 81, 93
filete 141
    de anillas 141
    de anillas pequeñas 141
    con palillos 141
    elevador 141
    en caucho 145
    de goma 145
    de olivas 141
    para uso con brida 141
    de pasta 145
fina
    cruz 25
    rodilla 29
firme 115
fístula de la cruz 49
flequillo 131
flexible 117
flexión
    directa 61
    de la nuca 61
flyer 119
fondista 119
foraje 127
forca 127
forma 65, 67, 121
formas 141
forraje
    seco 13
    verde 13
forzar el paso 121
foso 155
foso de agua 155
fosos 155
foto-finish 115

frac 153
fractura 55
fragua 43
franja 117, 119
franqueza 61
freno 101
freno (de inercia) 129
frente 17
frío 65
frontalera 141
frotar 131
frugal 67
fuera de forma 67, 121
fuerte 33, 65
  caña 29
  corvejón 33
  grupa 27
  lomo 25
  pierna 31
fuertes, riñones 25
fusta 101, 145
  de cacería 145
  de carreras 145
  de caza 105
  para doma 149
fustas y espuelas 145
fuste 137

gallo 149
galopar 77
galope 43, 85
  cambiado 85
  de carrera 85
  a la derecha 77, 85
  desunido 69, 85
  en trocado 77, 85
  ir al 77
  a la izquierda 77, 85
  largo 85
  lento 85
  a la mano 85
  medio 85
  refrenado 85
  reunido 85

salir al 77
  de trabajo 85
gamarra 145
gamuza 127
ganadería 9-11
ganadero 5
ganado 123
ganador 115
gancho 153
ganglios 49
garañón 9
garganta 17
garrapatas 51
gastrófilos 47
generación libre 7
gente del turf 109
gestación 11
gesto del caballo 93
gig 99
girar 81, 95
giratoria 101
giro
  abierto 95
  cerrado 95
giunda, castaño 39
globosa, rodilla 29
golosina 15
golpe con las espuelas 75
golpe de la fusta 75
gomas elásticas para trenzar
  129
grado 5
Gran Premio 93
granate 117
grande
  babilla 31
  cabeza 21
  corvejón 31
  rodilla 29
granos 13
gránulos 13
grasa para cascos 129
grieta 47
  en el casco 43, 51

gripe equina 49
groom 109
grueso 33
  cuello 23
grupa 17, 27
  alta 27
  ancha 27
  caída 27
  corta 27
  débil 27
  demasiado alto de la 37
  estrecha 27
  fuerte 27
  larga 27
  de mulo 27
  al muro 87
  oval 27
  plana 27
  tener desplazada 61
grupada 87
grupo 81
guadarnés 127, 137
guante 149
guardabarro delantero 101
guarnición
  inglesa 101
  con petral 101
guarnicionería 133-45
guarnicionero 137
guarniciones 99
guiar 99
guinda, alazán 39
guita 149
gymkhana 79

hacer
  la distancia 121
  un quiebro 69
  una variación 81
hackamore 141
hackney 103
handicap 111
handicapper 109
hebilla 101, 149

helecho 11
hemorragia 53
heno corto 13
heno (el primer corte) 13
heno (el segundo corte) 13
hepatitis 49
herencia 7
herida 51, 55
herida punzante 43, 49
heridas en las rodillas 47
hermana 5
hermano 5
hernia 49
herrador 43
herradura 43
  quitar la 45
herrar un caballo 45
herrería 43
heterogéneo 7
híbrido 7
hierba 13
  cana 13
  de San Juan 13
  de Santiago 13
hierro 11
hija 5
hijo 5
hilo para trenzar 129
hocico 17
hombreras 119
homogéneo 7
horizontal, cuello 23
horizontales, riñones 25
horma 153
hormiguillo 51
hormonas 55
horquilla 127
horse ball 79
hueco de corvejones 33
huella dactilar 41
hueso 15
  saca-brillo 153
hundida, cola 27
hundido, pecho 23

hundidos, riñones 25
huntsman 103

ictericia 49
ijada 17
impulsión 59
inbreeding 7
inbreeding incestuoso 7
incisivos 45
inclinada
  cuartilla 31
  espalda 27
inclinado, muslo 31
incurvación 61
incurvado 61
individuo 5
inflamación 55
  de articulación 47
influenza 49
infosura 49
iniciar 65
inmovilidad 59, 77
inscribir un caballo 113
inscripciones 111
inseminación artificial 9
inseminar 9
insensibilidad 55
inspección y examen de los
  caballos 97
inspeccionar el recorrido 95,
  97
instructor 91
  de alta escuela 91
insuficiente 93
Intermedia 93
ir en cabeza 121
ir al galope 77
ir al paso 77
ir al trote 77
irse de caña 69
isabelo 39
isquiones 73
izquierda 77, 115
izquierdo 33

jaboncillo 129
jefe en pista 95
jeringa 55
jinete
  de concurso completo 97
  estilo del 95
  experimentado 91
  licencia de 111
  de salto 93
  tirar al 69
  trajes de 149
  voltear al 69
jinetes 91
jockey 91, 109
jodphur 153
juaría 103
juego delantero 101
juegos ecuestres 79
juez 109
  de peso 109
  de salida 109
jurado de campo 99

la línea superior 61
lacayo 103
lactancia 11
lado
  cóncavo 61
  convexo 61
  derecho 59
  exterior 59
  interior 59
  izquierdo 59
laminitis 49
lanza 101
larga
  caña 29
  cruz 25
  cuartilla 31
  espalda 27
  grupa 27
  pierna 31
  rodilla 29
largas, costillas 23

largo 33
  antebrazo 29
  brazo 29
  corvejón 31
  cuello 23
  galope 85
  lomo 25
  muslo 31
  paso 85
  trote 85
largos
  aires 43
  riñones 25
látigo 101
latiguilla 137
latiguillo 149
lavado, alazán 39
lavar 131
  con esponja 131
lazo 97
lejos 115
leñera 155
lento, galope 85
león, pecho de 23
lesiones pulmonares por larvas
  de estróngilos 49
letras 93
'levade' 87
levantar la cama 131
levita
  de caza (francesa) 149
  roja 105
libre, paso 85
libres, aires 43
licencia
  de aprendíz 111
  de entrenador 111
  de jinete 111
  de jockey 111
liebre, vientre de 25
ligamento 15
ligera, cabeza 21
ligeramente pesado 117
ligereza 65

ligero, cuello 23
limfangitis 49
limitado en forma 121
limonera 99, 101
limpiacascos 127
limpiar 131
  las botas 153
  el caballo 131
  los cascos 131
  con esponja 131
linaje 5
linaza 13
línea 5, 7
  de centro 81
  de llegada 113
  principal 7
  recta 81
  sanguínea 5
liso 117, 119
llamada 109
llave 101
llegada 113
  en un pañuelo 123
lobero 41
loción 55
lombrices 51
lomo 17, 25
  convexo 25
  corto 25
  débil 25
  ensillado 25
  fuerte 25
  largo 25
  de mulo 25
  recto 25
losange 119
lote 113, 123
lucero 41
lumbres 43
lunar 41
  entre ollares 41
lunares 119
lupino 13
luz

intermitente 129
  de pare 129
  de la placa de matricula 129
  trasera 129

machete 105
macho 133
madre 5
maíz 13
mal 51, 93
mala unión cabeza-cuello,
  cabeza 23
malva 117
mama 21
mamar 11
manchado 39
mandil 101
manejabilidad 101
mangas 117, 119
mano
  cambiar de 77, 81, 85
  contacto con la 61
  contracambio de 81
  delante de la 69
  descenso de 65
  detrás de la 69
  doblar y cambiar de 81
  en la 61
  galope a la 85
  riendas en una 75
  trabajo a la 91
mano delantera 59
manos
  acción de las 73
  sostener las riendas con las
    dos 75
manta 127
  impermeable 127
  de Nueva Zelandia 127
  para desudar 127
mantenimiento 131
marathón 101
marcha atrás automática 129
marrón 117

martingala 145
  fija 145
  irlandesa 145
martingalas 145
más peso 115
masajes 131
maslo 17
master 103
matices 37
matricular un caballo 113
matrículas 111
media
  hermana 5
  parada 75
  pirueta 87
  vuelta 81
media-sangre 3
medianos 45
medicamento 53
medición 45
  con el bastón 45
  con la cinta 45
medidas 45
  inglesas 47
  métricas 47
medio
  cuello 115
  cuerpo 115
  galope 85
  hermano 5
  paso 85
  trote 85
medir 95
mejorar una raza 7
melaza 13
menudillo 17
mesa 155
meta 113
metodo de enjuiciamiento 95
metritis contagiosa 47
metro 47
mezcla de pienso 13
mezcladas, capas 37
miembro

apoyado 59
elevado 59
miembros 15, 59
    anteriores 59
    posteriores 59
milla 47
millero 121
mioglobinuria 47
miorelajante 55
mitad de carrera 113
modo de sostener las riendas
    75
molares 45
monitor 91
monta 9, 11, 113
montante 141
montar 73
    a la amazona 81
    en concursos 79
    contra reloj 95
    a la jineta 81
    a pelo 81
montura 133-5
    adaptar la 137
    de amazona 137
    cacería 133
    de carreras 137
    de doma 133
    mixta 133
    partes de 137
    de polo 137
    quitar la 137
    rozadura de 47
    de salto 133
    sintética 137
    'Western' 137
moquillo 49
morcillo, negro 37
morder 69
    el hierro 69
mordisquear 69
morfología 15
moro 39
mosqueado, tordo 39

mover 131
movilidad 61
movimiento 41-3, 59
movimientos 93
mozo 11
    de caballos 131
    de perros 103
    principal 131
mudarse 153
muermo 49
mula 3
mulo 3
    grupa de 27
    lomo de 25
muro 81
    de ladrillos 155
    de piedras 155
músculos 15
muserola 141
    alemana 141
    'flash' 141
    irlandesa 141
    mejicana 141
muslo 21, 31
    bien musculado 31
    inclinado 31
    largo 31
muslos 73
muy bien 93
muy mal 93
muy oscuro, tordo 39
muy pesado 117

nacimiento de la cola 133
nalga 21
naranja 117
narices 17
nariz 115
negrilla 45
negro 37, 117
    azabache 37
    morcillo 37
    pío 39
nemátodos 51

nervio 55
nervios 15
nervioso 65
neumonía 49
nieta 5
nieto 5
nítida, babilla 31
nítido, corvejón 31
nivel de doma 65
no colocado 113
no ejecutado 93
no en forma 67
no participante 113
no respectar 95
no útil para carreras 111
noble 37
noria 131
normal
    aplomos 33
    cadera 27
    castaño 39
    vientre 25
nuca 17
    flexión de la 61
nudo blanco 41
número de sorteo 113
nutrición 55

obediencia 65
obediente a las ayudas 6
obesidad 49
oblicua, espalda 27
oblicuo
    brazo 29
    cuello 23
obstáculo 93
    doble 155
    en escalera 155
    fijo 95
    de fondo 155
    simple 155
    sin dificultades 95
    triple 155
    vertical 155

obstáculos 93-7, 155
    de cross 97
ocho de cifra 85
ojo 17
    de perdiz 41
ollares 17
ombligo 17
operar 55
oreja 17
organización de las carreras
    113
órganos 15
origen 5
origen de una raza 9
oscuro
    alazán 37, 39
    castaño 39
    tordo 39
outsider 123
oval, grupa 27
overo 39
overo y roano 39
oxer
    de barras desiguales 155
    quadrado 155
oxiuros 51

pacemaker 121
padre
    de un producto 9
    de una raza 7
paja 13
    corta 13
palafrenero 11, 109
palancas 33, 145
palas 45
palma 43
    plana 43
palmada 73
palmear 73
palmitieso 43
palo de guardia 101
palomino 39
palos 113

pando 33
paño 127
pantorrillas 73
paperas 51
para la comida 67
parada 59, 77, 85
    de diez minutos 99
paradista 11, 109
parálisis 49
parar 77
    el entrenamiento 121
pararse 95, 121
parásitos 55
pared 43
partants 115
parte
    inferior 37
    superior 37
partición 129
participantes 115
particularidades 41
partida 103
partido 111
parto 11
pasaporte 111
pasar
    el hueso saca-brillo 153
    la lengua por encima del
        hierro 6
paseo 79
pasivo 73
paso 43, 85, 121
    en alto 155
    de andadura 43
    atrás 77
    de caminos 155
    de escuela 87
    ir al 77
    largo 85
    libre 85
    medio 85
    con riendas largas 85
    con riendas sueltas 85
    reunido 85

salir al 77
pasos de costado 87
'passage' 87
pastar 11
pasto 11-13
pastosa
   cabeza 21
   espalda 27
patear 69
patiabierto 33
pechina 101
pecho 17, 23
   amplio de 33
   ancho 23
   de cabra 23
   estrecho 23
   hundido 23
   de león 23
   profundo 23
   proporcionado 23
   en punta 23
pecho-petral (sujeto a la
   cincha) 137
pecho-petral (sujeto a la
   montura) 137
pedigree 7
pegar 73
pegarse 69
peinar 131
peine 129, 133
pelaje 15
pelham 145
pelo 15, 131
   de la cerneja 21
   de la cuartilla 131
   de invierno 131
   uniforme 41
   de vaca 37
   de verano 131
pelotón 103
pelouse 115
pelvis 15
penalidad
   por obstáculo 97

por tiempo 97
penalización 97
pene 21
pensión 131
pequeña, cabeza 21
pérdida de forma 121
pereza 61
perezoso 65
perilla 137
perímetro de la caña 45
períodos 45
peritonitis 49
permeabilidad a las ayudas 65
perrera 103
perro 103
persecución 103
pesada, cabeza 21
pesado 117
   cuello 23
pescante 101
pesebre 127
pesebre del heno 127
peso 115
   acción del 73
   antes de la carrera 115
   después de la carrera 115
   kilos 115
   máximo 129
   neto 129
   según la edad 111
pestaña 43
peste equina 47
piafe 87
'piaffer' 87
piano 155
picadero 81, 93
picadura 49
picazo, tordo 39
pico de gavilán 45
pie 21, 47, 143-5, 155
   interior 87
piel 15
pienso 13-15, 131
   caliente 15

compuesto 13
pierna 31
   acción de una sola 75
   activa 75
   bien definida 31
   bien musculada 31
   calzado alto hasta la 41
   cesión a la 87
   delante de la 69
   detrás de la 69
   fuerte 31
   inactiva 75
   larga 31
   passiva 75
piernas 145
   acción de las 73
   acción simultánea de las 75
   cesar la acción de las 75
pieza 103
pilares 145
pinchar 43
pinzas 45
pío 39
   alazán 39
   negro 39
piojos 49
pirueta
   directa 87
   inversa 87
   media 87
piruetas 87
pisada 59
piso 115-17
pista 59, 81, 115
   de arena 115
   de doma 93
   de entrenamiento 115
   de hierba 115
   a mano derecha 115
   a mano izquierda 115
   de verde 115
pizarra, tordo 39
placa de matricula 129
plana

cruz 25
grupa 27
rodilla 29
planas, costillas 23
plano, antebrazo 29
plantado 33
plantas venenosas 11
plastrón 149
plaza 127
pliegue lateral 61
poder hereditario 7
polo 79
polvo 55
pomada 55
pomo 137
poner
   flexible 95
   una reclamación 111
   en el remolque 129
ponerse las botas 153
poni club 79
pony 3
porta-baras 101
porte de la cola 27, 133
posada 87
posición 61, 73
poste de salida 113
postes de llegada 113
potencia genealógica 7
potra 9
potras 111
potrero 11
potrillo 11
   macho 9
potro 9, 67
potros 109
prado 11
premio 97
premios 109, 113
preparador 109
prestancia 59
primer mozo 11
primera
   ayuda 55

carrera 111
cura 55
primitivas 37
principiante 91
procrear 9
producto 5
   intermedio 7
productos 9
profundo, pecho 23
programa 115
prolífico 9
prominente, cadera 27
pronunciada, espalda 27
propia hermana 5
propio hermano 5
proporcionado 37
   cuello 23
   pecho 23
proporcional 37
proprietaria 109
proprietario 109
proprietario-entrenador 109
protectores 127
protegedorso 153
protestar con la cola 69
prototipo de especie 7
prueba 79
   abierta 97
   a la americana 97
   de campo 101
   combinada 79
   contra reloj 95
   de cross 79, 97
   de doma 91, 93, 97
   'elija sus puntos' 97
   en dos fases 97
   en dos mangas 97
   de la flexión 55
   de fondo 97
   funcional 81
   nacional 97
   de obstáculos al tiempo 101
   por equipos 97
   de potencia 97

de salto 79
de salto contra reloj 97
de salto de obstáculos 95,
    97
de seis barras 97
pruebas de salto 97
prurito 55
puerta lateral 129
puerta de servico 129
pulgada 47
punta
    cadera en 27
    de espalda 17
    pecho en 23
puntos 119
    de fuego 55
    de penalidad 97, 99
    de penalidad por tiempo 99
punzamiento 43, 49
pura sangre árabe 3
pura sangre (inglés) 3
púrpura 117
pus 55

quemadura 53
quijada inferior 17
quitameriendas 11
quitar
    la brida 141
    la herradura 45
    la montura 137
quitarse las botas 153

raceador 7
ración
    de crecimiento 15
    diaria 15
    de entretenimiento 15
    de mantenimiento 15
    de trabajo 15
radiografía 55
raid 79
rampa 129
ramplón 45

ranilla 43
    podrida 51
ranúnculo 11
rapar las crines 133
rasqueta 127
rastreo 103
rata, cola de 27
ratonero 39
    oscuro 39
raya 41
    de mulo 41
raza 5
    crear una 7
    indígena 3
    mejorar 7
    padre de una 7
razas 3
reacciones del caballo
    montado 67-71
recela 9
rechinar los dientes 6
recibirse 95
recinto
    del público 115
    de salida 99
recompensar 73
recorrido 95, 155
    de campo 97
    de obstáculos 101
recortar 45, 131-3
recta 115
    cabeza 21
    de enfrente 113
rectangular 37
rectitud 59
recto 59
    brazo 29
    corvejón 31
    de cuartilla 33
    cuello 23
    lomo 25
reculante 101
recular 77
red del heno 127

redonda, caña 29
refrescamiento 7
refugio 11
registro matrícula 11
regularidad 59
rehusar 95
relajado 65
remeter los posteriores 61
remetido
    de atrás 33
    de delante 33
remolacha 13
remolcar 129
remolino 41
remolque 129
rendaje
    deslizante 145
    lateral 145
rendajes y equipo para el
    trabajo a la cuerda 145
renovación de sangre 7
'renvers' 87
reparo 155
reprise 59, 93
    de enganches 103
    libre con música 93
    libre (Kür) 93
    nivel 91-3
    San Jorge 93
resabio 53
reseña 11
respectar 95
resultados 121-3
retirar 99
    el caballo del entrenamiento
    121
retrotar 69
reunión 65, 103
    de información 97
reunir el caballo 61
ría 155
rienda
    de abertura 75
    activa 75

de apoyo 75
de bocado 141
exterior 75
de filete 141
indirecta de oposición
    delante de las espaldas 75
indirecta de oposición
    détras de las espaldas 75
interior 75
de oposición 75
passiva 75
suelta 75
riendas 141
    abrir las 75
    acortar las 75
    ajustar las 75
    alargar las 75
    alemanas 145
    apoyarse en las 69
    de atar 145
    Chambon 145
    Gogue 145
    largas 145
    en una mano 75
    modo de sostener las 74
    sueltas 85
rígido 65
rincón 81
riñones 17, 25
    anchos 25
    caídos 25
    cortos 25
    estrechos 25
    fuertes 25
    horizontales 25
    hundidos 25
    largos 25
ritmo 59
roano 39
rodado, tordo 41
rodela 149
rodilla 17, 21, 29
    acodada 29
    ancha 29

ben definida 29
estrechamiento debajo de la
    29
fina 29
globosa 29
grande 29
larga 29
plana 29
rodillas
    cerrado de 33
    marcadas 47
rodilleras 127
rombo 117, 119
ronzal 127
rosa 117
rozadura de montura 47
rozaduras de la silla 51
rozar 95
rueda
    delantera de guía 129
    delantera de timón 129
    de recambio 129
ruedas 101

saca-botas 153
sacar
    el estiércol 131
    la lengua 69
    del remolque 129
sacudir la cabeza 69
sal 15
    bola de 15
sala de balanzas 115
salida 113
    con bandera 113
    con cajones 113
    con gomas 113
    falsa 113
salir
    al galope 77
    al paso 77
    al trote 77
salpicadero 101
saltar 95

ajustado 95
salto 9, 11, 79
  atrás hereditario 7
saltos de escuela 87
salud 9, 53
saludo 93
salvado 13
sarna 49
  sarcóptica 51
sastre 153
satisfactorio 93
seca
  cabeza 21
  espalda 27
secar 131
secreción 53
secretario de hipódromo 109
segundo caballo 103
selección 7
semental 9
señal de partida 99
señales 103
sensibilidad 55
  ecuestre 77
serpentina 85
serretón 129
servicio 9, 11
seto 155
silbido laríngeo 51
silla 133-5
sillín 101
simples 37
sindicato 109
sistema
  circulatorio 53
  músculo-esquelético 53
  nervioso central 53
sobreaguja 101
sobrecargo de peso 115
sobrecincha 127, 137, 145
sobrehueso 51
sobremano 49
sobrepie 49
sociedad hípica 79

solano furioso 11
soltar y coger 65
soltura 61
sombrero
  de copa 149
  forrado de seda 149
  hongo 149
sorpresa 123
sostener
  las riendas con las dos
    manos 75
  sólo las riendas del bocado
    75
stayer 119
steeplechase 97, 111
subasta 111
subastador 109
sudadero 137
  para llevar el sobrepeso 137
suela 43
suelo 81
suficiente 93
sumisión 61
supplemento 15
suspensión 61
sustentación, base de 61

tabla 45
tablilla 153
tacógrafo 129
talón 43
talones 73
  agrietados 47
tampón 55
tándem 99
tapizado 101
tara hereditaria 7
taras 47-51
tascar 67
técnicas de equitación 73-7
tejo 11, 13
temperamento 9, 65-7
temperatura corporal 53
tendones 15

tener
  condiciones 121
  la grupa desplazada 61
tenias 51
tensión 75
tenso 65
terapia por laser 55
tercio
  anterior 37, 59
  posterior 37, 59
terminología de entrenadores
  119-21
términos veterinarios
  generales 51-5
terreno 115-17
test sanguíneo 53
testera 141
testículos 21
tétanos 51
texto 93
tiempo 59
  óptimo 99
  de suspensión 61
tienda de hípica 137
tijeras 133
tijerillas 145
tiña 51
típico 7
tipo 5
  inglés 153
tirante 101
tirar al jinete 69
tiro
  de cuatro 99
  de tres a la larga 99
tirón 75
tocar 95
  con la fusta 73
tomar distancia 121
topino 43
toque
  de campana 93
  de timbre 93
tórax 15, 33

torcido 61
tordo 39
  atruchado 39
  mosqueado 39
  muy oscuro 39
  oscuro 39
  picazo 39
  pizarra 39
  rodado 41
tos 47
tostado, alazán 37
trabajo
  a la cuerda 67
  a la mano 91
  en los pilares 91
  en dos pistas 87
  a riendas largas 67, 91
tragarse la lengua 6
trailla 103
traje
  de amazona 149
  de caza 105, 149
  a la inglesa 149
trajes de jinete 149
trakehnen 155
tralla 101, 145
tranco 59
tranquilizante 55
tranquilizar 73
tranquilo 65
transcorvo 33
transición 61
transporte de caballos 129
trapo 129
'travers' 87
trébol 13
trenzar 133
tresillo 99
tricornio 149
triple barra 155
triscar 11
triturado 13
trofeo 103
trofeos 113

trompa de caza 105
tronco 15, 37, 59, 99
trotar 77
  sobre la diagonal derecha
    77
  sobre la diagonal izquierda
    77
trote 43, 85
  de escuela 87
  en extensión 85
  ir al 77
  largo 85
  levantado 77
  medio 85
  reunido 85
  salir al 77
  sentado 77
  de trabajo 85
trotón 3
tumefacción 55
tumor 51
turismo ecuestre 79

ubre 21
úlcera 51
última curva 113
ungüento 55
unidad de medida 45
urticaria 51
utensilios 125-55

vaca, vientre de 25
vacunación 55
vaho 47
vaina 17
vallado 11
vara de guardia 101
variedad 5
vejiga 51
vejiga debajo del tendón de
  Aquiles 51
velocidad 121
velocista 119
vendaje compresivo 55